T0339803

FOUNDATIONS OF
CULTURAL DIPLOMACY

FOUNDATIONS OF CULTURAL DIPLOMACY

Politics Among Cultures
and the Moral Autonomy of Man

NICOLAS LAOS

Algora Publishing
New York

Library of Congress Cataloging-in-Publication Data —

Laos, Nicolas K., 1974-
    Foundations of cultural diplomacy: politics among cultures and the moral autonomy
of man / Nicolas Laos.
        p. cm.
    Includes bibliographical references and index.
    ISBN 978-0-87586-831-8 (soft: alk. paper) — ISBN 978-0-87586-832-5 (hard: alk.
paper) — ISBN 978-0-87586-833-2 (ebook) 1. Diplomacy. 2. Cultural relations. I. Title.
    JZ1305.L36 2011
    327.2—dc22
                            2010053022

Printed in the United States

To the United Nations

A need
To see
How the Aeons of Humans structured
their cosmos
To gather
architectural plans
solutions to stability problems
rabbets, and corners, and difficult connections
To select the best materials.

—Christina Ch. Florou, poem "Architecture I"

And for the want of a word
I renew my life
For I was born to know you
To name you

Liberty.

—Paul Éluard, poem "Liberty"

TABLE OF CONTENTS

The channels by which we assess and understand the affairs of nations and peoples are manifold. Set in the context of international relations, the pursuit of determining the individual and collective Good within and among nations and, more expansively, on a global scale, has tested the most commanding of history's political theorists, philosophers, and statesmen. Reflection on the course of human events to this very day suggests that there is a timely and timeless quality to this enterprise.

In *Foundations of Cultural Diplomacy*, Nicolas Laos has captured and elucidated the labors and polemics of political thinkers and philosophers, from the ancients to post-modernists, in an effort to propose the philosophical platform upon which common theories of and ambitions for justice and human rights can be set. Tackling such a formidable agenda is no easy feat, as the reader will come to know. The pursuit of such a weighty quarry demanded both a sufficiently broad intellectual and theoretical net as well as the acuity of and balanced exposure to versed analysis, thus permitting the author to course through the many tempting but ultimately wanting avenues of thought.

It is clear, as the text progresses, that Laos finds Plato's philosophical framework to be the most satisfactory of the normative theoretical approaches for assessing the purpose, propriety, and utility of international relations. This is as it should be. Certainly the Dialogue of the *Republic* was largely devoted to illuminating the nature and form of the Ideal State.

Whether our interests now or in the past are local or global, or whether our view is cosmopolitan or communitarian, we are compelled to ask the ultimate Platonic question, "What is the responsibility of the individual to the community and, in turn, what is the attendant responsibility of the community for the welfare of the individual?"

The complex and fluctuating relations between peoples and nations over the range of history have thwarted the well-intentioned efforts of the most transcendent of thinkers and world leaders to envision and even create a global community which is just, protective of human rights, and ready to peacefully resolve conflicts. One merely has to look at contemporary overtures to fashion a better global future, the United Nations and the World Court, to see how painfully ineffectual we can be in pursuing our aspirations for a peaceful and just world.

As Laos points out, although formidable, the works of Medieval scholastics, philosophers of the Renaissance and Enlightenment, or Hegel, Feuerbach, Nietzsche and the post-modernists, are inadequate, individually or in tandem, to set the stage for a comprehensive understanding and exposition of normative international relations analysis as a means of providing practical guidance for decisions about a global future. In the arena of international relations, the mélange of world cultures, ethnic identities, religions, political systems, and levels of socio-economic development create for the philosopher, policy-maker, as well as the diplomat, bewildering hurdles to establishing norms not only for a good and just world order, but even for the keys and protocols for engaging in meaningful dialogue. That Laos finds some of our greatest political thinkers and philosophers unequal to the task of establishing a necessary comprehensive framework for envisioning and, ultimately, constructing a universal "truth-centered" civilization is not a surprise.

It is Plato, whose dialogues and lessons precede all others considered by the author, whose body of work is most adaptable and targeted to Laos' purpose: that is, the introduction of an "effective humanistic approach to international politics". In the Platonic philosophy, one discovers that the search for the truth has many faces: empirical, mythical, rationalist, spiritual. Plato's strength lies in his culling of these various elements in the course of attaining the forth level, that is the quest for the truth (the Good), through which the "best" systems, that is those promoting justice and human rights, can be conceived and justified. In a contemporary world uncertain both of its moorings and its bearings, it is not difficult to share Laos' enthusiasm, even passion, for "transforming the exercise of political power into the application of a higher civilizing programme".

Laos sees "humanistic cosmopolitanism" as an essential principle in the application of normative theory to international relations. A certain — very special — sort of human being can exercise such a humanistic approach: this is a person with "deeper relations with the truth". As a result, this individual is freed from the traps of a particular logical conception of the world (be it religious, legalistic, or nationalistic). Yet, such a person possesses a certain "spiritual 'Archimedean point' outside himself".

Unfortunately, the modern world, squeezed between radicals and nihilists, inevitably — again and again — finds itself at conflict, somewhat casually seen as "a political act, a political instrument, a continuation of political relations, a carrying out of the same by other means". Karl von Clausewitz' view on politics survived centuries, but the time has come, and Nicolas Laos emphasizes this throughout his book, to take a different approach. In essence, it is a stand that acknowledges the "innate, trans-historical value" of human beings and, as such, leaves no room for a war which is antithetical to this value.

Although, within the framework of Platonic philosophy, truth cannot be fully formalized, Laos provides a comprehensive description of what it means to be "in the quest for truth". In remaining loyal to Plato's tradition, the author seeks to reveal the relation between the object and its absolute truth, and not just provide descriptions of its empirical manifestations in abstract terms. According to Laos, by moving from opinions, through concepts and ideas towards the theory of the Good, a human being internalizes responsibility and develops moral (spiritual) autonomy. Such a transformation prepares the way for the emergence and flowering of some of the most valued of civil tenets and ambitions (i.e., human rights, justice, sustainable development). Embracing such a scenario, we, as well as our societies and institutions, become, as, Plato suggests, "beings-in-the-process-of-perfection".

On the matter of human rights, the author stresses the universalistic character of such rights. In principle, Laos states that the character of these rights derives from the recognition of a human being as a partaker of the absolute being (the truth) uniting all people within itself. Such an approach envisages the creation of a society in which there co-exist absolute individualism and absolute universalism. This is an opposition to a society based solely on either of the -isms.

The quest for truth is also the ultimate source of Laos' idea of "justice as harmony", which argues, per se, against cognitive and moral relativism in international relations. As such, the individual or national actor must be active in confronting injustice; harmony should not be equated with non-intervention, when necessary. In the sphere of sustainable development, the author proffers that such development is best achieved via a qualitative, rather than a quantitative, way of thinking. This is so, he suggests, as qualitative programming is an intrinsic manifestation of spiritual autonomy and the intentionality of human conscience.

Moving along Platonic lines, the author concludes his work with a normative assessment of some of the most pressing problems of today: economic inequality and terrorism. The latter issue, he believes, is a manifestation of the enslavement of the spirit by historical necessities. Overcoming or simply confronting these and other global issues demands a collective approach best envisioned and ultimately shaped through the lens of humanistic cosmopolitanism. Efforts at European integration, Laos argues, are laudable, but will remain incomplete without fully embracing the unifying power of human rights (the spiritual dimension) in tandem with the economic integration now underway.

Through *Foundations of Cultural Diplomacy*, Nicolas Laos undeniably shares the position of the English businessman and founder of the Colony (later, State) of Pennsylvania, whom he quotes: "... justice is the purpose and the fruit of government". Whether our vision is of a new world order, of the fellowship of nations, or the dealings of independent nations and their component jurisdictions, the author's contributions to the scholarship of international relations are most prominent in his proposal (p. 142-143) for the three steps of "an effective humanistic approach to international politics". The components of this proposed triad are: (1) specifying a normative inner order of each international actor; (2) determining the relation between normative inner orders among and between nations; and (3) based upon the knowledge derived from the preceding activities, educating and acculturating the world community so as to create a foreign policy environment among all members of the international system through which civilization and the prospects for universal human rights are continuously advocated and advanced. The attainment of the resulting global future promised by Laos' protocols should be foremost among our fondest hopes for humanity.

George J. Hagerty
Provost and University Professor
Hellenic American University
Athens, Greece

Chapter 1. Introduction: Culture, Norms and International Relations

Existence means the continuity of a being. Consciousness, as consciousness of existence, aims at the preservation of the existence of a given being under the best possible terms. Thus, a conscious being aims not only at the preservation of its existence, but also at the improvement of its existential conditions. Therefore, the intentionality of consciousness operates as an impulse to participate in the world (since consciousness absorbs the world) and also as pure self-knowledge. These functions take place at three different levels — namely: instinct, experience and intellect.

At the level of instinct, conscious activity is minimal, and existence reduces to the two basic instincts — namely, those of survival and reproduction. Instinct is a highly formalized behavioural code which reflects the logic of organic nature. At the level of experience, the intentionality of consciousness is expressed through the functioning of the senses. The senses are oriented towards the external world, with which they connect existence. Experience is about the person finding himself in some situation, and being aware of it. At the level of intellect, reason plays an active role. Thus, the conscious mind perceives and thinks in non-linear ways and it influences perception.

Through reason, conscious beings achieve their spiritual autonomy from nature. However, the spiritual maturity of humankind, i.e., its emancipation from natural/historical necessities, has been purchased at a high cost. When the human being became fully aware of its freedom and responsibility to give meaning (i.e., a reason) to each and every object of consciousness, it came across a crucial question: on the basis of which criteria should one give meaning to things? In other words, which is the original source of the meaning of things? Thus, the drama of humanity's spiritual emancipation from the natural order of things was followed by the drama of the quest for the meaning of being, the ultimate purpose of existence.

The quest for the meaning of being is the essence of culture. In other words, I understand the term 'culture' as a human community's attempt to live meaningfully, i.e., as a community of people who are characterized by a consensus on the significance of certain things. Thus, culture endows people with criteria by which they can evaluate things and they can decide on how things ought to be. Hence, culture is intimately related to the articulation of moral and normative judgments.

The fundamental issues which characterize a culture are the manner in which it understands truth as well as the manner in which it offers access to truth, i.e., knowledge. Therefore, culture underpins and determines the political and economic structures created by human beings. From this perspective, at the most fundamental level, cultural diplomacy signifies an attempt of the practitioner of cultural diplomacy to influence the manner in which other members of the international system make moral and normative judgments and, therefore, the manner in which they behave as social-political beings. As a conclusion, every discussion about the foundations of cultural diplomacy reduces to a discussion about moral and normative issues, which are the basis of cultural diplomacy. In fact, there is a deep, reciprocal relationship between culture and norms.

The need for the development of a global cultural diplomacy was stressed in Milan, on 7 October 2010, by the Director-General of UNESCO, Irina Bokova, on the occasion of the award ceremony for the honorary diploma in European and International Politics, as follows:

> Culture is the best gateway to the human heart and mind... We must build a lasting universal community of human beings drawing on values — culture first and foremost — that are the essence of humanity. This is the task of the new humanism... Globalization is no longer a matter of 'contact', as it was in the sixteenth century, but of sharing. How can we build a universal community in view of the diversity of peoples?

In the present book, based on Plato's philosophy, I attempt to provide answers to the ontological, epistemological and moral questions which emerge from the quest for a global cultural diplomacy and, more generally, from the quest for the articulation and deployment of a new humanism.

1.1 Normative political thought

Some of the most influential contributions to normative International Relations (IR) theory are due to Chris Brown[1], Mervyn Frost[2], Terry Nardin[3], and Nicholas Rengger[4]. Chris Brown has proposed the following definition of normative international relations theory:

> By normative international relations theory is meant that body of work which addresses the moral dimension of international relations and the wider questions of meaning and interpretation generated by the discipline. At its most basic it addresses the ethical nature of the relations between communities/states, whether in the context of the old agenda, which focused on violence and war, or the new(er) agenda, which mixes these traditional concerns with the modern demand for international distributive justice.[5]

Normative theory manifests the inextricable link between philosophy and international relations. Chris Brown has explained this relationship as follows:

> International relations relates to philosophy via the sub-disciplines of political and moral philosophy, and... political philosophy is itself best seen as a sub-division of moral philosophy.[6]

However, echoing modern normative IR theory (as opposed to classical normative political theorists, such as Plato and Aristotle), Chris Brown argues that a serious problem with the term 'normative' theory is that "normative theorists claim to possess some special knowledge which enables them to solve the difficult moral dilemmas of the day"[7]. Brown argues that this

---

1 C. Brown, *International Relations Theory — New Normative Approaches*, New York: Harvester-Wheatsheaf, 1992.

2 M. Frost, *Ethics in International Relations — A Constitutive Theory*, Cambridge: Cambridge University Press, 1986.

3 T. Nardin, *Law, Morality, and the Relations of States*, Princeton: Princeton University Press, 1983.

4 C. Brown, T. Nardin, and N. Rengger (eds), *International Relations in Political Thought*, Cambridge: Cambridge University Press, 2002.

5 C. Brown, op. cit. (ref. 1), p. 3.

6 C. Brown, op. cit. (ref. 1), p. 84.

7 C. Brown, op. cit. (ref. 1), p. 3

prejudice causes "resistance to normative theory" and that "clearly no such claim could be sustained"[8]. Brown's opinion about the scholars who work in the field of normative political theory is the following:

> [I]t can only be by virtue of their role as citizens who happen to have thought about a particularly difficult issue for longer than most of their fellows, and who have at their disposal knowledge of the ways in which similar problems have been thought about in the past — none of which amounts to any kind of right to prescribe.[9]

Therefore, Brown argues that the term "interpretive theory"[10] should substitute for the term normative theory.

Inherent in the attempt to dissociate normative theory from prescription and to reduce 'normative' theory to 'interpretive' theory is a specific attitude towards truth and knowledge: truth is a matter of interpretation, and the uncertainty of knowledge leads to skepticism. Hence, before one accepts the reduction of 'normative' theory to 'interpretive' theory and the dissociation of normative theory from prescription, he must accept the epistemological and ontological presuppositions of these arguments. It is not necessary to do so, and, in fact, I will argue in this book that an alternative approach to epistemology and ontology, and, therefore, to normative theory is possible and more creative than the one which deprives normative theory from the ability to prescribe and limits its scope to interpretation.

Another serious problem with the term 'normative' theory is the distinction between 'empirical' and 'normative' theory. Most positivist IR scholars draw a sharp distinction between empirical and normative theory. They argue that normative theory is prescriptive, which, according to them, connotes an arbitrary idealistic activity, whereas empirical theory is a theory of facts, of what actually happens. Thus, again, we realize that the antithesis between empiricist and normative theories leads us to the problems of truth and knowledge.

Many normative theorists have argued that normative theory is empirical in its own way. In fact, many normative theorists have argued that normative theory deals with the existential conditions (i.e., with 'facts') which have 'normative' content, e.g., rules about the conduct of war, or about human rights. Hence, "some so-called normative questions ought more ac-

---

8 C. Brown, op. cit. (ref. 1), p. 3.
9 C. Brown, op. cit. (ref. 1), p. 3.
10 C. Brown, op. cit. (ref. 1), p. 4.

curately to be seen as empirical"[11]. In the present book, I shall propose a different way of approaching the unity between empirical and normative theories. I shall argue that, even though empirical theory and normative theory are not identical, they are united because of what I shall call the 'critical' operation of human consciousness in history (see Section 3.5). Thus, normative theory necessarily leads us to the study of the problems of truth and knowledge.

1.2 On the value and the validity of norms

In general, normative international relations theorists attempt to clarify the basic moral issues of international relations. One noteworthy attempt is that of Chris Brown[12]. According to C. Brown, the contending approaches to normative IR theory can be reduced to two rival moral outlooks which are known as 'cosmopolitanism' and 'communitarianism'. Cosmopolitanism is a moral doctrine according to which the individual bears an inherent value, independently of one's participation in a political community, and it treats the whole community of human kind as the basic right- and duty-bearing agents of the international political system. On the other hand, communitarianism is a moral doctrine according to which value stems from the particular political community to which the individual belongs, and, moreover, "the individual finds meaning in life by virtue of his or her membership of a political community"[13]. For Chris Brown, the essence of contemporary normative theory consists in the assessment of cosmopolitanism and communitarianism. From this viewpoint, the major questions of normative theory are: Which rights do states have? Should they be allowed to exert rights which are in conflict with human rights or even jeopardize the existence of humankind (e.g., in case of the possession of weapons of mass destruction)? Which rights do individuals have? Do individual rights come before state rights and why? Are individuals and their rights formed by states? These questions determine C. Brown's approach to normative IR theory.

An alternative approach to normative IR theory has been set forth by Mervyn Frost[14]. The first step in Frost's theory is to identify the settled body of norms in international relations. Frost defines a norm as settled "where

---

11 C. Brown, op. cit. (ref. 1), p. 2.
12 C. Brown, op. cit. (ref. 1).
13 C. Brown, op. cit. (ref. 1), p. 55.
14 M. Frost, op. cit. (ref. 2).

it is generally recognized that any argument denying the norm (or which appears to override the norm) requires special justification"[15]. According to Frost, normative theory should be directed in the first place to the question: "What should I, as a citizen (or we the government, or we the nation, or we the community of states), do?" Moreover, Frost argues that, in order to answer the previous question, we must have already answered a more fundamental question which refers to the moral standing of the institutions within which we (and others) live. Thus, Frost argues that the moral autonomy of the state depends on the extent to which "the citizens experience the well-being of the state as fundamental to their own well-being"[16], and, in such a state, people recognize the state's constitution as a set of rules in terms of which they constitute each other. As a conclusion, for Frost, the aim of normative theory is to clarify "the ethical standing of institutions" in relation to each other[17]. Thus, Frost's theory attempts to reconcile human rights with state sovereignty by requiring that states must satisfy extremely demanding terms.

A third, alternative approach to normative IR theory is linked to the 'International Society School'[18], and it focuses on the ethics of international law[19] and the ethics of statecraft[20]. According to this approach, the core of international ethics consists in the moral choices of statesmen. R.H. Jackson emphasizes that, in every sphere of human life, ethics develops within the activity itself and is adapted to the characteristics and restrictions of human conduct in the corresponding sphere[21]. Terry Nardin defends a traditional notion of 'international society', and combines it with ideas on the

---

15 M. Frost, op. cit. (ref. 2), p. 121.

16 M. Frost, op. cit. (ref. 2), p. 179.

17 M. Frost, op. cit. (ref. 2), p. 4.

18 According to C. Brown, op. cit. (ref. 1), p. 123, the notion of 'international society' is the following: "The idea of 'international society' plays a major role in traditional international theory. The proposition is that relations between states do not simply create an international *system* but a *society*, the implication being that there is a normative content to these relationships, a 'morality of states' which may be different from the morality that governs individuals, but which is not simply a cloak for self-interest and instrumental behaviour. International society is not based on member states with common or compatible domestic structures, but on the willingness of its members to behave towards each other in ways that conform to its norms, that is, in accordance with international law and custom".

19 T. Nardin, op. cit. (ref. 3).

20 R.H. Jackson, "The Situational Ethics of Statecraft", in: C.J. Nolan (ed.), *Ethics and Statecraft — The Moral Dimension of International Affairs*, Westport: Praeger, 1995.

21 R.H. Jackson, op. cit. (ref. 20).

nature of politics and society developed by Michael Joseph Oakeshott[22]. In his book *On the Human Conduct*, Oakeshott argues that the aim of political philosophy is to analyze the ideal character and postulates of human conduct. According to Oakeshott, every human association is structured in terms of practices, which are different types of interdependent rules which he calls *respublica*. In Oakeshott's words, "what relates *cives* to one another and constitutes civil association is the acknowledgment of the authority of *respublica* and the recognition of subscription to its conditions as an obligation"[23]. Thus, for Oakeshott, law is morally binding because it is made by authorized men according to established procedures. Therefore, from the viewpoint of this approach to normative IR theory, the nature of the international society is pluralist, since states are assumed to have different goals and different notions of what is good and bad, and, therefore, only a form of association that does not assume common purposes is morally legitimate. However, this approach does not provide a criterion by which one can distinguish between international pluralism and moral relativism, and it does not explain "why diversity should be respected *morally* simply because it is a fact about the modern international system"[24].

1.3 Norms and international law

By the term 'international law', one may refer to any of the following somewhat different things, singly or in combination:

(i) Positive international law: the corpus of specific agreements (treaties, conventions, declarations, protocols) that states have made between or among themselves and to which they have formally consented to conform.

(ii) Customary international law: the unwritten corpus of behavior customs known by historical record and followed by informal consensus.

(iii) The principles of international law: ideal principles, such as 'humanity' in the law of war, that are held to underlie both positive and customary international law.

(iv) The theory of international law: the realm of the publicists.

According to Article 38 of the Statute of the International Court of Justice, the previous four categories of international law are four definitive sources for the determination of law in the adjudication of particular cases.

---

22 M.J. Oakeshott, *On Human Conduct*, Oxford: Clarendon Press, 1975.
23 M.J. Oakeshott, op. cit. (ref. 22), p. 149.
24 C. Brown, op. cit. (ref. 1), pp. 125-126.

However, these four categories are not, in any case, formally equal, since the principles of international law are held to underlie both positive and customary international law and the writings of the publicists are theoretical, or interpretive, contributions to the entire corpus of international law.

The original sources of international law reach back into the classical era, and especially to Roman law. In the Middle Ages, civil and canon lawyers founded their contributions to legal thought on the ideas of natural law (*jus naturale*) and law of nations (*jus gentium*) inherited from the Roman legal thought. The ideas of jus naturale and jus gentium inspired modern legal thought, and early naturalistic publicists[25] such as Francisco de Vitoria, Francisco Suarez and Hugo Grotius formulated the conceptual framework of modern international law on the basis of the ideas of jus naturale and jus gentium.

In his *De jure praede* (1605), Grotius[26] argued (against contemporary skeptics such as Michel de Montaigne) that there could be universal moral standards on the basis of which questions of international conflict could be adjudicated. However, departing from the Platonic and the Aristotelian moral tradition, Grotius argued that the foundation of such a universal morality should be self-preservation, and, more specifically, the following two principles: (i) self-preservation must always be legitimate, and (ii) wanton injury of another (i.e., not for reasons of self-preservation) must always be illegitimate. Furthermore, he justified the acquisition of property as follows: the primary form of property appears whenever people seize from a natural world which is not owned by anybody the necessities of life and, gradually, develops through economic and technical change into a modern system of private property. However, Grotius' theory failed to provide satisfactory answers to the new skepticism of David Hume. Since Grotius had departed from the Platonic ontology of the idea of the Good, his naturalistic theory of law was vulnerable to criticism by Hume, who — in the absence of the Platonic idea of the Good — placed emphasis on the useful and agreeable consequences of an agent's action as they spark a spectator's moral approval[27] and, thus, opened an intellectual path to Jeremy Bentham's utilitarianism[28].

---

25 See: R. Tuck, *Natural Rights Theories*, Cambridge: Cambridge University Press, 1979.

26 See: R. Tuck, op. cit. (ref. 25).

27 See: J.L. Mackie, *Hume's Moral Theory*, London: Routledge & Kegan Paul, 1980.

28 See: H.L.A. Hart, *Essays on Bentham, Jurisprudence and Political Theory*, Oxford: Clarendon Press, 1982.

In the history of international law, Jeremy Bentham is primarily known as the person who first used the term 'international law'. It was in 1789 when "international law" first appeared in Bentham's influential *Introduction to the Principles of Morals and Legislation*[29] (printed in 1780 and published in 1789), which was intended to introduce a comprehensive penal code and focuses on the principle of utility. According to Bentham, 'good' is that which produces the greatest amount of pleasure and the minimum amount of pain. As P.J. Kelly argued, for Bentham, the law, in general, "provides the basic framework of social interaction by delimiting spheres of personal inviolability within which individuals can form and pursue their own conceptions of well-being"[30]. Bentham applied his general principle of utility to the conduct of nations, arguing that his principle should be observed even in times of war, when the force inflicted upon the enemy should not exceed that needed to achieve one's objective.

The emotive and consequentionalist morality of Bentham's utilitarianism emphasized 'quantity', as opposed to 'quality', so that he is considered to be the father of 'hedonistic arithmetic'. Indeed, according to Bentham, the quality of pleasures ultimately reduces to their quantity, or at least to their intensity, which consists in the price, or value assigned to them by consciousness. Hence, from such a utilitarian viewpoint, one should interpret each and every particular pleasure or sequence of pleasures in order to make sure that, ultimately, the sum total of experienced quantity of pleasure is equivalent to the energy which is dissipated by consciousness due to the pursuit of pleasure. Thus, Bentham's utilitarianism has two important defects: (i) it is based on the characterization of pleasures only in quantitative terms (in fact, Bentham is restricted only to quantitative classifications of pleasure); (ii) it assumes that, within the framework of all persons' participation in pleasures, individual interest is identified with general interest, but it fails to provide an inter-subjective criterion of pleasure. Additionally, Bentham's theory seems to ignore that — in the absence of a universal idea of the Good — a person can express a form of moral egoism and, thus, subordinate the 'general interest' to one's 'individual interest', or, conversely, the concept of the 'general interest' can become a cause of suppression of the individual will.

---

29 See: H.L.A. Hart, op. cit. (ref. 28).

30 P.J. Kelly, *Utilitarianism and Distributive Justice — Jeremy Bentham and the Civil Law*, Oxford: Oxford University Press, 1990, p. 81.

John Stewart Mill[31] attempted to save utilitarianism from the defects of Bentham's theory by arguing that the character of pleasure is qualitative and not quantitative. According to J.S. Mill, if we ignore the qualitative character of pleasure, we end up with a morality which is suitable for "pigs". Thus, Mill distinguishes pleasures into degrading ones and noble ones, and he argues that the latter are associated with spiritual goods and must be preferred to the first. Even though Mill's utilitarianism is an improved version of Bentham's morality, it remains defective, because it is characterized by antinomies inherent in utilitarianism. According to Mill, there is an empirical (as opposed to rational) criterion of the quality of pleasures. On the basis of this criterion, which, for Mill, is manifested in the noblest minds, experience teaches that — in the absence of other influences (e.g., obligations) — consciousness chooses, and should choose, the noblest pleasures. However, Mill seems to ignore that, on certain occasions, consciousness actually chooses pleasures which are generally considered to be degrading, and that the judgments which are made by those minds which Mill considers to be the 'noblest' ones are always questioned by other minds which pose the following question: on what grounds can a particular pleasure be imposed on another particular pleasure in the name of pleasure? If truth is reduced to pleasure, then we end up in a world where my pleasure simply competes with your pleasure, and there is no objective criterion by which one can evaluate pleasures.

Both the emotive and the consequentionalist aspects of hedonism are sources of significant antinomies, which rule out all versions of emotive and/or utilitarian versions of morality. The emotive character of hedonism presupposes the destruction of personality, since pleasure cannot be a criterion, or a rule by which one can achieve an integrated and unified conscious experience. Instead, from the viewpoint of utilitarianism, every particular pleasure, in order to be fully and most intensely experienced, must, even temporarily, be the unique object of consciousness (i.e., consciousness must be absolutely attached to it). When hedonistic morality is manifested as utilitarianism, it places excessive emphasis on individual interest, and, thus, the antithesis between competing interests is over-emphasized, making the goal of harmonizing competing interests look chimerical. Thus, within the framework of utilitarianism, interest emerges as the most significant aspect

---

31 See: A. Ryan, *J.S. Mill*, London: Routledge & Kegan Paul, 1974.

of pleasure, and, ultimately, it deprives pleasure from its qualitative aspect, even when this is not formally declared.

Hence, the challenges of normative thought urge us to tackle the fundamental moral questions at the level of reason, and not at the levels of experience and instinct. For, ultimately, law presupposes a truth which can safeguard the unquestionable validity of a legal order. As long as such a truth is absent, every legal order lacks a firm foundation and is unstable because it cannot prove its value by itself.

In the 19th century, the German jurist Georg Jellinek, following the philosophical legacy of G.W.F. Hegel, argued that the state expresses the highest values of the nation, and sovereignty is "the quality of a state in virtue of which it alone can be linked legally with its own will"[32]. For this reason, according to Jellinek, acts in which the state exercises its will are acts of self-obligation[33] (*Selbstverflichtung*), and, therefore, international law is the outcome of the state's self-restraint, and not of the imposition of external rules on the behavior of the state. Moreover, following G. Jellinek, the German jurist H. Triepel and the Italian jurists D. Anzilotti and A. Cavaglieri argued that international law is based on the existence of common will among the states and does not necessarily obey to external moral principles.

However, the First World War (1914-1918) destroyed the previous international order and influenced deeply the goals and the content of international law. After the tragic experience of the First World War, the major aim and the major intellectual problem of the publicists were to establish the obligatory character of international law. In the 19th century, international law was primarily a law of mutual deterrence — namely, its priorities were to safeguard and protect the territorial integrity and independence of states, to promote the principle of non-intervention and to safeguard the freedom of action in areas where states could not claim sovereign rights. After the First World War, and especially during the period 1918-1939, international law became primarily a law of international co-operation and co-ordination. The tendency of international law to be transformed from a law of mutual deterrence to a law of co-operation and co-ordination was maintained after the Second World War and culminated on 24 October 1945, when the United Nations officially came into existence upon the ratification of its Charter by the five permanent members of the Security Coun-

---

32 G. Jellinek, *Die Lehre von den Staatenverbindungen*, 1882, p. 34.
33 G. Jellinek, op. cit. (ref. 32).

cil — France, the Republic of China, the Soviet Union, the United Kingdom and the United States — and by a majority of the other 46 signatories.

The period around 1960 marks an increasing international awareness of issues which necessarily have an impact on all parts of the globe (e.g., the global ramifications of a nuclear war, the globalization of international political economy, the communications revolution, international crime, environmental questions and ecological concerns, etc.). Thus, "there was growing realization that an element of community interest was inseparable from self-interest"[34], and a new important development took place in international law. After the 1960s, international law tends to be transformed into a law of international solidarity, emphasizing common, international actions for development, the international, institutional protection of human rights, and the conformity of states to the regulations of the International Seabed Authority. Moreover, Charles R. Beitz[35] has argued that relativizing state sovereignty in favour of increased powers in the hands of international bodies or new global institutions is the only viable way to maintain peace and justice in a world of increasing globalization and complex interdependence.

The fundamental theoretical challenge faced by international law is the general antithesis between the positivist school and the natural law school:

> The positivist school, which developed so rapidly in the pragmatic, optimistic world of the nineteenth century, declared that law as it exists should be analysed empirically, shorn of all ethical elements. Moral aspirations were all well and good but had no part in legal science. Manmade law must be examined as such and the metaphysical speculations of Natural Law rejected because what counted were the practical realities, not general principles which were imprecise and vague, not to say ambiguous. This kind of approach to law in society reached its climax with Kelsen's 'Pure Theory of Law'. Kelsen defined law solely in terms of itself and eschewed any element of justice, which was rather to be considered within the discipline of political science.[36]

The antithesis between the positivist school and the natural law school implies that international law and, generally, normative political thought need to justify their norms, especially in an era when the emergence of glob-

---

34 A.J.R. Groom and D. Powell, "From World Politics to Global Governance — A Theme in Need of a Focus", in: A.J.R. Groom and M. Light (eds), *Contemporary International Relations: A Guide to Theory*, London: Pinter, 1994, p. 82.

35 C.R. Beitz, *Political Theory and International Relations*, Princeton: Princeton University Press, 1979, p. 69.

36 M.N. Shaw, *International Law*, fifth edition, Cambridge: Cambridge University Press, 2003, p. 48.

al problems calls for even more effective institutions and policies of global governance.

1.4 The purpose and the structure of the present book

The purpose of this book is double: first, to explain the interplay between culture and politics and, second, to propose a new approach to political philosophy in general and normative international relations theory in particular based on a new interpretation of Plato's ontology and epistemology.

In chapter 2, I examine the problem of truth and the validity of knowledge as well as the development of nihilism. In this way, I want to evaluate different approaches to truth and to the spiritual capacity of the human being. Furthermore, I place special emphasis on the analysis and the evaluation of Nietzsche's philosophy, because his nihilism has inspired various attacks against the intellectual achievements and ambitions of modernity on behalf of post-modernism and multiculturalism.

In order to understand the meaning of the term 'nihilism', it is useful to study its etymology. The word nihilism derives from the Latin word 'nihilismus', which consists from the Latin term 'hilum', which means cord, and the negative prefix 'ne'. Thus, nihilism refers to that condition in which something has no relation to anything. In such a condition, things being unrelated to each other, there is no 'cosmos', but chaos prevails. Furthermore, when things are unrelated to each other, they cannot be integrated into any spiritual hierarchy, and, thus, they cannot bear any value. Hence, nihilism nullifies values and norms.

The problem of the value and the validity of knowledge is the major cause of 'science wars'. The term 'science wars' is closely associated with the book *Higher Superstition*[37] which was published by the biologist Paul Gross and the mathematician Norman Levitt in 1994. Gross and Levitt blamed the academy for endorsing the Nietzschean position that there were no facts, only interpretations, and that the history of science is essentially a history of power relationships. Gross and Levitt identified their Nietzschean enemy as the "academic left", meaning the feminists, ecologists, sociologists of sci-

---

37 P. Gross and N. Levitt, *Higher Superstition: The Academic Left and Its Quarrels with Science*, Baltimore: Johns Hopkins University Press, 1994.

ence, etc. Moreover, Fromm[38] and Callon[39], supporting the arguments of Gross and Levitt, argued that the post-modernists, literary critics and new historians and anthropologists are also members of the Nietzschean 'camp'. In 1995, Gross, Levitt and Gerald Holton organized a conference called "The Flight from Science and Reason".

In 1996, the journal *Social Text* published, in response, a special issue on the 'science wars'. The aim of the editors of this special issue was to show that the attack on the so-called Nietzschean 'camp' was a symptom of a deeper anxiety in the scientific community. According to the editors of this special issue, the primary cause of this anxiety was the intellectual legitimacy crisis suffered by the Enlightenment ('modernity'). This crisis has been particularly emphasized by M. Horkheimer and T. Adorno[40].

Therefore, it is impossible to talk meaningfully about cultural diplomacy and normative political thought — which is concerned with how things ought to be — without addressing the problems of truth and knowledge, which are the most fundamental cultural issues. Every substantial contribution to cultural diplomacy and normative political thought is inextricably linked to the development of some answers to the following philosophical-cultural questions: Which are the sources of knowledge? Which are the sources of values?

In Chapter 3, I articulate what I consider to be a creative interpretation of Plato's myth of the cave in order to propose an original approach to the problems of knowledge and truth, and, therefore, to open new perspectives for cultural diplomacy, normative political thought and moral philosophy. The interpretation of Plato's philosophy that I propose and especially the emphasis I place on the distinction between the terms 'Platonic idea' and 'concept' imply that the conclusions of many scholars who treat Platonic ideas as concepts — irrespective of whether they feel that they agree or disagree with Plato — are open to serious criticism and that the contribution of Plato to philosophy and political thought can be placed within a more intellectually fruitful analytical framework than the one which dominated Platonic studies in the 19th and the 20th centuries.

---

38 B. Fromm, "Science Wars and Beyond", *Philosophy and Literature*, Vol. 30, 2006, pp. 580-589.
39 M. Callon, "Whose Impostures? Physics at War with the Third Person", *Social Studies of Science*, Vol. 29, 1999, pp. 261-286.
40 M. Horkheimer and T. Adorno, *Dialectic of Enlightenment — Philosophical Fragments*, Stanford: Stanford University Press, 2002.

In Chapter 4, I study the nature and the value of moral consciousness, and, then, building upon the arguments which I have articulated in Chapters 3 and 4, I propose an original approach to the universalistic character of human rights, to justice and to normative issues in international relations. Thus, I propose a post-nihilistic approach to politics based on my interpretation of Plato's theory of ideas.

In the present book, I follow a philosophical approach to international relations. By saying that I follow a 'philosophical approach', I mean a methodical and systematic investigation of the problems which result from the relationship of consciousness to the world and to itself; in other words, the problems which result from a conscious being's attempt to interpret the quality of the incorporation of consciousness, as consciousness of existence, in the reality of the world. These problems refer to the world itself, to consciousness and to the connection between the world and consciousness.

It goes without saying that, like the 'special' sciences, philosophy is also a science, only one of a more general character. For instance, as physics studies the specific structure of matter, so philosophy studies its general nature. However, there is an important difference between philosophy and the 'special' sciences. The 'special' sciences deal with the establishment of relations and laws which, arguably, can be used for the interpretation of the objects of scientific research. By the term 'relation', we mean a set of ordered pairs, usually defined by some rule, i.e., a *relation* is used to describe certain properties of things, whereas 'laws' establish relations between variables, i.e., they generalize sets of information. On the other hand, the aim of philosophy goes beyond the establishment of relations and laws, because it aims, additionally, at evaluating the objects of philosophical research in a unified manner. Thus, by explaining one of its objects, philosophy is in the position to explain all other objects of philosophical research by applying the same criterion. Furthermore, there is another difference between philosophy and science. When, during the course of scientific research, it becomes necessary to refute some scientific statements about the reality of the world and the reality of consciousness, scientists modify these statements in order to adapt them to those statements which have not been falsified yet. On the other hand, philosophers follow a more radical research path: whenever they have to refute a statement, they refute the entire philosophical system which includes the given statement and develop a new framework for the study of their problems. Thus, the difference between philosophy and science does not refer only to the level at which they study their problems, but also it refers to the manner in which these problems are experienced by the mind of the researcher and to consciousness itself.

Philosophy is not only a science, like the other sciences, but it is primarily a state of mind. The very meaning of the word philosophy (derived from the Greek compound philo + sophia = love of wisdom) indicates a special attitude of a philosopher as well as his objective. In particular, philosophy is a free and unprejudiced quest for truth, for the sake of seeking truth (i.e., theorizing) and for the sake of the human being whose consciousness is motivated, attracted and enriched by the quest for truth. Thus, even though philosophy can be considered as a science, i.e., as a systematic form of knowledge ('scientia'), its object is the set of all objects of the other sciences. Moreover, philosophy is the creation of a world of meanings which expresses the reality of the human being, since it is founded on human reason.

CHAPTER 2. THE ITINERARY OF THE EUROPEAN SPIRIT: THE QUEST FOR KNOWLEDGE VERSUS NIHILISM

2.1 From the medieval thought to the Renaissance

The medieval thought subordinated reason to faith and philosophy to theology, requesting from man to recognize afterlife as the purpose of his existence[41]. Characteristic of this thought is the view of Augustine of Hippo[42], according to which authentic knowledge is the knowledge of God and self. All other knowledge, such as the scientific objects of logic, metaphysics and ethics, has value only if and to the extent that it contributes to the knowledge of God. In his book *On the Trinity* (XII, 14), Augustine argues that intelligence is needed for understanding what faith believes, and faith for believing what intelligence understands, and he proceeds as follows: "Faith seeks, understanding finds... And yet again, understanding still seeks Him whom it finds". The function of this pursuit is insight or wisdom ('sapientia'), and it constitutes the highest function of reason when it is directed towards God, i.e., the creative principle (ibid). Thus, Augustine divided ratio into 'ratio scientiae', which seeks to find the elements or principles of

41 See: F.B. Artz, *The Mind of the Middle Ages*, Chicago: University of Chicago Press, 1980 (especially in chapters VII and VIII, Artz studies the development of medieval ideas).

42 See: H.I. Marrou, *St Augustine and His Influence through the Ages*, New York: Harper Torch, 1957; R. Martin, "The Two Cities of Augustine's Political Philosophy", *Journal of the History of Ideas*, Vol. 33, 1972.

nature by an analysis of what is given from the external world, and 'ratio sapientiae', which turns inward (in the world of consciousness), finding there both God and the soul. In his *De libero arbitrio* (II, 9), Augustine argues that 'ratio sapientiae' is superior to 'ratio scientiae' and must govern the latter. By being restricted to the truths of faith, the mental life of the early medieval man was entrenched in a deeply emotional world. The spiritual fruit of this attitude was the development of a mystical theology, which was based on an inner, apophatic experience of the divine.

After the 9th century AD, and especially during the 12th and the 13th centuries, the scholastic theologians initiated a new approach to knowledge — namely, they attempted to explain the truths of faith in a logical manner. In his books *Scripta super libros sententiarum* and *Summa theologiae*, Thomas Aquinas[43] argues that Augustine's ratio sapientiae is the correct method of theology, but he disagrees with Augustine on the distinction between ratio superior and ratio inferior, because, according to Thomas Aquinas, knowledge starts from the world of senses, which is the realm of the ratio inferior (e.g., natural science), and is completed in the mental world and the supernatural, which is the realm of the ratio superior. Thomas Aquinas argued that faith is a gift from the Creator, and it perfects a finite nature, which, without this gift, would remain in a state of spiritual scarcity. For Thomas Aquinas, man's finite nature has a supernatural purpose — namely, the love and direct knowledge of God. However, even though the finite nature of man ought to conform to this supernatural purpose, man's nature can never attain this purpose by itself, because this purpose is supernatural. Thomas Aquinas tackles this antinomy of human existence as follows: faith confers divine grace, which comes from the Creator; because the Creator is responsible for the existence of the human being, even though grace comes from outside, grace works internally, and, therefore, faith is intrinsic to the nature it perfects. Moreover, a nature perfected through faith has its intelligence (or reason) perfected by faith, too. Hence, according to Thomas Aquinas, faith confers on reason the ability to penetrate more deeply in its rational structure.

Thomas Aquinas' thought put cataphatic (rationalistic) theology within a philosophically rigorous setting. Whereas apophatic theology attempts to describe God in terms of what He is not, cataphatic, or natural theology

---

43 See: D.J. O'Connor, *Aquinas and Natural Law*, London: Macmillan, 1967; J. Weisheipl, *Friar Thomas D' Aquino — His Life, Thought and Works*, Oxford: Blackwell, 1974.

describes God 'positively', according to what He has revealed of Himself in Scripture and nature. Therefore, by making God an object of human reason — even under the Thomistic assumption that it is God's grace that perfects human reason — the cataphatic, natural theology of scholasticism explicitly recognizes the value of human reason. In particular, Thomas Aquinas argues that ratio (reason) governs the soul and that the highest characteristic of the human being is man's power of knowing as contemplation of God. Furthermore, Thomas Aquinas argues that love, as a characteristic of the human being, is inferior to ratio, because will is determined by the knowledge of good and evil and hence by ratio. The intellect, or ratio, does not conceive only the idea of the good, but also it knows what is good on every specific occasion, and therefore it determines will. In addition, according to Thomas Aquinas, freedom, as a characteristic of the human being, is inferior to ratio, because freedom needs to be underpinned by ratio, and, therefore, freedom is equivalent to the necessity which follows from knowledge based on reason. This development in the intellectual history of the West had very important spiritual consequences. The dominant role that logic started playing in the spiritual life of the West posed very crucial questions about the certainty/uncertainty of knowledge, which brought a series of cognitive issues into the philosophical foreground.

The 14th century is marked by philosophical controversies over universals. John Duns Scotus[44], in his essays which are organized in the *Opus Parisiense* and *Opus Oxoniense*, followed the Thomistic legacy about universals, according to which universals exist *before* things, as forms in the mind of God, *in* things, as the common nature of things, and *after* things, as abstract concepts in our minds. Hence, conceptual knowledge has a real object, there is a fundamental agreement between thought and reality, and logical notions are not mere acts of thought, but they correspond to reality. But it is not necessary that the correspondence between knowledge and the objects of knowledge be one of identity. According to Duns Scotus, the reality of the universals coexists with the uncertainty and the skepticism which characterize our knowledge about the mind and its functions. Thus, Duns Scotus argues that the proof of God's existence which was articulated by Thomas Aquinas on the basis of a chain of syllogisms which starts from the level of

---

44 See: P.V. Spade, *Five Texts on the Mediaeval Problem of Universals*, Indianapolis: Hackett Publishing, 1994; A.B. Wolter, *Duns Scotus on the Will and Morality*, Washington, DC: The Catholic University of America Press, 1986.

God's creatures (nature) and culminates in the Creator Himself is not certain. For Duns Scotus, 'revealed' truth is uncertain (because it transcends conventional logic), and certain truth is not 'revealed'. Thus, Duns Scotus distinguishes between two different types of truth: the truth of the material world and the truth of the spiritual world. Moreover, he argues that there are two different paths which lead to these two different types of truth: philosophy, which leads to the truth of the material world, and theology, which leads to the truth of the spiritual world. In other words, the supersensible world belongs to the authority of faith, and the sensible world is subject to reason. Hence, in the philosophy of Duns Scotus, natural sciences safeguard their autonomy from theology. This position is a consequence of Duns Scotus' view that knowledge is the outcome of the interaction between rational consciousness and objects which are external to it; this interaction gives birth to mental images of reality. These mental images are — according to Duns Scotus — blurred perceptions, which can be clarified if and to the extent that they become the object of the will. In other words, knowledge is an instrument of will. Contrary to Thomas Aquinas' deterministic rationalism, Duns Scotus argues that, before becoming clarified by the will, perception is merely a potentiality, which becomes an actuality not according to natural (deterministic) logical processes but according to a decision of the will, i.e., on the basis of the values which guide consciousness.

Whereas philosophical realism, as expressed for instance by Thomas Aquinas and Duns Scotus, is the view that universals are real, in the sense that they exist independently of consciousness, nominalism is the view that universals do not exist outside the mind and are not inherent in things. Duns Scotus — even though he did not lack confidence in human reason and he employed the methods of logic in theology and philosophy — emphasized that the articles of faith are capable of rational treatment only *after* we acquire them through revelation and that they cannot be acquired or demonstrated by natural reason alone. The philosophy of Duns Scotus reduced the size of the sphere of provable truth significantly. This shrinkage of the sphere of provable truth suggested to some thinkers a more radical path: no theological truth can be proved by natural reason. This is the view of nominalism, whose great leader was William of Occam[45]. According to William of Occam's *Sentences* and *Summa totius logices*, only particulars exist, and they are the only source of our knowledge. Therefore — he argues — it

---

45 See: C. Michon, *Nominalisme: La théorie de la signification d'Occam*, Paris: J. Vrin, 1994.

is through intuition, or perception, that we become aware of the existence of things. We form universals by abstracting from the particular objects the qualities common to them. Hence, from this viewpoint, universals exist merely as thoughts in the mind and are expressed in words or conventional signs which designate particular similar things. Additionally, for William of Occam, the object of science is only a set of terms, a 'term' being a word endowed with its meaning (i.e., with its conceptual definition).

The Renaissance introduces the Western civilization into 'modernity' by combining elements of the medieval world with new achievements of the Western collective consciousness. The term 'Renaissance' has been used to define a vast intellectual movement that spanned roughly the 14th through the 17th century, but it was originally used much later: the term 'Renaissance' was originally developed by Jules Michelet[46], who used this term in order to characterize the period of the 15th and the 16th centuries as one in which "man found himself. While Vesalius and Servetus revealed to him his physical life, Luther and Calvin, Dumoulin, Cujas, Rabelais, Montaigne, Shakespeare, Cervantes revealed his moral life". The guiding principle of the Renaissance is the revival of the classical ancient spiritual legacy, but this revival took place due to minds which were characterized by a new, anthropocentric spirit. Renaissance humanism was based on classical ancient literature in order to teach trust in education, art and science, to defend reason and the unity between reason and action (or between theory and practice), and to promote linguistic cultivation and the freedom of personal expression. Hence, Martin Luther[47] published a pamphlet entitled *On Christian Liberty* (1520), in which he wrote that the Christian is freed, liberated from bondage to impossible duties, false teachers and illegitimate authorities, and that the Church is a voluntary association.

Renaissance humanism is closely related to a revived interest in classical republicanism and the development of new ideas about 'power', 'sovereignty' and the 'state'. In fact, C.T. Davis[48] and N. Rubinstein[49], in their stud-

---

46 J. Michelet, *Histoire de France au XVIIᵉ Siècle*, Tome VII: Renaissance, Paris: Chamerot, 1857 (published in English by Elibron Classics, Adamant Media Corporation, in 2006).

47 Martin Luther, *Martin Luther: Selections from His Writings*, ed. J. Dillenberger, Garden City, NJ: Doubleday, 1961.

48 C.T. Davis, "An Early Florentine Political Theorist: Fra Remigio de Girolami", *Proceedings of the American Philosophical Society*, Vol. 104, 1960, pp. 662-676.

49 N. Rubinstein, "Political Theories in the Renaissance", in: A. Chastel et al.(eds), *The Renaissance: Essays in Interpretation*, London: Methuen, 1982.

ies of the development of Italian republican ideology after the translation of Aristotle's *Politics*, around 1260, show the manner in which the reversal of the guiding principles of the medieval political thought took place as a result of Renaissance writers such as Brunetto Latini, Ptolemy of Lucca and Remigio de Girolami. In the first book of Thomas Aquinas' *De regimine principum*, we see that, even though Aquinas was familiar with the classical Greek political thought, he was interpreting and using it in a way which was substantially different from the way in which Renaissance thinkers were interpreting and using the classical Greek political thought: Aquinas, inspired by Aristotle, was recognizing three types of government, but he preferred monarchy to the government of many, even though he was admitting that the latter has some advantages. On the other hand, Brunetto Latini, after his acquaintance with the classical Greek thought, came to the conclusion that communal government is better than monarchy, as he argued in his *Trésor*, written in exile in Paris in the 1260s, after his time in office as chancellor of Florence's first republican government. Moreover, Ptolemy of Lucca, in his own *De regimine principum* (ca. 1302-5), argues in favour of republican government and draws a close analogy between the Greek polis, "which is a plurality or city", and "the political rule" of Italian cities[50].

The progress in the natural sciences[51] and their combination with philosophy, the recognition of individual consciousness, the creation of republics and nation-states after the end of the religious wars (1648), and the

---

50 N. Rubinstein, op. cit. (ref. 49), p. 158.

51 We read in F.M.A. de Voltaire's *Essay on the Manners of Nations* (originally published in 1756), chapters 121 and 118: "True philosophy did not begin to shine on men until the end of the sixteenth century. Galileo was the first to make physics speak the language of truth and reason; it was shortly before this that Copernicus had discovered the true world-system... Philosophy, always hampered, could not, in the sixteenth century, make as much progress as the fine arts... The representation of light and shade in painting, developed by Leonardo. Charles V overturned the old world, discovered and conquered the new; trade between the East Indies and Europe was established by means of the ships and arms of Portugal... At that time Nature produced extraordinary men in almost every field, especially in Italy. What is still striking in that outstanding century is that despite the wars caused by ambition and the religious disputes which had begun to disturb European states, that same genius which made the fine arts flourish at Rome, Naples, Florence, Venice, Ferrara, and brought their light from Italy to Europe, first refined men's manners over almost all Christendom. This great change was due in part to the court of Francis I... Prosperity made its contribution... Industries were stimulated everywhere... in a word, Europe saw the birth of great days".

theory of natural law[52] by contrast with absolute monarchy gave rise to a new reality which is characterized by the debate between rationalism and empiricism and is always founded on the reflective man, i.e., on the 'subject'. In the 17th century, the dominant view among European philosophers was that consciousness is a philosophical category which is distinct from that of the world, and which, as pure thought, looks for the foundations of its own knowledge in order for its judgments to form a consistent and unified whole.

2.2 The controversy between rationalism and empiricism

According to rationalism, there are cognitively significant ways in which we can acquire knowledge through reason and independently of sense perception, i.e., there are cases where the content of our knowledge transcends sense experience and thus reason can provide additional information about reality. On the other hand, according to empiricism, experience is the ultimate source of all knowledge and concepts. In the 17th and the 18th centuries, the protagonists of rationalism were René Descartes, Baruch de Spinoza and Gottfried Wilhelm Leibniz, and the protagonists of empiricism were David Hume, John Locke and George Berkeley.

Descartes argues that knowledge requires certainty, but we can never be sure our sensory impressions are not part of a dream or a massive deception. Thus, Descartes proposes the intuition/deduction thesis, according to which intuition is a form of rational insight and deduction is a process in which we derive conclusions from intuited premises through valid arguments, so that intuition and deduction provide us with knowledge a priori, i.e., independent of sense perceptions. Descartes writes in his *Rules for the Direction of our Native Intelligence*: "all knowledge is certain and evident cognition"[53] and when we "review all the actions of the intellect by means of which we are able to arrive at a knowledge of things with no fear of being mistaken", we "recognize only two: intuition and deduction"[54].

---

52 Within the framework of Renaissance political thought, 'natural law' refers to a law which is normative as well as natural; in other words, it refers to some principle or principles of objectively right conduct whose rightness is immanent in the nature of man or things.

53 R. Descartes, *Rules for the Direction of our Native Intelligence (originally published in 1628)*, in: *Descartes: Selected Philosophical Writings*, trans. J. Cottingham, R. Stoothoff and D. Murdoch, Cambridge: Cambridge University Press, 1988, Rule II, p. 1

54 R. Descartes, op. cit. (ref. 53), Rule III, p. 3.

However, Descartes' thought created significant problems. First of all, his argument that knowledge requires certainty rules out a significant part of the knowledge we assume we have acquired in regular, everyday life. Second, intuition is not necessarily a source of necessary knowledge. Since it is possible for someone to deceive us, it logically follows that we should doubt not only our sense perceptions but also our intuitions. Indeed, a deceiver might cause us to have false empirical beliefs (i.e., sense perceptions about non-existent things) and intuit false judgments, too. Descartes' response to this criticism was given in his book *Meditations*, where he argued as follows: no such deceiver can interfere with our intuitions and with the deductions which are based on our intuitive premises because God, who is not a deceiver, guarantees the truth of intuition as innate knowledge, and hence the knowledge which is based on the intuition/deduction thesis is certain[55]. However, the problem with this argument — known as the Cartesian Circle — is that Descartes' explanation of the manner in which we acquire this certain knowledge begs the question, since it attempts to deduce the conclusion that all intuitive knowledge is true from intuited premises (truthful God). Furthermore, Descartes' explanation of the manner in which we acquire infallible knowledge does not tackle a problem Descartes himself noted in his *Rules*: Long deductions are determined by our fallible memory[56].

Spinoza rejects the Cartesian distinction between God and the natural world, but he completely agrees with Descartes' intuition/deduction thesis. Therefore, in Spinoza's philosophical system, God is identified with nature, God's reason is identified with natural necessities, theology reduces to the geometric method, and man's perfection reduces to a process according to which man conceives the truth of God within the natural world and conforms to the logical order of the universe[57]. Contrary to Descartes, Spinoza argues that the ego is not self-conscious, but it is mirrored in the logically consistent structure of the natural world (which Spinoza identifies with God), and, by mirroring itself in the logically consistent structure of the natural world — namely, by affirming a pantheistic unity of the world — the ego knows itself (acquires its image). Therefore, Spinoza develops a

---

55 R. Descartes, *Meditations*, in *Descartes: Selected Philosophical Writings (originally published in 1641)*, trans. J. Cottingham, R. Stoothoff and D. Murdoch, Cambridge: Cambridge University Press, 1988.

56 R. Descartes, op. cit. (ref. 53), Rule VII, p. 7.

57 See E. Curley, *Behind the Geometric Method*, Princeton: Princeton University Press, 1988.

mechanistic cosmo-conception which rules out both the subjective content (experience) of sense perceptions and the carrier of those personal experiences, i.e., the subject.

Leibniz reformulated the intuition/deduction thesis as follows:

> The senses, although they are necessary for all our actual knowledge, are not sufficient to give us the whole of it, since the senses never give anything but instances, that is to say particular or individual truths. Now all the instances which confirm a general truth, however numerous they may be, are not sufficient to establish the universal necessity of this same truth, for it does not follow that what happened before will happen in the same way again... From which it appears that necessary truths, such as we find in pure mathematics, and particularly in arithmetic and geometry, must have principles whose proof does not depend on instances, nor consequently on the testimony of the senses, although without the senses it would never have occurred to us to think of them.[58]

In other words, Leibniz defends the intuition/deduction thesis not in order to know the nature of knowledge itself (which was the purpose of Descartes' rationalism) but in order to know the nature of the object of knowledge. According to Leibniz, mathematics, metaphysics, logic and morality are areas in which our knowledge outstrips the knowledge that can be provided by the senses, because judgments in these areas involve forms of necessity which transcend experience. Indeed, in mathematics, for instance, many propositions are known to be necessarily true, even though none of our experiences warrants a belief in the necessity of such truths. On the other hand, Leibniz's argument becomes weaker and vaguer if we ask the following question: what is the source of the reliability of our intuitions about the external world? Does our intuition of a particular true proposition follow from some causal interaction between consciousness and the external world, and what is the nature of this causal interaction?

The previous questions have been emphasized by empiricists. In particular, Locke rejects rationalism in the form of any version of the innate knowledge or innate concept theses and ties all concepts to experience, even though he adopts the intuition/deduction thesis with regard to our knowledge of God's existence. Locke is attributed with developing the theory of "tabula rasa" (blank tablet), according to which the human mind is

---

58 G. Leinbiz, *New Essays on Human Understanding (originally published in 1704)*, in *Leinbiz: Philosophical Writings*, ed. G.H.R. Parkinson, trans. M. Morris and G.H.R. Parkinson, London: J.M. Dent & Sons, 1973, pp. 150-151.

at birth a blank slate and data are added and rules for processing data are formed as a consequence of one's sensory experiences[59].

Berkeley followed a more radical path to empiricism, by arguing that things only exist as a result of their being perceived or because they are the entity which perceives. According to Berkeley, the true cause of any phenomenon is a spirit, and most often it is the spirit of God, and thus it cannot be known as such, but the regularities we discover in the natural world provide the sort of explanation proper to science:

> If therefore we consider the difference there is betwixt natural philosophers and other men, with regard to their knowledge of the *phenomena*, we shall find it consists, not in an exacter knowledge of the efficient cause that produces them, for that can be no other than the *will of a spirit*, but only in a greater largeness of comprehension, whereby analogies, harmonies, and agreements are discovered in the works of Nature, and the particular effects explained, that is, reduced to general rules, which rules grounded on the analogy, and uniformness observed in the production of natural effects, are most agreeable, and sought after by the mind; for that they extend our prospect beyond what is present, and near to us, and enable us to make very probable conjectures, touching things that may have happened at very great distances of time and place, as well as to predict things to come.[60]

Hume divides all true propositions into two categories:

> All the objects of human reason or inquiry may naturally be divided into two kinds, to wit, 'Relations of Ideas', and 'Matters of Fact'. Of the first are the sciences of Geometry, Algebra, and Arithmetic, and, in short, every affirmation which is either intuitively or demonstratively certain. That the square of the hypotenuse is equal to the square of the two sides is a proposition which expresses a relation between these figures. That three times five is equal to half of thirty expresses a relation between these numbers. Propositions of this kind are discoverable by the mere operation of thought, without dependence on what is anywhere existent in the universe. Though there never were a circle or triangle in nature, the truths demonstrated by Euclid would forever retain their certainty and evidence. Matters of fact, which are the second objects of human reason, are not ascertained in the same manner, nor is our evidence of their truth, however great, of a like nature with the foregoing. The contrary of every matter of fact is still possible, because it can never

---

59 J. Gibson, *Locke's Theory of Knowledge and its Historical Relations*, Cambridge: Cambridge University Press, 1968.

60 G. Berkeley, *Of the Principles of Human Knowledge*, in: *The Works of George Berkeley, Bishop of Cloyne*, eds A.A. Luce and T.E. Jessop, London: Thomas Nelson and Sons, 1948-1957, Vol. 2, p. 105.

imply a contradiction and is conceived by the mind with the same facility and distinctness as if ever so conformable to reality.[61]

According to Hume, intuition and deduction can, indeed, provide us with certain knowledge (such as the knowledge of mathematical and logical truths), but this knowledge is not substantive knowledge of the external world; instead, this knowledge is only knowledge of the relations of our own ideas. Moreover, Hume argues that, contrary to what rationalists argue, even knowledge in morals is not the result of infallible intuition and deduction, but it is empirically gained:

> Morals and criticism are not so properly objects of the understanding as of taste and sentiment. Beauty, whether moral or natural, is felt more properly than perceived. Or if we reason concerning it and endeavour to fix the standard, we regard a new fact, to wit, the general taste of mankind, or some other fact which may be the object of reasoning and inquiry.[62]

In addition, Hume attempts to deconstruct the rationalist appeals to our knowledge in metaphysics as follows:

> If we take in our hand any volume — of divinity or school metaphysics, for instance — let us ask, Does it contain any abstract reasoning concerning quantity or number? No. Does it contain any experimental reasoning concerning matter of fact and existence? No. Commit it then to the flames, for it can contain nothing but sophistry and illusion.[63]

2.3 The Enlightenment

The 18th century is mainly the age of the Enlightenment. In fact, the Enlightenment spans roughly the historical period between the English and the French Revolutions (1688-1789), and its characteristic values are the following: (i) independence of thought, (ii) freedom of the individual to use its reason in all areas of life and doubt traditional patterns of thought and social organization, and (iii) cultivation of moral sensitivity towards a transcendental source of values, which was encouraged by the Protestant pursuit of a personal, direct relationship between man and God. In 1784, in

---

61 D. Hume, *An Inquiry Concerning Human Understanding (originally published in 1748)*, Indianapolis, IN: Bobbs-Merrill, 1955, Section IV, Part 1, p. 40.
62 D. Hume, op. cit. (ref. 61), Section XII, Part 3, p. 173.
63 D. Hume, op. cit. (ref. 61), Section XII, Part 3, p. 173.

his famous essay "Answering the Question: What Is Enlightenment?", Immanuel Kant defined the Enlightenment as follows:

> Enlightenment is man's emergence from his self-imposed immaturity. Immaturity is the inability to use one's understanding without guidance from another. This immaturity is self-imposed when its cause lies not in lack of understanding, but in lack of resolve and courage to use it without guidance from another. *Sapere Aude!* [dare to know] 'Have courage to use your own understanding!' — that is the motto of Enlightenment. Laziness and cowardice are the reasons why so great a proportion of men, long after nature has released them from alien guidance, nonetheless gladly remain in lifelong immaturity, and why it is so easy for others to establish themselves as their guardians. It is so easy to be immature... Perhaps a revolution can overthrow autocratic despotism and profiteering or power-grabbing oppression, but it can never truly reform a manner of thinking; instead, new prejudices, just like the old ones they replace, will serve as a leash for the great unthinking mass. Nothing is required for this enlightenment, however, except freedom; and the freedom in question is the least harmful of all, namely, the freedom to use reason publicly in all matters. But on all sides I hear: 'Do not argue!' The officer says, 'Do not argue, drill!' The tax man says, 'Do not argue, pay!' The pastor says, 'Do not argue, believe!'... In this we have examples of pervasive restrictions on freedom. But which restriction hinders enlightenment and which does not, but instead actually advances it? I reply: The public use of one's reason must always be free, and it alone can bring about enlightenment among mankind; the private use of reason may, however, often be very narrowly restricted, without otherwise hindering the progress of enlightenment. By the public use of one's own reason I understand the use that anyone as a scholar makes of reason before the entire literate world. I call the private use of reason that which a person may make in a civic post or office that has been entrusted to him.[64]

The most influential philosophers of the Enlightenment were David Hume and Immanuel Kant. The philosophy of Hume is characterized by a reaction against the Enlightenment's steady faith in the human reason. Hume discusses skepticism in his *Treatise of Human Nature*, Book I, Part IV, and in his *Inquiry Concerning Human Understanding*, Section XII, in order to undermine ordinary claims to knowledge. However, skepticism is neither a

---

64 Kant's essay "Answering the Question: What Is Enlightenment?" (German: "*Beantwortung der Frage: Was ist Aufklärung?*") was originally published in the December 1784 publication of the *Berlinische Monatsschrift (Berlin Monthly)*, edited by Friedrich Gedike and Johann Erich Biester, as a reply to the question posed a year earlier by the Reverend Johann Friedrich Zöllner, who was also an official in the Prussian government. See: H.J. Reiss (ed.), *Kant's Political Writings*, Cambridge: Cambridge University Press, 1979, p. 54.

new phenomenon in the history of philosophy — since the father of skepticism is the ancient Greek philosopher Pyrrho (ca. 360 BC – ca. 270 BC) — nor an unavoidable conclusion of the investigation of the problem of knowledge.

If truth — whether it is assumed that it exists objectively or that it is a creature of the intellect — is a value, then access to truth — namely, knowledge — consists a value, too. The successive stages of the interaction between (external) reality and consciousness, as this interaction is structured by the logical confirmation of truth, do not constitute an automatically given or self-evident series of operations; instead, they are consequences of cognitive operations which are often highly dramatic and complex mental voyages. The value of the different results of such a dramatic and complex mental voyage is often an object of doubt, and thus the evaluation of knowledge in general is susceptible to doubt. Hence, the problem of doubt about the value of knowledge (i.e., skepticism) plays an important role in the history of philosophy and it was justly emphasized by both rationalist and empiricist philosophers in the 17th and the 18th centuries. However, absolute skepticism, i.e., an extreme version of doubt about the value of knowledge, is self-contradictory, and even moderate skepticism, such as the skepticism of Hume, can be effectively opposed.

The different skeptical arguments can be divided into four groups: (i) The first form of skepticism emphasizes that we can know only very few of the qualities of any object of our consciousness, and thus the substance of every object of our consciousness remains unknown. However, in opposition to this argument, one can point that limited knowledge does not mean invalid knowledge and that the knowledge of specific, significant qualities of an object of our consciousness is a valid, significant form of knowledge of the given object. (ii) The second form of skepticism emphasizes that the senses and reason can provide us with false impressions. Indeed, our senses are imperfect, i.e., fallible, and, under different circumstances, they can present the same sensible objects in different ways and with the same level of plausibility every time. Similarly, our intellect can confuse dreams with reality. However, in opposition to this argument, one can point that the fallibility of sensible knowledge as well as dreams are susceptible to control by reason and that there are, at least within certain conceptual communities, evident truths and principles, such as the principle of contradiction[65] (i.e., contradictory statements cannot both at the same time be true). (iii) The third form of skepticism points that morality and legislation are different from one society to another, and hence knowledge in the areas of morality and legislation is uncertain. However, one may counter-argue that these differences are due to different partial circumstances. (iv) The fourth form of skepticism consists in the argument that our reason operates based on tautologies, i.e., logical statements in which the conclusion is equivalent to the premise. However, this skeptical argument can be opposed in two ways. First, one can counter-argue that the sin of being committed to a tautology is smaller than the sin of completely refusing to give any value to reason, since the latter is an obvious contradiction. Second, following Michael Nicholson, one can point that:

> Apart from the rather obvious uses of mathematical statements which are tautological, there is still a use for tautologies in the development of science. That they occur is clear enough... However, the development of tautological frameworks is only one stage in the process of trying to develop a theory of some phenomenon... and a preliminary stage at that. It is a useful stage nevertheless. The conceptual frameworks, tautological though they are, determine the categories which are deemed relevant to the argument... The tautological theory is only the beginning. If a theory is found to be tautologous (and it may not be obvious at first sight) then the next stage is to restate the theory in a non-tautologous form, either in its entirety or by breaking it down into sub-theories which are themselves non-tautologous even if the group itself is tautologous.[66]

The fundamental epistemological question posed and studied by Kant is: 'how are synthetic judgments a priori possible?' Kant is focused on this question because he believes that one can arrive at certain knowledge only if he proves the validity of synthetic judgments a priori. In particular, Kant writes in his *Critique of Pure Reason*: "In the solution of the above problem is comprehended at the same time the possibility of the use of pure reason in the foundation and construction of all sciences which contain theoretical

---

65 However, according to Lucien Lévy-Bruhl, the primitive mind does not address contradictions, since, according to Lévy-Bruhl's "law of participation", in the mind of primitive people, the same thing or phenomenon may at the same time be several entirely different forms of being. See: L. Lévy-Bruhl, *Primitive Mentality* (originally published in 1922), New York: AMS Press, 1978.

66 M. Nicholson, *Causes and Consequences in International Relations — A Conceptual Study*, London: Pinter, 1996, pp. 96-97.

knowledge a priori of objects"[67]. Additionally, he writes in his *Prolegomena*: "Upon the solution of this problem depends the existence or downfall of the science of metaphysics"[68]. In his *Critique of Pure Reason*, Kant introduced the distinction between 'analytic' and 'synthetic' judgments. He characterizes an analytic judgment as one in which the predicate merely expresses something which is already contained (though hidden) in the subject (e.g., "all bachelors are unmarried"), and, therefore, analytic judgments tell us nothing about the way the world is, but merely clarify what is involved in our concepts. Additionally, analytic truths are a priori — namely, knowable independently of any particular experience. By contrast, a synthetic judgment is one in which the concept of the predicate brings to the concept of the subject something which lies completely "outside" the subject, "although it stands in connection with the subject"[69].

Kant defines real knowledge as one which is achieved through judgments which add one concept to another in such a way that the content of the second was not already contained — at least for the knowing subject — in the first. Such judgments are called synthetic, and hence, according to Kant, theoretical knowledge is possible if and only if the connection between predicate and subject is synthetic in this sense. However, the fundamental epistemological question posed by Kant has a second part: it demands that these judgments (synthetic) must be acquired a priori, i.e., without any reference to empirical data (in order to be certain). In other words, the previous Kantian epistemological question contains two presuppositions: first, that we need other means of attaining knowledge besides experience, and, second, that all knowledge attained through experience is approximately valid. Kant does not doubt the existence of such judgements (i.e., synthetic a priori). In fact, Kant, like Hume, rejected metaphysics as a theoretical knowledge of non-empirical ('transcendental') subjects (e.g., God, freedom and immortality) but, unlike Hume, he accepted metaphysics as a theoretical knowledge of knowledge (i.e., as an epistemological attitude).

---

67 I. Kant, *Critique of Pure Reason*, Introduction to 2nd edition, Section VI. The standard German edition of Kant's works is: Königlichen Preussischen (later Deutschen) Akademie der Wissenschaften (ed.), *Kants gesammelte Schriften*, Berlin: Georg Reimer (later Walter De Gruyter). The best English edition of Kant's works is: P. Guyer and A. Wood (eds.), *The Cambridge Edition of the Works of Immanuel Kant*, Cambridge: Cambridge University Press.

68 I. Kant, *Prolegomena*, Section V.

69 I. Kant, op. cit. (ref. 67), Introduction to 2nd edition, Section VI.

Kant soon realized that the British empiricism, even though it is useful as a tool against intellectual laziness, is not a product of sharp analytical skills, but it is a consequence of poor imagination. Thus, Kant's epistemology has the character of a critique of both empiricism and rationalism. He disagrees with empiricism on the grounds that the mind is not a "tabula rasa" which passively receives knowledge of the world through the senses, and he disagrees with rationalism on the grounds that reason is not a sufficient source of knowledge because knowledge demands both concepts and sensible data. In the *Critique of Pure Reason*, he argues:

> Experience no doubt teaches us that this or that object is constituted in such and such a manner, but not that it could not possibly exist otherwise. Experience never exhibits strict and absolute, but only assumed and comparative universality (by induction).[70]

In *Prolegomena*, the following version of the previous argument is used:

> Firstly, as regards the *sources* of metaphysical knowledge, the very conception of the latter shows that these cannot be empirical. Its principles (under which not merely its axioms, but also its fundamental conceptions are included) must consequently never be derived from experience, since it is not *physical* but *metaphysical* knowledge, i.e., knowledge beyond experience, that is wanted.[71]

Moreover, Kant argues as follows:

> Before all, be it observed, that proper mathematical propositions are always judgments *a priori*, and not empirical, because they carry along with them the conception of necessity, which cannot be given by experience. If this be demurred to, it matters not; I will then limit my assertion to *pure* mathematics, the very conception of which implies that it consists of knowledge altogether non-empirical and a priori.[72]

Kant was of course aware of the fact that most synthetic judgments are *a posteriori*, i.e., their truth value can be determined only by reference to empirical data. However, he held the metaphysical position that there is a special class of synthetic judgments whose truth value can be determined a priori, i.e., independently of experience.

The starting point of Kant's epistemology is experience, i.e., any phenomenal object or system of phenomenal objects. The opening sentence of the Introduction to the second edition of the *Critique of Pure Reason* is: "There

---

70 I. Kant, op. cit. (ref. 67), Introduction to 2nd edition, Section II.
71 I. Kant, *Theorie der Erfahrung*, pp. 90ff.
72 I. Kant, op. cit. (ref. 67), Introduction to 2nd edition, Section V.

can be no doubt that all knowledge begins with experience". According to Kant, any object of experience can be analyzed into three constituents: (i) discrete qualities (called "impressions" by Hume), (ii) spatial and temporal continua (the so-called "forms of intuition"), and (iii) the pure concepts or categories. In his *Transcendental Aesthetic*, Kant explains that his purpose is to "isolate" ingredient (ii) from ingredients (i) and (iii), i.e., to isolate sensibility by taking away from it everything which the intellect thinks through concepts and also everything that belongs to sensation, so that the only thing that remains is "pure intuition". After this preliminary analysis of experience, Kant proceeds with the theory of sense perception.

In his *Transcendental Aesthetic*, Kant argues that, in order to perceive, we must have sensations (e.g., color, sound, etc.), but mere sensation is not real knowledge. Mere sensation is equivalent to a modification of consciousness, i.e., a mere subjective state produced in us by something external to our consciousness. Hence, if our mind were a "tabula rasa" which merely received impressions from outside, then the subject should be isolated in his or her own subjectivity and would be unable to perceive the reality of the world. For Kant, real knowledge requires sense qualities, referring to the content of experience, and the forms of space and time, constituting the form of experience. The forms of arranging sensations in space and time are not sensations themselves, because they are not empirical (a posteriori) forms of intuition but are inherent (a priori) in the nature of the mind. Thus, our sensations are objectified by being related to external objects, by being projected into space and by being ordered in time. According to Kant, it is due to this peculiar human way of perceiving that there is an objective ('external') world at all. Kant's theory of sense perception is based on a dialectical relationship between subjectivity and objectivity: space and time are subjective in the sense that we know only the products of our peculiar way of perceiving things (a way that need not characterize all creatures), and also space and time are objective in the sense that all phenomena are arranged in space and time.

However, real knowledge is not equivalent to the spatio-temporal organization of experience. Percepts must somehow be related to each other, instead of being disconnected elements of space-time. For instance, the perception of fire followed by the perception of cooked meat is not the same as knowing that the fire can be used in order to cook food. We must somehow connect these two experiences in thought in order to be able to form the judgment that the meet was cooked by the fire. In his *Transcendental Analytic*, Kant argues that real knowledge would be impossible without a synthetic, thinking mind, without reason. On the one hand, sensibility is receptive, and the forms of sensibility are intuitional. On the other hand, reason is active and conceptual. By the term 'reason' (rational understanding), Kant and his followers, mean a pre-existent (a priori) structure within the framework of which there exist various functions of categories[73], which, when they are adequately activated, can connect isolated segments of sensation (i.e., empirical data) into a whole, thus allowing the formulation of synthetic statements, and leading to a creative outstripping of the level of experience. Our world of experience becomes possible due to these categories. Kant argues that the phenomenal order, i.e., nature as we perceive it, depends on the forms of our intellect, not vice versa, as the empiricists argue. Therefore, within the framework of the Kantian philosophy, the rational human understanding prescribes its laws to nature, safeguarding the spiritual autonomy of man.

To explain the manner in which categories (i.e., pure, non-empirical concepts), which are intellectual entities, are applied to precepts, which are sensible entities, Kant introduces a third mediating entity which he calls the "transcendental schema". By the term schema, Kant means the procedural rule by which a category is associated with a mental image of an ob-

---

73 Kant finds that there are twelve kinds of pure concepts or categories of the understanding based on reason; these are arranged in four groups of three each as follows: The first group expresses the categories of quantity: totality, plurality, unity. It includes the following judgments: (1) the universal judgment (e.g., all dogs are animals), (2) the particular judgment (e.g., some fruits are sweet), and (3) the singular judgment (e.g., Isaac Newton was a natural scientist). The second group expresses the categories of quality: reality, negation, limitation. It includes the following judgments: (1) the affirmative judgment (e.g., electrical energy is a form of potential energy), (2) the negative judgment (e.g., the intentionality of consciousness is not extended), and (3) the infinite judgment (e.g., the intentionality of consciousness is unextended). The third group expresses the categories of relation: inherence and subsistence (or substance and accident), causality and dependence (or cause and effect), community/reciprocity between the active and the passive. It includes the following judgments: (1) the categorical judgment (e.g., the body is heavy), (2) the hypothetical judgment (e.g., if temperature increases, then entropy increases), and (3) the disjunctive judgment (e.g., energy forms are either potential or kinetic). The fourth group expresses the categories of morality: possibility and impossibility, existence and non-existence, necessity and contingency. It includes the following judgments: (1) the problematical judgment (e.g., this may be hot), (2) the assertory judgment (e.g., this is hot), and (3) the apodictic judgment (e.g., every effect must have a cause). These twelve rules function like a filter between our minds and the external world.

ject. According to Kant, it is produced by the imagination through the pure form of time. The category of quantity is expressed in the schema of time-series. The category of quality is expressed in the schema of time-content. The categories of substance, causality, and reciprocal action are expressed in the schema of time-order (permanence, succession, and simultaneity). The categories of possibility, actuality, and necessity are expressed in the schema of time-comprehension.

Kant has shown that knowledge involves perception, and, since things-in-themselves cannot be perceived by the senses, it follows that, in sense perception, we know only the way things appear to consciousness, not what they are in themselves. Moreover, things-in-themselves cannot be perceived or intuited by the intellect because the mind's eye cannot see things directly, as they really are. Hence, if we apply categories to such a thing-in-itself, we cannot prove the validity of this knowledge. For instance, we cannot prove that every existing thing corresponds to a substance in an intelligible world. In general, metaphysics is impossible when it refers to non-empirical entities. However, even though we cannot rationally understand things-in-themselves, we can think things-in-themselves as things to which none of the predicates of sense perception applies. In other words, even though the thing-in-itself is essentially *unknowable*, the concept of the thing-in-itself — called "noumenon" (plural: "noumena") — as something not knowable by the senses, but as something which can be known by intellectual intuition, is *thinkable*, and it operates as a limiting concept, i.e., as the border of the mental capabilities of the human being.

2.4 Kantian accounts of politics and cosmopolitanism

Kant's political philosophy is part of his practical philosophy, which he exposed in his book *Groundwork for the Metaphysics of Morals*. His *Metaphysics of Morals* has two distinct parts: the "Doctrine of Right" and the "Doctrine of Virtue". Kant separates political rights and duties from what we might call morals in the narrow sense. In particular, Kant[74] argues that 'right' (i.e., public legal justice) has the following characteristics: (i) it is related only to actions that have influence on other persons (i.e., duties to the self are excluded), (ii) it is not related to the wish but only to the choice (i.e., decisions which bring about actions) of others, and (iii) it is not related to the

---

74 I. Kant, *Groundwork for the Metaphysics of Morals*, p. 230.

substantive content ('matter') of the other's act but only to its form. In order to explain condition (iii), Kant mentions the example of trade, which, from the viewpoint of right, must have the form of being freely agreed by both buyers and sellers, but it can have any substantive content or purpose the agents want. Furthermore, Kant[75] argues that both right and virtue relate to freedom but in different ways: right concerns outer freedom and virtue concerns inner freedom (governing passions), or, in other words, right concerns acts themselves independent of the motive an agent may have for performing them, whereas virtue concerns the proper motive for dutiful actions.

According to Kant, "there is only one innate right", and this right is "freedom (independence from being constrained by another's choice), insofar as it can coexist with the freedom of every other in accordance with a universal law"[76]. The right of freedom is, for Kant, the only basis of the state, and he adds that the welfare of citizens cannot be the basis of state power. In particular, Kant[77] argues that a state cannot legitimately impose any particular conception of happiness (welfare) upon its citizens, because to do so would be equivalent to treating citizens as children, assuming that they are unable to understand what is truly useful or harmful to themselves. Moreover, Kant[78] distinguishes an ethics of autonomy — whose prescriptions are based on will, or practical reason itself — and an ethics of heteronomy — in which something independent of the will, such as welfare, is the basis of the law.

Given the tension between virtue and right, or between a morality and a public legal justice, Kant uses the concept of 'ends' in order to connect the moral to the political-legal realm. In fact, Kant originally used the concept of 'ends' in his *Critique of Judgment*, in which he argues that nature can be approximately (never exactly) known through purposes and functions which transcend mechanical causality, that persons as free agents have purposes which strive to realize, and that art has a "purposiveness without purpose" which makes it the symbol of morality. Therefore, since 'ends' can link nature, human freedom and art, it logically follows that they can operate as a bridge connecting morality to the political-legal system (morality and the political-legal system being two forms of human freedom).

---

75 I. Kant, op. cit. (ref. 74), pp. 406-407, 218-221.
76 I. Kant, op. cit. (ref. 74), p. 237.
77 I. Kant, op. cit. (ref. 74), pp. 290-291.
78 I. Kant, op. cit. (ref. 74), pp. 440-441.

According to Kant's *Metaphysics of Morals*, in the moral realm, "good will" means never universalizing a maxim which would not treat humanity (whether in your own person or in the person of any other) as an end in itself. This is Kant's formula of autonomy. Within the framework of Kantian teleology, morality and politics-law can be connected as follows: If all persons had good will, then they would treat all others as ends in themselves, thus giving rise to a "kingdom of ends". Even though this is man's moral duty, this is not actually the case, because of the pathology of man's moral condition. Hence, if good will means treating other persons as ends in themselves, and if public legal justice is equivalent to the observance of some moral ends, then public legal justice is a partial realization of the state of affairs which would be created if all wills were good.

In his *Metaphysical Principles of Virtue*, Kant explains his view of politics as the legal realization of moral ends as follows:

> Man in the system of nature... is of little significance and, along with the other animals, considered as products of the earth, has an ordinary value... But man as a person, i.e., as the subject of a morally practical reason, is exalted above all price. For as such a one (*homo noumenon*) he is not to be valued merely as a means to the ends of other people, or even to his own ends, but is to be prized as an end in himself.[79]

Therefore, the notion that persons are ends in themselves provides 'good will' with an objective end, on which the categorical imperative is founded, and determines what politics can legitimately do. As a result, Kant's philosophy and political thought do not reduce to what Hegel called a formal doctrine based on chill duty, but it endows humanism with a philosophically rigorous structure.

In his theory of international politics, Kant distinguishes the term "Völkerrecht", which means the right of peoples or nations, and which he discusses as cosmopolitan right, from the term "Staatenrecht", which means the right of states. Kant argues that states must be considered to be in a state of nature relative to one another and that, like men in a state of nature, they must be considered to be in a state of war with each other. According to Kant's normative theory of international relations, like individuals, the states ought to leave this state of nature in order to form an international society, under a social contract, which, in this case, is equivalent to a league of states. However, before the creation of such a league of states, a state

---

79 I. Kant, *Metaphysical Principles of Virtue*, pp. 96-97.

does have a right to go to war against another state, if the latter threatens or follows an aggressive policy against the first[80]. Moreover, Kant argues that any declaration of war ought to be approved by the people "as co-legislating members of a state"[81]; for, rulers who wage war without their subjects' consent treat their subjects as mere means, instead of treating them as ends in themselves. In Kant's words: citizens "must therefore give their free assent, through their representatives, not only to waging war in general but also to each particular declaration of war"[82]. In addition, according to Kant, once war has been declared, states ought to conduct war in accordance with certain principles which safeguard the possibility of the creation of a league of nations in the future. Thus, Kant emphasizes that those actions which impede the building of mutual trust between states — such as the use of assassination — must be prohibited.

States are morally obliged to leave this natural, self-help and warlike inter-state system in order to enter into a league, or congress, of states. In particular, in his *Metaphysics of Morals*, Kant argues that such an international league must be a viable, stable and voluntary coalition among states. In his essay *Towards Perpetual Peace*, he added that the best possible relation between states is the creation of a state of nations, thus raising the issue of a world government[83]. This super-state, or state of nations, means that states ought to subject themselves to public coercive laws. Kant admits that it is not easy for states to surrender their sovereign power, and, therefore, he proposes that, until nations are convinced — either through their moral progress or through the experience of chaos — to create such a super-state, the second best option is the creation of a league of states in which each state retains the right to leave.

In the essay *Towards Perpetual Peace*, Kant proposes a set of six "preliminary articles", which are a set of rules that ought to be applied in the absence of the international peace which could, and should, be established by bringing the states in constitutional relationships with each other within the framework of an international state. These six articles are:

> 1. No conclusion of peace shall be considered valid as such if it was made with secret reservation of the material for a future war.

---

80 I. Kant, op. cit. (ref. 74), p. 346.
81 I. Kant, op. cit. (ref. 74), p. 345.
82 I. Kant, op. cit. (ref. 74), pp. 345-346.
83 I. Kant, *Towards Perpetual Peace*, p. 357.

2. No independently existing state, whether it be large or small, may be acquired by another state by inheritance, exchange, purchase or gift.

3. Standing armies (*miles perpetuus*) will gradually be abolished altogether.

4. No national debt shall be contracted in connection with the external affairs of the state.

5. No state shall forcibly interfere in the constitution and government of another state.

6. No state at war with another shall permit such acts of hostility as would make mutual confidence impossible during a future time of peace. Such acts would include the employment of assassins (*percussores*), or poisoners (*venefici*), breach of agreements, the instigation of treason (*perduellio*) within the enemy state, etc.[84]

Obviously, the previous six articles are not sufficient by themselves to establish a peaceful order, since article six assumes that wars will still occur. To institute an international order that can lead to peace, Kant proposes three "definitive articles". The first of these "definitive articles" is that every state shall have a republican civil constitution, i.e., a constitution based on the civil rights of the individual. Republicanism is desirable for its own sake — since the right of freedom is the only basis of the state — but here Kant adds that a republican constitution will be conductive to international peace, because, "under this constitution, the consent of the citizens is required to decide whether or not war is to be declared", and, unlike rulers, who treat war as a project whose costs will be mainly paid by others or even as a sport, the citizens of a republic, knowing that they will have to bear the costs of the war themselves, "will have great hesitation in embarking on so dangerous an enterprise"[85]. The second definitive article is that "the right of nations shall be based on a federation of free states"[86]. The third definitive article states that "cosmopolitan right shall be limited to conditions of universal hospitality"[87].

To understand Kant's concept of "cosmopolitan right", we must bear in mind that, for Kant, relations among states are not the same as relations among the peoples (nations, *Volk*) of the world. In particular, individuals

---

84 I. Kant, op. cit. (ref. 83), pp. 343-347.
85 I. Kant, op. cit. (ref. 83), p. 348ff.
86 I. Kant, op. cit. (ref. 83), p. 354.
87 I. Kant, op. cit. (ref. 83), p. 357.

are considered "citizens of a universal state of human beings" with corresponding "rights of citizens of the world"[88], since individuals can relate to states of which they are not citizens as well as to other individuals who are citizens of other states. This right is equivalent to free international trade and free international communication and transportation. Kant points that the "cosmopolitan right" facilitates the trust and cooperation necessary for the establishment of a peaceful inter-state order.

2.5 The German idealism and the opening of a romantic path to nihilism

In the intellectual history of Europe, the Enlightenment was succeeded by the German idealism. The protagonists of the German idealism are Johann Gottlieb Fichte, Friedrich Wilhelm Joseph Schelling and Georg Wilhelm Friedrich Hegel.

According to Kant, thinking ego does not create experience and nature, but it is a transcendental condition for knowing experience and nature. Fichte's starting point was the Kantian concept of the category, but he combined it with the thought of the self-conscious ego, thus giving rise to a new concept of the ego, according to which the ego is creative activity and the ultimate source of reality. Fichte's goal was to analyze all categories of thinking with respect to their genesis, not to deduce them, like Kant, from a priori forms of knowledge. Abolishing Kant's things-in-themselves, Fichte, in his *Foundation of the Entire Science of Knowledge* (1794), argued that object, matter and noumenon depend on the activity of the pure ego. Thus, the reality of the world is not something extraneous to the thinking subject; instead, it is a raw material projected by the thinking ego and subdued by the intentionality of the ego, i.e., a moment in the ego's development. As a consequence of Fichte's theory of the pure ego, epistemology (i.e., every form of knowledge of knowledge) necessarily coincides with the knowledge of the pure ego, and the absolute affirmation of the pure ego is effected by nullifying everything extraneous to it[89]. Thus, the modern form of nihilism was born, since, due to Fichte's philosophy, reason becomes the product of an absolute ('pure') subject, whose infinite will nullifies objective reality, thus marking a radical departure from the Enlightenment, which was recognizing a reality external to consciousness.

88 I. Kant, op. cit. (ref. 83), p. 349.
89 See also: J.G. Fichte, *The Popular Works of Johann Gottlieb Fichte*, trans. W. Smith, 2 vols, London: Thoemmes, 1999.

Fichte's political thought evolved as a logical consequence of the imperatives of his philosophical system and in response to the wounded German pride at defeat by Napoleon[90]. Thus, according to Fichte's *Treatise on Natural Law* (1796) and *Ethics* (1798), the purpose of the state is to actively promote the welfare of its citizens, and freedom is the right and duty to develop one's higher, rational self. Moreover, in Fichte's *The Closed Commercial State* (1800) and *Characteristics of the Present Age* (1806), the ends of state power become identical with the existence of consciousness itself. Thus, finally, in his *Address to the German Nation* (1807/8), Fichte develops the doctrine of modern nationalism, according to which the German must be adequately guided to see that his nation — defined primarily by language and an organic collective character — is his own extended self, in which he realizes his freedom.

In his 1799 *Letter* to Fichte, Friedrich Heinrich Jacobi endorsed an even more radical version of nihilism by arguing that rationalism must end in a complete egoism, or solipsism, or what he called "nihilism" (*Nihilismus*). Before Jacobi, nihilism was mainly connected with a moral crisis caused by the Christian's despair that life is meaningless because there is no God, divine providence, or immortality. In Jacobi's philosophy, nihilism — namely, doubt about the existence of everything — is primarily connected with the skeptical argument that we have no reason to believe in the existence of anything apart from our own passing impressions.

The genealogy of the Fichtean ego influenced Schelling[91], who considered the entire reality to be the idea of the absolute divine Ego. In his *System of Transcendental Idealism*, Schelling — like Fichte before him and Hegel after him — argues that there is a dialectical process at work in the world, and in this process, two opposing activities — thesis and antithesis — are reconciled in a higher synthesis. Moreover, he develops a genealogy of self-consciousness, from primary sensation to creative imagination, from creative imagination to reflection, and from reflection to the absolute act of will. According to Schelling, since all forms of life obey the same dialectical process, it follows that the activities of mind correspond to those found in nature. Art represents, for Schelling, the highest stage in the development of

90 See: R. Aris, *History of Political Thought in Germany from 1789 to 1815*, London: Allen & Unwin, 1936; H.S. Reiss (ed.), *The Political Thought of the German Romantics 1793-1815*, Oxford: Blackwell, 1955.
91 See: C.J. Murray (ed.), *Encyclopedia of the Romantic Era: 1760-1850*, vol. 2, New York: Fitzroy Dearborn, 2004.

self-consciousness, because the creative artist, following the creative action of nature, becomes conscious of the activity of the Absolute.

Although Hegel agrees with Fichte and Schelling that there is a dialectical process at work in the world (thesis–antithesis–synthesis), he follows a radically different line of thought. By contrast with Fichte and Schelling, Hegel, in his *Phenomenology of Spirit* (1807) and *The Science of Logic* (1812), departed from the sphere of the ego and focused his attention on the active spiritual reality itself. He historicized idealism[92], and, in his philosophical system, he described the activity of thinking as something which exists by itself and in itself, reflecting — as another form of subject — on itself. Hegel speaks as though thoughts or notions think themselves. In fact, he treats thoughts or notions like a growing organism that gradually unfolds its capacities and becomes a "concrete universal". According to Hegel, reality is equivalent to logic, in the sense that reality, being a moving dynamic process, is equivalent to a logical course which follows the triple dialectic of thesis-antithesis-synthesis. In his *Philosophy of Right*, Hegel wrote that "what is rational is actual, and what is actual is rational"[93]. Furthermore, in Hegel's philosophy, truth, like rational reality, is a living logical process. The core of Hegel's concept of logic is the absolute idea (universal reason, which Hegel

---

92 Historicism abolished the Enlightenment faith in the universality and impartiality of reason. Whereas the Enlightenment believed that there are principles which hold for all people — independently of history — as intelligent beings, the fundamental methodological principles of historicism are the following: (i) History: everything in the social and political world has a history, in the sense that all social and political principles and institutions are the result of a specific historical development and subject to change (nothing is eternal). (ii) Context: all human beliefs, practices and institutions must be studied within a specific historical context, which shows the manner in which they arose of historical necessities (e.g., political, economic, cultural and geographic conditions). (iii) Organicism: society is an organism (an indivisible whole), in which all aspects of social life (e.g., politics, religion, law, etc.) are necessarily intertwined, and which, like all organisms, undergoes a process of development. Hence, historicism is characterized by relativism, in the sense that, for a historicist, all values are equally legitimate because they are a necessary response of a people to specific historical conditions. However, even though Hegel introduced historicism in epistemology, he substituted nihilistic egoism for nihilistic relativism, by transcending the subject (individual "ego") of the earliest German idealism (Fichte and Schelling) in order to ascend to a quantitatively 'higher' (larger), and hence spiritually safer, subject — namely, the historical subject (i.e., the nation). See: K. Mannheim, "Historicism", in: *Essays on the Sociology of Knowledge*, London: Routledge & Kegan Paul, 1952, and C. Taylor, *Hegel*, Cambridge: Cambridge University Press, 1975.
93 G.W.F. Hegel, *Philosophy of Right* (originally published in 1821), trans. T.M. Knox, Oxford: Oxford University Press, 1942, p. 10.

identifies with God), which is the potential universe, i.e., the trans-temporal totality of all the possibilities of evolution, and which is historically objectified in the state, philosophy, art, and religion. Hegel calls the realized absolute idea spirit (Geist).

In the philosophical system of Hegel, spirit is understood as the highest essence of everything, and all else is considered mere appearance (Schein), as the self-projection of the idea into itself. Hegel calls spirit the ground (Grund) of appearance, and he argues that the more appearance expresses spirit (i.e., essence) the more it collapses into spirit. Finite things decline into the absolute idea and thereby reveal it. Thus, according to Hegel, 'being' is the idea which moves far away from itself, i.e., it gives rise to a contradiction, in order finally to return to itself enriched by its voyage.

Hegelianism leads to nihilistic historicism. History is meaningful when it is not the realm of necessity, i.e., when it can be rejected in the same way that a free consciousness can reject the idea of God. Historical action is creative to the extent that man tends to transcend himself (in order to arrive at a higher self, instead of returning to himself) and looks for truth in being. On the other hand, historical action reduces to nihilism to the extent that man tends to transcend only established historical conditions and looks for truth in becoming. Nihilistic historicism is committed to a linear concept of time[94], which implies that the transient present can be placed in time if and only if it satisfies the need for continuous change in the perspective of some pre-determined end or an eternal becoming. Hence, the present as such is essentially nullified, leaving behind an ontological gap.

---

94 When Hegel refers to "absolute knowledge", he endorses a linear concept of time, i.e., the time in which the subject "sees itself as a passing moment", and alienation-externalization (Entäusserung) is disclosed as linear time itself. For, according to Hegel, the purpose of this succession is "the revelation of the depth of spirit" ("the absolute concept"), which is equivalent to "the raising up of its depth... the negativity of this withdrawn I". This "negativity" is the externalization of its substance, and "this revelation is also the concept's time, in that this externalization is in its own self externalized, and just as it is in its extension, so it is equally in its depth, in the self". Hence, for Hegel, "time appears as the destiny and necessity of spirit that is not yet complete within itself, the necessity to enrich the share which self-consciousness has in consciousness, to set in motion the immediacy of the in-itself" (G.W.F. Hegel, *Phenomenology of Spirit* (originally published in 1807), trans. A.V. Miller, Delhi: Motilal Banarsidass, 1998, Paragraph 801).

2.6 Hegelian accounts of politics and communitarianism

The essence of Hegel's political thought is to be found in his *Philosophy of Right*. In this book, he argues that the state — in general, the political community — is not an instrument developed by human reason in order to safeguard and promote individual interests. Hegel contends that the state contains elements of "subjective freedom", but it is primarily an ethical entity whose purpose is related to the network of interpersonal relationships, thus transcending individually-oriented goals.

According to Hegel, this ethical nature (*Sittlichkeit*) is characterized by a triple dialectic, in which the thesis ("first moment" of the ethical nature of social existence) is the family, the antithesis ("second moment" of the ethical nature of social existence) is the civil society, and the synthesis ("third moment" of the ethical nature of social existence) is the state. Hegel defines the family as the kind of human relationships based on particularistic altruism[95] — namely, the willingness to act not in one's own interest but for the good of a particular set of people (the rest of the family) — and the civil society as the realm of selfishness[96]. In particular, by contrast with the family, in the civil society, persons are related to each other on the basis of individual interests, and private property is the objectification of a person's existence for others. Furthermore, Hegel maintains that the civil society — even though it is the realm of selfishness — needs certain institutions, e.g., laws, courts of justice and police, in order to operate effectively. Hence, the civil society "may be prima facie regarded as the external state, the state based on need"[97], but also it provides a framework for the mediation of individual wills through social interaction and a means whereby individuals are educated (*Bildung*) through their itinerary towards a higher universal consciousness. Within the dialectical structure of Hegel's political thought, the state is a synthesis of the constitutive elements of the family and the civil society, and it is based on universal altruism[98]. The self-consciousness of the synthesis between particularity and universality — a synthesis achieved through the political constitution of the state — is expressed by the citizens' belief that their freedom is equivalent to the objective laws and institutions provided by the State. The aspect of universality is related to the

---

95 G.W.F. Hegel, op. cit. (ref. 93), Paragraphs 158-159.
96 G.W.F. Hegel, op. cit. (ref. 93), Paragraphs 181-182.
97 G.W.F. Hegel, op. cit. (ref. 93), Paragraph 183.
98 G.W.F. Hegel, op. cit. (ref. 93), Paragraph 260.

recognition on the part of all citizens that they "do not live as private persons for their own ends alone, but in the very act of willing these they will the universal in the light of the universal, and their activity is consciously aimed at none but the universal end"[99]. The aspect of particularity is related to "the right of individuals to their particular satisfaction", the right of subjective freedom on which civil society is founded, and, therefore, according to Hegel, "the universal must be furthered, but subjectivity on the other hand must attain its full and living development"[100]. Hegel concludes that "it is only when both these moments subsist in their strength that the state can be regarded as articulated and genuinely organized"[101].

The core of Hegel's account of international relations is to be found in Paragraphs 321-340 of the *Philosophy of Right*. First of all, Hegel explains the concept of individuality in the sphere of international relations:

> Individuality is awareness of one's existence as a unit in sharp distinction from others. It manifests itself here in the state as a relation to other states, each of which is autonomous vis-à-vis the others. This autonomy embodies mind's actual awareness of itself as a unit and hence it is the most fundamental freedom which a people possesses as well as its highest dignity.[102]

By becoming conscious of what is not, a nation-state achieves a negative relation to itself, and "this negative relation is that moment in the state which is most supremely its own, the state's actual infinity as the ideality of everything finite within it"[103]. This negative relation is externally expressed as the relation of one nation-state to the other. According to Hegel, there can be no higher authority than the state, and war is an "ethical moment" in the life of a nation-state. Thus, war is neither an external accident nor an absolute evil, but a necessary feature of a world in which the individualities of states are unlimited. Moreover, for Hegel, "sacrifice on behalf of the individuality of the state is the substantial tie between the state and all its members and so is a universal duty"[104]. War provides the framework within which individuals prove their courage, which involves a transcendence of selfishness for the sake of the state, which is the source of the value and the identity of its members:

99 G.W.F. Hegel, op. cit. (ref. 93), Paragraph 260.
100 G.W.F. Hegel, op. cit. (ref. 93), Paragraph 260.
101 G.W.F. Hegel, op. cit. (ref. 93), Paragraph 260.
102 G.W.F. Hegel, op. cit. (ref. 93), Paragraph 322.
103 G.W.F. Hegel, op. cit. (ref. 93), Paragraph 323.
104 G.W.F. Hegel, op. cit. (ref. 93), Paragraph 325.

> The intrinsic worth of courage as a disposition of mind is to be found in the genuine absolute, final end, the sovereignty of the state. The work of courage is to actualize this final end, and the means to this end is the sacrifice of personal actuality.[105]

By treating the state as sovereign in the full sense, Hegel argues that "international law springs from the relations between autonomous states" and that, therefore, what is absolute in international law "retains the form of an ought-to-be, since its actuality depends on different wills each of which is sovereign"[106]. In the civil society, individuals (private persons) pursue their self-interest in the context of universal interdependence based on civil institutions, but, in the international system, individuals (states) are in the full sense sovereign and thus their individuality is not limited by relations of private right or morality. However, since states are obliged to have relations with other states, they need to recognize each other in a formal manner. Therefore, Hegel maintains, international law prescribes that states ought to respect and keep the international treaties which are ratified by them; but, since the rights of states "are actualized only in their particular wills and not in a universal will with constitutional powers over them", it necessarily follows that "this universal proviso of international law... does not go beyond an ought-to-be"[107]. If states disagree about the interpretation of their treaties and a compromise between them is impossible, then they will decide to settle their disputes by war.

At this point, it is important to emphasize that Hegel's political theory is a branch of his logocentric philosophical system. In Paragraphs 340-360 of the *Philosophy of Right*, Hegel argues that the march of reason in history is a dialectical process in which private persons and states are mere, unconscious tools in the hands of the "cunning of reason", i.e., they are mainly unaware of the significance of their historical action. Hegel recognizes that "world-historical individuals", such as Alexander the Great, Caesar and Napoleon, introduced changes in history. But Hegel argues that their historical significance does not derive from the intentionality of their consciousnesses, since they shared similar motives with the rest of humanity, i.e., ambition, quest for glory and greed. Their historical significance derives from the objective consequences of their historical action. Thus, the purpose of

---

105 G.W.F. Hegel, op. cit. (ref. 93), Paragraph 328.
106 G.W.F. Hegel, op. cit. (ref. 93), Paragraph 330.
107 G.W.F. Hegel, op. cit. (ref. 93), Paragraph 333.

Hegel's philosophy of history is to go behind phenomena in order to bring to light the rationality which determines historical becoming.

2.7 Opposition to Hegel's philosophy

The first reactions against Hegelianism came from within — namely, from the so-called Left Hegelians, who attempted to restore the relationship between truth and actuality within the framework of the dialectical system of thesis-antithesis-synthesis and to influence politics. Ludwig Andreas von Feuerbach, a prominent Left Hegelian, criticized Hegel's philosophy of religion by arguing that:

> The Hegelian philosophy is the last magnificent attempt to restore Christianity, which was lost and wrecked, through philosophy and, indeed, to restore Christianity — as is generally done in the modern era — by identifying it with the negation of Christianity.[108]

According to Feuerbach, the 'I' becomes aware of itself by distinguishing itself from another self, the 'You' of this 'I', and, in this process of self-realization (the 'I-You' relationship), the 'I' realizes that it is a member of a species. By arguing that man is the only reality and by elevating *feeling* over *reason*, Feuerbach contended that God is merely a projection of man's desire for a different self (e.g., for an immortal one):

> Man — this is the mystery of religion — objectifies his being and then again makes himself an object to the objectified image of himself thus converted into a subject... God is the idea of the species as an individual... freed from all limits which exist in the consciousness and feeling of the individual.[109]

Feuerbach was focused on the world of senses:

> To-be-here [*Dasein*] is the primary being, the primary determination. Here I am — this is the first sign of a real, living being... The sensuous is not, in the sense of speculative philosophy, the immediate; namely, it is not the profane, obvious, and thoughtless that is understood by itself. Immediate, sensuous perception comes much later than the imagination and the fantasy. The first perception of man is merely the perception of the imagination and the fantasy. The task of philosophy and of science in general consists, therefore, not in leading away from the sensuous, that is, real, objects, but rather in leading towards them, not in transforming objects into ideas and

---

108 L.A. Feuerbach, *Principles of the Philosophy of the Future* (originally published in 1843), trans. M.H. Vogel, Library of Liberal Arts, Indianapolis: Bobbs-Merrill, 1966, p. 34.
109 L.A. Feuerbach, *The Essence of Christianity* (originally published in 1854), trans. G. Eliot, Amherst, NY: Prometheus Books, 1989, pp. 29, 153.

conceptions, but rather in making visible, that is, in objectifying objects that are invisible to ordinary eyes. Men first see the objects only as they appear to them and not as they are... Only now, in the modern era, has mankind arrived again...at the sensuous, that is, the unfalsified and objective perception of the sensuous, that is, of the real.[110]

Thus, Feuerbach attempted to substitute the self-consciousness of the emancipated man for God (treating the latter as an outcome of 'false consciousness') without negating the rational unity of the world which underpins Hegel's dialectic.

Karl Marx, influenced by Feuerbach's materialism, attempted to transcend the idealist theses according to which the subject and the object, or man and the natural world, are united in the pure spirit. In fact, Marx maintained Hegel's dialectical way of thinking, but — as Marx said — he turned over the dialectic of Hegel in order to place it upon its feet. The result of Marx's decision to turn over the dialectic of Hegel was the thesis that "the nature of individuals depends on the material conditions determining their production"[111]. Within the framework of Marx's materialist conception of history, the relations of production constituted the real basis of society, on which there arose a legal-political and cultural superstructure which was expressed by definite forms of social consciousness.

Karl Marx, being committed to the rational core of Hegel's dialectical philosophy, believes that historical becoming is the gradual unfolding of a necessary reason, which — for Marx — is equivalent to material conditions:

> In the social production which men carry on they enter into definite relations that are indispensable and independent of their will; these relations of production correspond to a definite stage of development of their material powers of production... It is not the consciousness of men that determines their existence, but, on the contrary, their social existence determines their consciousness.[112]

From the viewpoint of Marxism, the historian must examine "the economic structure of society" in order to understand the driving force of history. In Marx's words: "With the change of the economic foundation, the entire immense superstructure is more or less rapidly transformed"[113].

---

110 L.A. Feuerbach, op. cit. (ref. 108), pp. 62, 59.

111 This argument was put forward by Karl Marx and Friedrich Engels in their book *The German Ideology* (1845). See: K. Marx, *Selected Writings*, ed. D. McLellan, Oxford: Oxford University Press, 1977, p. 161.

112 K. Marx, *A Contribution to the Critique of Political Economy* (original edition of 1859), trans. N.I. Stone, New York: International Library Publishing, 1904, pp. 11-12.

113 K. Marx, op. cit. (ref. 112), p. 12.

However, Marx's theory has a serious problem in explaining historical change. If the intentionality of consciousness could not be imposed on
material conditions, and if the relations of production determined consciousness, then, after the establishment of the first economic structure in
the history of humanity, men would be unable to introduce change in their
material conditions, because their minds would be determined by the established relations of production. If economic change is not explained as
a consequence of the imposition of the intentionality of human consciousness on material conditions in order for human consciousness to improve
its existential conditions, then historical becoming acquires autonomy from
human consciousness and the latter becomes a victim of a necessary historical becoming. The emphasis which Marx placed on the element of necessity in historical becoming gave an eschatological character to his political
thought, nullified the historical significance of individuality and cultivated
a peculiar form of authoritarianism, which later, in the hands of Marxist
political movements and regimes[114], became ruthless totalitarianism.

It is only because consciousness does not reflect the material conditions
of life mechanically that a revolutionary movement can exist, i.e., people
who are ready to fight and even die for their ideas, whereas, if they adapted
to the established state of affairs, they could survive. The reason that consciousness does not reflect the material conditions of life mechanically is
because it endows them with significance, i.e., with a meaning which transcends material conditions, and does not accept them pathetically. If the
spirit were pathetically determined by the material conditions of life, there
would not exist people willing to die for any cause, even for their own food.
Within human consciousness, material conditions do not exist as such but
they are always united with a meaning given to them by consciousness, and,
therefore, the human spirit is creative and can improve its existential conditions in history. It is for this reason that there are people who jeopardize
their lives by struggling for the general good instead of working only for the

---

114 Joseph Stalin says: "Whatever is the mode of production of a society, such in the
main is the society itself, its ideas and theories, its political views and institutions.
Or, to put it more crudely, whatever is man's manner of life, such is his manner
of thought" (J. Stalin, *Dialectical and Historical Materialism*, New York: International
Publishers, 1977, p. 29). In the name of historical necessity, Stalin's government
sent millions to forced labour camps, forcibly collectivized the peasantry and deprived workers of all socio-economic rights.

sake of their individual good. In other words, consciousness does not live by bread alone but also by principles and visions.

Whereas the Left Hegelians did not diverge from Hegel's dialectical way of thinking, this was not the case with other philosophers who opposed Hegel's spiritualism. In particular, Arthur Schopenhauer attempted to describe reality in such a manner that would allow the deep sources of the consciousness of existence to come to light[115]. Schopenhauer turned his attention, from questions about God, being, and the subject-object distinction, to the human person itself in order to explain man's experiences and perceptions. If man, he says, were merely an intellectual being, an outward looking subject, then he should perceive only phenomena arranged in spatio-temporal and causal relations. However, according to Schopenhauer's *World as Will and Idea*, when consciousness submerges into its innermost self, it comes face to face with its true, basal self. It is in the consciousness of activity, for Schopenhauer, that one becomes aware of the thing-in-itself, and the thing-in-itself is will. In Schopenhauer's philosophy, will is identified with life, and, in opposition to Hegel's philosophy, will is not spirit, but it is an indeterminate condition which, like the unconscious, determines the activities of man. Schopenhauer understands will as a blind life impulse, an uncaused activity, which is naturally imperfect and unsatisfied, and it can find tranquillity only in an ascetic way of life and in art, i.e., beyond selfish everyday goals which trigger ambition and generate needs.

Søren Aabye Kierkegaard, "the father of existentialism", played a protagonistic role in the development of philosophical opposition to Hegelianism. Kierkegaard examined Hegelianism's promise that it could provide man with absolute knowledge by virtue of a science of logic. In fact, according to Hegel, anyone who could follow the dialectical progression of the concepts of his logic would have access to the mind of God, which, for Hegel, was equivalent to the logical structure of the universe. According to Kierkegaard, Hegelianism is a hubristic and paranoid attempt to build a dialectical ladder by which humans can easily climb up to heaven. Kierkegaard's attempt to refute Hegelianism starts from the study of the experience of the ego and the personal struggle of human consciousness. The philosophy of objective knowledge, he argues, is a deceptive idol which alienates man from himself. He argued in *Concluding Unscientific Postscript to Philosophi-*

---

115 See: A. Schopenhauer, *Essays of Schopenhauer*, ed. S.H. Dircks, The Floating Press, 2010.

cal Fragments that "subjectivity is truth" and "truth is subjectivity". For Kierkegaard, the only knowable reality is the reality of ourselves, and therefore the only truth is that which follows from our relationship of fear with a God who continuously hides Himself. Hence, every man struggles for truth in a personal manner, seeking eternal salvation. In Kierkegaard's *Either-Or* and *Life's Way*, existence is equivalent to the categorical approval or disapproval of one of the three "stages" of life which are available to us: (i) the "aesthetic stage", which means a way of life based on sensuous experience, egoism, fragmentation of the subject of experience, nihilistic wielding in irony and skepticism, and attempts to overcome boredom; (ii) the "ethical stage", which means a way of life based on norms which are a substitute for the hedonism of the aesthetic stage, since the moral consciousness sees this aestheticism to be meaningless, escapist and a despairing means of avoiding commitment and responsibility; (iii) the "religious stage", which means a life of religious faith in which man becomes aware of his freedom as well as of his limits, and the aesthetic *"transfiguration"* of the actual world into the ideal is transformed into the religious *"transubstantiation"* of the finite world into a reconciliation with the infinite. Man exists in time, but his passion for the infinite, by giving him a deeper inner life, allows him to transcend the world of necessity and be regenerated in the world of faith.

Kierkegaard's political thought is based on his subjectivism. Kierkegaard criticizes modernity for attempting to subdue "the single individual" to "the crowd". In the *Two Ages: A Literary Review*, Kierkegaard attacks conformity and assimilation of the individual into the crowd, which becomes the standard of truth as a result of a deceptive transformation of the quantitative into qualitative. He criticizes modernity for being "devoid of passion" and promoting a kind of uniformity which nullifies the passion of the individual soul[116].

However, the philosophy of Kierkegaard does not transcend Hegelianism in an absolute way, because the role that reason as history plays in Hegel's philosophy is played by the individual's inner life (i.e., psychology) in Kierkegaard's philosophy. In fact, in Kierkegaard's philosophy, the spirit becomes aware of itself by progressing though three necessary stages of life, and thus the spirit becomes an objectively determined rhythm of individual

---

116 See *A Literary Review*, novella by the author of "An Everyday Story", reviewed by S. Kierkegaard (*En literair Anmeldelse af S. Kierkegaard*), and S. Kierkegaard, *The Kierkegaard Reader*, ed. J. Chamberlain and J. Rée, Oxford: Blackwell, 2001.

existence. Within the framework of a deterministic transition from nature (aesthetic stage) to knowledge (ethical stage) and from knowledge to faith (religious stage), man's freedom to follow his authentic self is equivalent to individual self-assurance, and thus it does not signify the liberation of man from the illusion of his ontological autarchy. Therefore, the philosophy of Kierkegaard leads us to a Hegelian way of thinking about the absolute: the absolute is the idea which finds itself in the reconciliation of its content with material reality.

In Kierkegaard's philosophy, the relation between the 'I' and God is totally private (i.e., autonomous vis-à-vis the common experience and symbolic system of the Church as a historical entity and vis-à-vis the authority of reason), and, therefore, even though it can help us avoid the evils of conformist morality and assimilation into the crowd, it cannot save us from the evils of an emotional religious life. Within the framework of Kierkegaard's emotional religiousness, faith reduces to a powerful human passion. The private character of the relationship between man and God in Kierkegaard's system implies the decision of man to live the passion of a relationship with an unsubstantiated romantic ideal and to call this relationship faith. Faith as passion transforms the faithful person into a romantic knight who, like Cervantes' Don Quijote de la Mancha, lives a solitary life and is accountable only to God. The God of religious passion is experienced by the religious consciousness as presence because the God of religious passion is not a distant metaphysical substance (like the God of the rationalists), but this close contact between man and God has a psychological character, and, therefore, within the framework of a totally private relationship between man and God, man reproduces himself.

2.8 Nietzsche, nihilism, and post-modernism

Friedrich Nietzsche became familiar with the anti-Hegelianism of his age through the philosophy of Schopenhauer. For Nietzsche, Hegel's philosophy, by introducing the idea of the dialectical progress of spirit towards a privileged perspective, inhibits the European civilization from developing its forces freely. Nietzsche rejects every theological/teleological interpretation of history, every reduction of historical issues to a truth which transcends time and space, and simultaneously he feels alien to rationalism, the Enlightenment, and idealism. However, Nietzsche adopted Leibniz's view that consciousness derives from a richer primordial psychological world, Kant's criticism of the principle of causality, which limited the validity of logic, as well as Hegel's decision to give priority to becoming over being, but he did so in order to support an atheistic perspective of philosophy, which consists in an attempt to nullify the idea of truth.

In the first aphorism of Nietzsche's book *Beyond Good and Evil*, we read:

> The will to truth which is to tempt to many a hazardous enterprise, the famous truthfulness of which all philosophers so far have spoken with respect — what questions has this will to truth not laid before us?

Thus, he starts his work by posing the fundamental philosophical problem of truth. In his book *Beyond Good and Evil*, Nietzsche follows a radical philosophical path. He severely criticizes reason (i.e., a rational motive for a belief or action) and particularly instrumental rationality. Instrumental rationality is focused on the most efficient or cost-effective means to achieve a specific end, but it does not itself reflect on the value of that end, nor is it concerned with goals of higher value, such as the promotion of human understanding on a more general level and the improvement of the human condition. However, Nietzsche is not an unqualified enemy of reason. Instead, he argues that reason, and therefore truth, have not been adequately investigated by his predecessors in the history of philosophy. In Nietzsche's own words:

> What in us really wants 'truth'?... Suppose we want truth: why not rather untruth? And uncertainty? Even ignorance?... The problem of the value of truth came before us — or was it we who came before the problem? Who of us is Oedipus here? Who the Sphinx? It is a rendez-vous, it seems, of questions and question marks. And though it scarcely seems credible, it finally almost seems to us as if the problem had never even been put so far — as if we were the first to see it, fix it with our eyes, and risk it.[117]

By the term truth, Nietzsche refers to a façade of power which is equivalent to the established 'science' in the Western world. Hence, a new question emerges: is knowledge evil in general? Furthermore, Nietzsche's syllogism obliges one to think about the concepts of genealogy and validity. There is a difference between the genealogy of an argument and its validity for the same reason that there is a difference between the validity of a proposition and its content. Without truth, every authority (scholar, political,

---

117 F. Nietzsche, *Beyond Good and Evil* (originally published in 1886), trans. W. Kaufmann, New York: Vintage Books, 1989, Aphorism 1.

etc.) is based only on power. However, according to Nietzsche, even the traditional concept of truth — which refers to the set of all presuppositions which constitute the terms under which the knowledge of reality is in agreement with the nature of reality, i.e., it corresponds to the presence of reality — is a manifestation of the "will for power"; for, according to Nietzsche, all elements of reality are phenomena which call for interpretation and do not exist in themselves. This Nietzschean thesis plays a protagonistic role in the so-called post-modern approach to epistemology. Michel Foucault, one of the most influential post-modern scholars, argues that "nothing in man — not even his body — is sufficiently stable to serve as the basis for self-recognition or for understanding other men"[118]; therefore, there is no escape from the functioning of power and contingency, and struggle is always necessary to avoid domination.

Is the will for truth a truth, or is it simply another name for the will for power (and authority)? "What in us really wants 'truth'?" Nietzsche's answer is the will for power. However, within the framework of Nietzsche's philosophy, the will for power is not an interpretation of a phenomenon, but it is truth itself. But why do not we want "untruth", "uncertainty" and "ignorance"? Nietzsche is not the first philosopher who posed this question. Let us recall that the Platonic Socrates considers philosophy as a methodical quest for knowledge based on ignorance — namely, as the wisdom of asking questions. For the Platonic Socrates, philosophy is moral wisdom and a form of knowledge which is equivalent to self-knowledge and moral progress.

Moreover, Nietzsche is not the first philosopher who questioned the value of truth. Nietzsche's thought is compatible with the thought of Callicles[119], a character in the Platonic dialogue *Gorgias*. In the Platonic dia-

---

118 M. Foucault, *Language, Counter-Memory, Practice*, ed. D.F. Bouchard, Ithaca, NY: Cornell University Press, 1977, p. 153. The term 'post-modern' appeared for the first time in Jean-François Lyotard's *La Condition Postmoderne* (*The Post-modern Condition*) in 1979. Lyotard argues: "Lamenting the 'loss of meaning' in postmodernity boils down to mourning the fact that knowledge is no longer principally narrative" (J.-F. Lyotard, *The Postmodern Condition: A Report on Knowledge*, trans. G. Bennington and B. Massumi, Minneapolis: University of Minnesota Press, 1984, p. 26). According to Lyotard, as a result of the de-realization of the world, narrative elements disintegrate into "clouds" of linguistic combinations and collisions among innumerable, heterogeneous language games.

119 For Callicles' influence on Nietzsche's own thought, see: E.R. Dodds (ed.), *Plato: Gorgias*, Oxford: Oxford University Press, 1959 (text, introduction and commentary).

logue *Gorgias*, 483b, 492a-c, Callicles defends nature's own justice, where the strong exercise their advantages over the weak, and additionally he argues that the natural man has large appetites and the means to satisfy them and that only a weakling praises temperance and justice. Callicles, like Nietzsche, argued that truth is a matter of interpretation (as opposed to objective proof), and the strong impose their truth-interpretation on the weak. Nietzsche added the following argument to Callicles' theory of truth: as a value, truth is a kind of delusion without which our form of life would be impossible. Therefore, in order to avoid using the concept of truth as a pretense for the will for power, we must reject the idea of truth which is based on the correspondence between reality and intellect. This is Nietzsche's project.

In the second aphorism of the book *Beyond Good and Evil*, Nietzsche studies the following question:

> How could anything originate out of its opposite? For example, truth out of error? Or the will to truth out of the will to deception? Or selfless deeds out of selfishness? Or the pure and sunlike gaze of the sage out of lust?

He argues that, according to metaphysicians,

> such origins are impossible... the things of highest value must have another, peculiar origin — they cannot be derived from this transitory, seductive, deceptive, paltry world from this turmoil of delusion and lust.[120]

Nietzsche rejects this metaphysical attitude by arguing that values should not be identified with reality and that faith in opposite values (on the grounds of the principle of distinction between truth and deception) is a matter of temporary interpretations ("provisional perspectives"); in his own words:

> it is on account of this 'faith' that they trouble themselves about 'knowledge', about something that is finally baptized solemnly as 'the truth'. The fundamental faith of the metaphysicians is the faith in opposite values... one may doubt, first, whether there are any opposites at all, and secondly whether these popular valuations and opposite values on which the metaphysicians put their seal, are not perhaps merely foreground estimates, only provisional perspectives.[121]

Thus, according to Nietzsche,

---

120 F. Nietzsche, op. cit. (ref. 117), Aphorism 2.
121 F. Nietzsche, op. cit. (ref. 117), Aphorism 2.

> for all the value that the true, the truthful, the selfless may deserve, it would still be possible that a higher and more fundamental value for life might have to be ascribed to deception, selfishness, and lust.[122]

At this point, again, Nietzsche follows the philosophical legacy of the sophists[123]. For both the sophists and Nietzsche, deception may deserve a high value, especially when it is presented as truth in order for the deceiver to gain power and prestige. If deception is presented as truth, on the basis of necessities which call for such a radical transcendence of established, traditional values, then it follows that: (a) the order of things is determined by power and, more specifically, by a hierarchy of power; and (b) power and power hierarchies themselves are only temporary, or provisional perspectives, given that there is no higher principle, or goal, to inspire and guide life. However, Nietzsche wanted a higher principle, or goal, to inspire and guide life, and thus he constructed one by himself ('arbitrarily') on the basis of his theory of the will for power and his radical skepticism on values. Nietzsche's theory of the will for power and his radical skepticism on values were his proposals for a higher goal of life, for a better life contrasted to common life, and for an authentic knowledge discriminated from the established, dominating knowledge. In fact, a quest for authenticity underpins Nietzsche's criticism of morality.

In the third aphorism of his book *Beyond Good and Evil*, Nietzsche articulates an original argument:

> by far the greater part of conscious thinking must still be included among instinctive activities, and that goes even for philosophical thinking. Behind all logic and its seeming sovereignty of movement, too, there stand valuations or, more clearly, physiological demands for the preservation of a certain type of life.[124]

But what lies outside the realm of instinct? Nietzsche's answer is the following: creative thought, since creative thought does not recur, whereas instinct is characterized by recurrence. Within the framework of Nietzsche's philosophy, knowledge as truth is not determined only by logic, but it is

---

122 F. Nietzsche, op. cit. (ref. 117), Aphorism 2.
123 The protagonists of the sophistic movement were Protagoras of Abdera, called the individualist, and Gorgias of Leontini, surnamed the nihilist: the first is famous for his argument that "Man is the measure of all things", and the latter is famous for his argument that "nothing exists: even if anything existed, we could know nothing about it, and, even if we knew anything about anything, we could not communicate our knowledge". For more details, see: G.B. Kerferd, *The Sophistic Movement*, Cambridge: Cambridge University Press, 1981.
124 F. Nietzsche, op. cit. (ref. 117), Aphorism 3.

primarily determined by man's will to impose his power on nature. This Nietzschean thesis is the foundation of Michel Foucault's post-modern approach to epistemology. In fact, in his book *The Order of Things*[125], Foucault undertook "an archaeology of the human sciences" to show the manner in which the human sciences were not "natural" modes of inquiry, but they evolved according to an underlying structure of thought, and, in his "Nietzsche, Genealogy, History"[126], Foucault sought to show that academic "discourses" are not a neutral result of scholarly inquiry, but they emerged as the direct consequence of power relations, and, therefore, epistemology is determined by underlying power structures.

In the act of walking, one moves his feet without thinking, i.e., he makes automatic movements. In general, according to Nietzsche, the forms of perception are not only logical, but also they include impulsive systems and necessities. Nietzsche, like Leibniz[127], identifies consciousness with rational thought and representation of external things. Moreover, Nietzsche argues that rational thought and representation are secondary components of perception (since impulsive systems and necessities play the primary role in perception), and they are consequences of a Kantian way of understanding space-time. According to Nietzsche, motion and space-time serve the will for power. At this point, Nietzsche leaves the following question open: if truth as value has no content, being an arbitrary result of the will for power, then how can conscious beings communicate with each other and create a society? In other words, if truth is delusion and discursiveness, and therefore if the world is deprived of any meaning, then how can conscious beings communicate with each other and create a society?

In the fourth aphorism of *Beyond Good and Evil*, Nietzsche argues that "the falseness of a judgment is for us not necessarily an objection to a judgment", and he emphasizes that this argument reflects the innovative charac-

125 M. Foucault, *The Order of Things — An Archaeology of the Human Sciences*, trans. A. Sheridan, New York: Pantheon, 1970.

126 M. Foucault, "Nietzsche, Genealogy, History", in: P. Rabinow (ed.), *The Foucault Reader*, Harmondsworth: Peregrine Books, 1986, pp. 76-100.

127 Leibniz's theory of mind is a *representational* theory of mind: perception is not understood in terms of awareness, but rather in terms of the substance's "representing external things". The fundamental principles of Leibniz's logic are: (1) All our ideas are compounded from a very small number of simple ideas, which form the alphabet of human thought. (2) Complex ideas proceed from these simple ideas by a uniform and symmetrical combination, analogous to arithmetical multiplication. See: R.S. Woolhouse and R. Francks, *Leibniz: Philosophical Texts*, Oxford: Oxford University Press, 1998.

ter of his thought. Nietzsche believes that the main philosophical problem is not the consistence of a logical structure, but "the question is to what extent it is life-promoting, life serving, species-preserving, perhaps even species-cultivating"[128].

According to Nietzsche, false judgements (which include the set of synthetic a priori statements) are "the most indispensable for us", because man could not live "without accepting the fictions of logic, without measuring reality against the purely invented world of the unconditional and self-identical, without a constant falsification of the world by means of numbers"[129]. Within the framework of Nietzsche's philosophy, the renunciation of false judgments is equivalent to the renunciation of life. Nietzsche argues that, by recognizing "untruth as a condition of life", we undertake the risk of "resisting accustomed value feelings" and that "a philosophy that risks this would by that token alone place itself beyond good and evil"[130].

Nietzsche persistently fights against truth, recognizing untruth — namely, the arbitrary interpretation of logical values — as "a condition of life". He is based on the idea that knowledge as truth is primarily determined by the will for power and not by our reason. This is, for instance, the case with phenomena, like walking, which are determined not only by our reason but also by the parasympathetic nervous system and by unconscious operations.

When Nietzsche renounces logical knowledge, he refers to the positivist concept of knowledge. The positivist mind aims at dominating nature through abstract logical categories, which include the Kantian synthetic a priori judgments (e.g., the Pythagorean theorem), which are constituted by logical concepts and underpin scientific and philosophical knowledge. Nietzsche juxtaposes "untruth" with the positivist concept of knowledge, and he argues that, given that life is equivalent to the will for power, the knowledge which stems from will is the source of the value and the validity of "untruth". According to Nietzsche, values based on will are superior to knowledge based on reason. However, at this point, Nietzsche makes the mistake of identifying positivist knowledge with knowledge based on reason in general.

---

128 F. Nietzsche, op. cit. (ref. 117), Aphorism 4.
129 F. Nietzsche, op. cit. (ref. 117), Aphorism 4.
130 F. Nietzsche, op. cit. (ref. 117), Aphorism 4.

Indeed, the purpose of positivist knowledge is domination through the knowledge of natural laws and through generalizations about social phenomena. Carl Hempel argued that, from the viewpoint of positivism, an event is explained by 'covering' it under a general law. Usually, this takes the form of a deductive system in which (1) a general law is postulated, (2) antecedent conditions are specified, and (3) the explanation of the observed event is deduced from (1) and (2). This model is known as the "deductive-nomological model", and, according to Hempel, it can be applied to both the natural and the social sciences[131]. Additionally, Hempel articulated an alternative model, known as the "inductive-statistical model", whereby probabilistic laws are established through induction and are used to show the manner in which the event under consideration is highly likely given the established law[132]. Thus, by focusing on positivist knowledge alone, Nietzsche keeps only the ultimate purpose of the positivist knowledge — namely, domination — and he recognizes the will for power as truth.

On the other hand, knowledge based on reason does not mean only positivist knowledge. Another kind of knowledge based on reason is the knowledge of substances, which was originally developed by Plato[133] and Aristotle[134]. The purpose of positivist knowledge is domination through

---

131 C. Hempel, "Reasons and Covering Laws in Historical Explanation", in: P. Gardiner (ed.), *The Philosophy of History*, Oxford: Oxford University Press, 1974, pp. 90-105.

132 C. Hempel, *Philosophy of Natural Science*, Englewood Cliffs, NJ: Prentice-Hall, 1966, p. 11.

133 According to Plato's *Republic* and *Phaedro*, looking for the "idea" means some kind of synopsis. In fact, Plato conceives of a general geometric figure as the synopsis of all the material representations of the specific general geometric figure. From this viewpoint, the work of the philosopher consists in a series of reductions of phenomena to the unity of the corresponding idea.

134 According to Aristotle's *Categories*, the study of being in general (being qua being) crucially involves the study of substance, and, additionally, in his *Metaphysics*, Aristotle argues for the ontological priority of substance. Aristotle explains that metaphysics is the study of being as being, i.e., a general theory of being. However, 'being' — as Aristotle pointed out in the third book of his *Metaphysics* — is "said in many ways". For instance, consider the following analogy: there are business tables and statistical tables. A business table is a table in the sense of an open, flat surface supported by legs or by a base, whereas a statistical table is a table of statistical data. Hence, since there is not a single sense of 'table' which simultaneously applies to a business table and a statistical table, there is not a general science of tables. In other words, tables do not constitute a single kind, and, therefore, there is not a single science whose objects would be all objects that are correctly called 'tables'. If the level of ambiguity which characterizes the term 'table' in the previous example characterized also the term 'being', then Aristotle's

the application of the covering-law model on natural and social systems. Positivist knowledge is indifferent to substances which transcend space-time and which are the primary object of Plato's and Aristotle's thought. Positivist knowledge is focused on the knowledge of nature for the purpose of domination, whereas Plato's and Aristotle's thought is focused on the acquisition of that knowledge which can answer the following question: 'What is it?' — namely, it can offer a solution to the problem of substances.

An elementary form of positivist knowledge exists even in animals; for instance, a chimpanzee can use some elementary tools in order to organize its life in a more effective way. Thus, it is not positivist knowledge that differentiates the kind of knowledge that human minds can achieve from the kind of knowledge that animals can achieve. The unique characteristic of human knowledge consists in the use of a priori judgments about substances within the framework of a higher process of thought. For instance, the bees build bee-hives by instinct, and thus bee-hives are always the same, since instinct is based on the accumulation of unlimited experiences by the species, but, on the other hand, architects, first, conceive the designs of their constructions freely in their minds and afterwards they build them. The knowledge of substances expresses an open-minded attitude towards the 'absolute' — not the conquest of the absolute — and its purpose is to contemplate the absolute for the sake of the human being whose conscious-

---

general science of being would be impossible. Aristotle admits that the term being is said in many ways, but he argues that it is not merely ambiguous. According to Aristotle, the various senses of 'being' have an ambiguity "in relation to one" ("pros hen"), i.e., they are related to a single central sense. For instance, let us consider the term 'health': it does not have a single definition that applies uniformly to all cases (e.g., there are many different things that can be called 'healthy': organisms, diets, exercise, geographical locations, etc., but not all of these are healthy in the same sense); yet, these various senses have something in common: they all refer to one central thing — namely, health — which is actually possessed only by some of the things that are called healthy — namely, by healthy organisms — and these are said to be healthy in the primary sense of the term. Other things can be characterized as healthy only to the extent that they are adequately related to things that are healthy in this primary sense of the term. The situation is the same — Aristotle argues — with the term being. 'Being' has a primary sense as well as related senses whereby it applies to other things, to the extent that they are adequately related to things that are 'beings' in the primary sense of the term. The beings in the primary sense are substances, whereas the beings in other senses are the qualities, quantities, etc. that belong to substances. For instance, consider a white horse: a horse is a substance — i.e., a being in the primary sense — and the color white (a quality) is a being only in a secondary sense because it qualifies some substance. See: A. Code, "Aristotle's Metaphysics as a Science of Principles", *Revue Internationale de Philosophie*, Vol. 51, 1997, pp. 357-378.

ness is motivated, attracted and enriched by the contemplation of a mental prototype of the world of experience. Thus, the philosophical goal of Plato and Aristotle was not the achievement of that type of knowledge which leads to a violent conquest of the object of knowledge by consciousness; instead, the philosophical goal of Plato and Aristotle was the satisfaction of their desire to intensify the experience of their love for the absolute good ('divine'). Thus, Aristotle, in *Nicomachean Ethics*, 1178b 28-32, argues that:

> Happiness extends... just so far as contemplation does, and those to whom contemplation more fully belongs are more truly happy, not accidentally, but in virtue of the contemplation; for this is itself precious. Happiness, therefore, must be some form of contemplation.

Within the framework of the classical Greek philosophy, the characterization of the divine as the absolute good is due to its perfection which makes it infinitely lovable. According to Plato, order, harmony, justice, measure, and beauty manifest the life of the absolute good, and every sensible being which desires to acquire a permanent form and structure as well as every supersensible being which can be used as a general mental prototype for the accomplishment of specific human tasks are related to the absolute good. In the Platonic philosophy, the idea of the absolute good is the end, the ultimate purpose of the universe, since it is the order of the constitution of every creation and reality and their integrated expression. Within the framework of the Platonic theory of ideas which I defend in this book, the *raison d'être*, the very being or existence of events, is neither in their happening itself, i.e., it is not in their becoming, nor in their own essence. The *raison d'être*, the very being or existence of events, is in the end, the ultimate purpose, for which they happen, i.e., in their participation in a significance which transcends them, the Idea.

The actualization of the idea of the absolute good is the purpose of the divine architect's work in the Platonic dialogue *Timaeus*, of the painter's, the doctor's and the teacher's works in the Platonic dialogue *Gorgias*, and of the statesman's work in Platonic dialogue *Politicus*. Plato argues that every being exists due to the end (ultimate purpose) towards which it is directed, and, therefore, the beings which exist in accordance to their end obey a universal love whose object is the divine perfection. Furthermore, Aristotle, in his *Physics*, E1, 265a, argues that the celestial bodies, obeying the universal love, imitate the perfect being of the divine by moving along orbits which are "perfect and eternal". Hence, we realize that, in the classical Greek philosophy, the philosophical quest for substances leads to a form of knowledge which transcends the empirical form of the existence of the objects of consciousness, and thus knowledge becomes connected with imagination, even though it is knowledge based on reason. The empirical form of the objects of consciousness impedes their identification with consciousness, and, thus, it implies that the structure of consciousness is not identical with the structure of the world. But imagination, by transcending the empirical form of the objects of consciousness, allows the imposition of the intentionality of consciousness on the world. Platonic love — being an impulse towards the Truth and the Good — can be approached as a way of understanding the will for power different from the way in which Nietzsche understands the will for power.

From the viewpoint of Nietzsche's approach to the will for power, a false judgment can be seen as an expression of creativity, and, hence, it can be interpreted as a consequence of a dynamic attitude to life. But, when philosophy recognizes untruth as a condition of life and therefore it moves beyond every distinction between good and evil, identifying will as such with truth, then it is necessarily indifferent as to whether an untrue judgment underpins injustice and violence. In other words, Nietzsche respects creativity as such, without any further qualifications. But, in this way, contrary to the classical Greek philosophers' approach to creativity, Nietzsche's approach to creativity is unable to provide a solid foundation of life.

If one refuses to distinguish between good and evil, then the will for power obliges him to be always on the side of the victimizer and never on the side of the victim. Contrary to Nietzsche's argument, evil is not merely a synonym to prejudice. It is untruth that allows evil to take place and be justified. Untruth is a necessary foundation of evil, and, on the other hand, truth is a necessary foundation of good, as Plato argues in his dialogue *Apology of Socrates*.

In the fifth aphorism of Nietzsche's *Beyond Good and Evil*, we read that:

> What provokes one to look at all philosophers half suspiciously, half mockingly, is not that one discovers again and again how innocent they are — how often and how easily they make mistakes and go astray; in short, their childishness and childlikeness — but that they are not honest enough in their work.

In particular, Nietzsche argues that philosophers pretend to have

> discovered and reached their real opinions through the self-evolving of a cold, pure, divinely indifferent dialectic (in contrast to all sorts

of mystics, who, fairer and more foolish, talk of 'inspiration'); while at bottom it is an assumption, a hunch, indeed a kind of 'inspiration' — most often a desire of the heart that has been filtered and made abstract — that they defend with arguments sought out after the event.[135]

Furthermore, Nietzsche argues that the "stiff" hypocrisy of Kant, with which he misleads us to into his "categorical imperative", "makes us fastidious ones smile, we who find no small amusement in spying out old moralists and ethical preachers"[136]. Nietzsche adds that "the hocus-pocus in mathematical form, by means of which Spinoza has... clad his philosophy in mail and mask" in order to fortify his opinions (i.e., his love for *his own* 'sophia') by intimidating (through mathematical structures) all those who "would dare to cast a glance on that invincible maiden, that Pallas Athena" is a "masquerade" which betrays "personal timidity and vulnerability"[137].

In summary, according to Nietzsche, philosophers are dishonest because they pretend that their thoughts echo objective reality, whereas, for Nietzsche, what they really do is to reduce their prejudices, their ideas, to "the truth". In reality — Nietzsche contends — philosophers defend judgments which are equivalent to advocates' tricks or their own hearts' desires but they present them in abstract forms and by means of arguments which they have articulated after (not before) the original conception of their ideas. It is useful to mention that this Nietzschean thesis underpins Richard Rorty's post-modern approach to epistemology, according to which philosophers should give up on the idea that our knowledge 'mirrors' nature and instead adopt a pragmatic theory of truth which is compatible with Rorty's self-description as a "postmodern bourgeois liberal"[138].

For Nietzsche, the truths of Kant and Spinoza are equally deceptive because they hide that their purpose is to establish a "desire" of their heart and not an objective truth. However, naturally, one could ask Nietzsche: why does it matter that they try to establish their truths, or "desire"? It matters — Nietzsche would say — because one's truth, or "desire", may not be appealing to others, and, therefore, it loses its value. However, at this point, Nietzsche makes a mistake: the validity of truth does not depend on

---

135 F. Nietzsche, op. cit. (ref. 117), Aphorism 5.
136 F. Nietzsche, op. cit. (ref. 117), Aphorism 5.
137 F. Nietzsche, op. cit. (ref. 117), Aphorism 5.
138 R. Rorty, *Objectivity, Relativism and Truth: Philosophical Papers*, Vol. I, Cambridge: Cambridge University Press, 1991, pp. 197-202.

its genealogy but on its logic, its consistence, and the logic of truth depends on the fact that it can harmoniously unite a multitude of data towards a specific perspective[139]. Therefore — at least when they do not have the arrogance of Hegel to declare that their philosophies mark the end of the history of philosophy — philosophers are not as dishonest as Nietzsche contends.

In the sixth aphorism of *Beyond Good and Evil*, Nietzsche argues that every great philosophical system is a kind of confession of the philosophers' intensions, something like the philosopher's "involuntary and unconscious autobiography". Hence — Nietzsche contends — philosophy is not the outcome of a knowledge impulse, but it is the outcome of a will which uses knowledge as a tool (independently of whether or not knowledge is true). The philosopher is inspired by his personal impulses — "in the philosopher... there is nothing impersonal"[140] — and his impulses attempt to rule over the others' impulses. According to Nietzsche, the philosopher's passion is to dominate, and the philosopher projects this passion outwardly by presenting it as truth. In other words, the philosopher's passion is a rationalization of an impulse, which, for Nietzsche, is an instinctive power.

At this point, Nietzsche uses a psychological category — rationalization — in an ambiguous manner. Rationalization is a psychological category, which was formally defined by the psychoanalyst Alfred Ernest Jones as "the inventing of a reason for an attitude or action the motive of which is not recognized"[141], and which was already known by the 18th century as an attitude according to which, when a man has to consider his actions, he realizes "that such of them, as strong inclination and custom have prompted him to commit, are generally dressed out and painted with all the false beauties which a soft and flattering hand can give them"[142]. However, Nietzsche uses the psychological category of rationalization as if it were an instinctive power. Thus, Nietzsche fails to see that, if impulses were determining

---

139 It is useful to add that, in the theory of propaganda, the attempt to link the validity of a premise to a characteristic or belief of the person advocating a premise is known as "argumentum ad hominem". This tactic is logically fallacious, because insults and even true negative facts about the opponent's personal character or about the genealogy of an idea do not prove anything about the logical merits of the opponent's truth.

140 F. Nietzsche, op. cit. (ref. 117), Aphorism 6.

141 See: A. Phillips, *On Filtration*, Cambridge, Mass.: Harvard University Press, 1994, p. 109.

142 L. Sterne, *The Life and Opinions of Tristram Shandy, A Gentleman* (originally published in 1759-1767), Middlesex: Penguin, 1976, p. 147.

and choosing the purposes of human action, then humans would not need truth at all. In other words, the very fact that people address the problem of truth and debate about truth indicates that their actions are not merely the outcome of impulsive forces. Furthermore, if truth were identical with will, then the communication among humans would be impossible. Hence, what philosophers look for is truth as the foundation of society, for society and justice are impossible without truth, i.e., without a reason that can harmoniously unite a multitude of sensible data towards a specific perspective.

In the fourteenth aphorism of *Beyond Good and Evil*, Nietzsche leaves philosophers aside in order to criticize natural scientists. According to Nietzsche, natural science is not an explanation of the world, but an interpretation and rationalization of phenomena. However, Nietzsche argues, such a natural science, which is an interpretation of phenomena "and not a world-explanation", is regarded as a world-explanation, i.e., as a 'true' interpretation, because "eyes and fingers speak in its favour, visual evidence and palpableness do, too"[143]. Thus, Nietzsche continues, natural science attracts and fascinates "an age with fundamentally plebeian tastes", since natural science "follows instinctively the canon of truth of eternally popular sensualism"[144]. Following this Nietzschean epistemological argument, Jacques Derrida[145], one of most influential post-modernists, developed the theory of deconstruction, according to which texts collapse under their own weight once it is demonstrated that their 'truth content' is merely the "mobile army of metaphors" identified by Nietzsche.

In fact, in the fourteenth aphorism of *Beyond Good and Evil*, Nietzsche starts — indirectly — from the Kantian principle that the noumenal world is essentially unknowable. Hence, all the thoughts of natural scientists are interpretations. From this viewpoint, the world as such should be a matter of indifference to us, and we should be interested only in the world which we have constructed by putting things in an order which reflects our own will. In other words, Nietzsche rejects the distinction between subject and object and identifies truth with the will for power. However, if we take Nietzsche's syllogism seriously, then we have no reason to accept it, because, if every judgment about the world is an 'interpretation' — where 'interpretation' means an act of the will for power — then the theory of the

143 F. Nietzsche, op. cit. (ref. 117), Aphorism 14.
144 F. Nietzsche, op. cit. (ref. 117), Aphorism 14.
145 See: C. Norris, *Derrida*, London: Fontana, 1987.

will for power is also an 'interpretation' of the world, and simultaneously it contests the role of a fundamental reality which underpins the creation of cognitive categories, which is a contradiction.

In addition, since — as Nietzsche admits — interpretation is based on the senses, it *naturally* urges the 'interpreter' to consider the results of his work as a 'discovery' of an objective truth and not only as a 'construction' of a subjective truth. Hence, contrary to what Nietzsche contends, people have legitimate reasons to regard natural science as a world-explanation. Nietzsche fails to see that an important issue about truth is the impact that truth has on the manner in which the person who seeks truth understands life. In other words, we should study the quest for truth not only from the aspect of the validity of knowledge, but also from the aspect of the impact that the relationship between man and truth has on one's understanding of life.

In the seventeenth aphorism of *Beyond Good and Evil*, Nietzsche criticizes the "superstitious" belief of logicians, like Descartes, that the event of "cogi-to" ('I think') is an "immediate certainty", since their sort of reasoning had the following form: *I* am the one who 'thinks', thinking is one of *my* activities, and *I* am the agent–master of this activity. At this point, Nietzsche raises the following counter-arguments: (i) Whenever someone seeks an idea, the idea comes to him — if it comes — not because this is his wish, but because this is the idea's own wish. Hence, the Cartesian "cogito" is nullified, or, at least, it is shown that the activity of thinking cannot be manipulated by the subject. (ii) Furthermore, Nietzsche rejects the old logicians' belief that there is no predicate without a subject to which it is related within a sentence. Nietzsche's thought is oriented towards the 'interpretation' of events and not towards events themselves:

> After all, one has even gone too far with this 'one thinks' — even the 'one' contains an interpretation of the process, and does not belong to the process itself. One infers here according to the usual grammatical formula — 'To think is an activity; every activity requires an agency that is active; consequently...'. It was pretty much on the same lines that the older atomism sought, besides the operating 'power', the material particle wherein it resides and out of which it operates — the atom. More rigorous minds, however, learnt at last to get along without this 'earth-residuum', and perhaps some day we shall accustom ourselves, even from the logician's point of view, to get along without the little 'one' (to which the worthy old 'ego' has refined itself).[146]

---

146 F. Nietzsche, op. cit. (ref. 117), Aphorism 17.

(iii) If a thought comes when *it* wishes, then *thought itself* is the one who thinks inside me, and not *I*. Thus, if thought itself — and not I — thinks, i.e., if the predicate is the verb (to think), then the subject is the activity of thinking, and not a personal actor ('I'). In other words, the activity of thinking is described by Nietzsche as a process without a personal subject. Nietzsche understands the sentence '*I* think' in the same way that he understands the sentence '*it* rains'.

In order to nullify the Cartesian ego, i.e., in order to deconstruct the subject of the Cartesian statement 'I think therefore I am', Nietzsche goes back to the Homeric "Sing in me, Muse, and through me tell the story of that man..."[147], where thought/inspiration offers itself to the poet. At this point, it is useful to mention that Nietzsche's attempt to deconstruct the Cartesian ego has inspired many post-modernists' (e.g., M. Foucault's) desire to undermine the notion that there is such thing as a natural self as well as many utilitarian philosophers' (e.g., Derek Parfit's) attempt to show that we are simply physical and/or psychological continuity (a set of embodied memories which fade over time, and many of which are shared by many people) and that there is no "further fact" about identity, no deeper irreducible sense of 'ego'[148].

Nietzsche (like the post-modernists and the utilitarians who also attempted to undermine the 'I' after him) seems to ignore that thought is not something given or immediately available and also that it is always a question that generates a thought as a conceptual framework within which the given question is handled. The subject which poses a question has a self before the 'I' of the sentence 'I think'. Therefore, contrary to what Nietzsche maintains, a thought does not come by itself, but when one asks a question. Moreover, every question is always posed according to the terms of the person who asks, and it is a combination of logic and imagination. Imagination is an absolutely personal and open way of thinking, and, at some stage of its development, it is objectified as a logico-grammatical phenomenon. The activity of asking questions does not nullify the 'I', but it allows the 'I' to exist in a dynamic manner, instead of remaining closed in its static substance.

---

147 Homer, *Odyssey*, trans. R. Fitzgerald, New York: Vintage, 1961, verse 1.
148 D. Parfit, *Reasons and Persons*, Oxford: Clarendon Press, 1984. According to John Rawls, the core of utilitarianism is that society is to be arranged so as to maximize (the total or average) aggregate utility or expected well-being, and, thus, utilitarianism fails to "take seriously the distinction between persons" (J. Rawls, *A Theory of Justice*, Oxford: Oxford University Press, 1972, p. 24).

In the nineteenth aphorism of *Beyond Good and Evil*, Nietzsche argues that willing is "something complicated, something that is a unit only as a word — and it is precisely in this one word that the popular prejudice lurks". According to Nietzsche, every act of the will is characterized by multiplicity: "the will is not only a complex of sensation and thinking, but it is above all an affect, and specifically the affect of the command"[149]. Moreover, Nietzsche contends that a philosopher is obliged to connect willing with a form of morality which consists in a theory of the power relationships which determine the phenomenon of life.

Nietzsche attempts to depart from the "popular prejudice" about willing as well as from Schopenhauer's approach to willing, by arguing that willing is something more complex than a mere rational pursuit of goals; it is an emotional state prior to any goal:

> In short, he who wills believes with a fair amount of certainty that will and action are somehow one; he ascribes the success, the carrying out of the willing, to the will itself, and thereby enjoys an increase of the sensation of power which accompanies all success. 'Freedom of the will' — that is the expression for the complex state of delight of the person exercising volition, who commands and at the same time identifies himself with the executor of the order — who, as such, enjoys also the triumph over obstacles, but thinks within himself that it was really his will itself that overcame them. In this way the person exercising volition adds the feeling of delight of his successful executive instruments, the useful 'under-wills' or under-souls. [150]

Thus, the will for power nullifies every concept of meaning, by rejecting all questions and debates about 'why' and 'purposes', and, ultimately, it rejects God, as the transcendental source of the meaning of being, and divinizes the 'superman' (Übermensch). Nietzsche studies volition only with respect to the subject which exercises volition, without dealing with the object of volition, i.e., without making any reference to what the subject wills. Therefore, willing reduces to an impulsive state and blocks the sociability of human consciousness. From Nietzsche's viewpoint, society is determined by a hierarchy of power, and the happiness of the commander is identified with social happiness. In the absence of truth, the spirit is identified with power, and power is ultimately identified with the exercise of force by the 'supermen' on the 'under-souls'.

---

149 F. Nietzsche, op. cit. (ref. 117), Aphorism 19.
150 F. Nietzsche, op. cit. (ref. 117), Aphorism 19.

Nietzsche rejects all questions and debates about 'why' and 'purposes' in order to keep the will pure, i.e., separated from every purpose and from the rational mind in general. In this way, he deprives human life from significant elements. If we are concerned with the quality and the value of our life, we cannot will without thinking, i.e., inherent in every act of will is a purpose, an object. In fact, it is in questions and debates about 'why' and 'purposes' that quality and value lie. Louis Lavelle has pointed out that there are two emotional attitudes underlying philosophy: First, surprise at "the perpetual miracle of initiative"[151], or "my own insertion into the world"[152]. According to Lavelle, the mystery of the insertion of myself into the world resides less in the performance of this act than in my inner decision-command whereby this act is brought about, i.e., in my active presence in myself, and, therefore, in my feeling of responsibility towards myself and the world. This ongoing initiative, which consists in the insertion of myself into the world, is the stuff of being, and it cannot be separated from action. The second striking factor of experience, for Lavelle, is "that ever actual presence from which I never succeed in escaping", and which corresponds to the 'cogito' (thinking), which enables me to chose from the totality of being a being that is my own[153]. A value, as it has been shown by Lavelle, is a principle that legitimizes a price, and, if all values are reduced to the commander's delight, then we cannot talk meaningfully about freedom and justice.

A society of freedom, justice and personal responsibility is possible only if it is related to truth, as a universal principle which unites all persons in itself, because truth can transmute the impulse for domination into a spiritual quest for justice and creative communication with others. Truth impedes the transformation of man into an instrument, or a means, manipulated by commanders (this has been stressed, among others, by I. Kant), because it spiritualizes the passion for life and, thus, every action is guided by and evaluated according to a universal end, which Plato has called the Good.

In the twenty-first aphorism of *Beyond Good and Evil*, Nietzsche fights against the ideas of "causa sui" and "freedom of the will":

> The causa sui is the best self-contradiction that has been conceived so far, it is a sort of rape and perversion of logic; but the extravagant pride of man has managed to entangle itself profoundly and frightfully with just this nonsense. The desire for 'freedom of the

151 L. Lavelle, *De l'être*, Paris: Aubier, 1947, p. 9.
152 L. Lavelle, *De l'acte*, Paris: Aubier, 1937, p.10.
153 L. Lavelle, op. cit. (ref. 151), p. 9.

will' in the superlative metaphysical sense, which still holds sway, unfortunately, in the minds of the half-educated; the desire to bear the entire and ultimate responsibility for one's actions oneself, and to absolve God, the world, ancestors, chance, and society involves nothing less than to be precisely this causa sui and, with more than Münchhausen's audacity, to pull oneself up into existence by the hair, out of the swamps of nothingness.[154]

According to Nietzsche, the antithesis between freedom and determinism is "a misuse of cause and effect", and he continues this argument as follows:

> One should not wrongly reify 'cause' and 'effect' as the natural scientists do (and whoever, like them, now 'naturalizes' in his thinking), according to the prevailing mechanical doltishness which makes the cause press and push until it 'effects' its end; one should use 'cause' and 'effect' only as pure concepts, that is to say, as conventional fictions for the purpose of designation and communication — not for explanation. In the 'in itself' there is nothing of 'causal connections', of 'necessity', or of 'psychological non-freedom'; there the effect does not follow the cause, there is no rule of 'law'. It is we alone who have devised cause, sequence, for-each-other, relativity, constraint, number, law, freedom, motive, and purpose; and when we project and mix this symbol world into things as if it existed 'in itself', we act once more as we have always acted — mythologically... It is almost always a symptom of what is lacking in himself when a thinker senses in every 'causal connection' and 'psychological necessity' something of constraint, need, compulsion to obey, pressure, and unfreedom; it is suspicious to have such feelings — that person betrays himself... And as a matter of fact, the fatalism of the weak-willed embellishes itself surprisingly when it can pose as 'la religion de la souffrance humaine'; that is its 'good taste'.[155]

Thus, Nietzsche reduces the antithesis between freedom and determinism to the antithesis between the possible and the impossible, or between strong and weak wills. In this way, he fights the spirit (the dialectic between necessity and freedom) with the instinct (will for power). For Nietzsche, there is no 'free will', since none can be fully responsible for his existence and actions, and, therefore, there is no 'unfree will' either. In real life, Nietzsche contends, we have to do only with possible and impossible wills, and the authentic nature of the human being is the state of the realization of its will for power (i.e., the super-human) by creating causes, relations, laws, motives, and goals. Therefore, Nietzsche understands the authentic nature

154 F. Nietzsche, op. cit. (ref. 117), Aphorism 21.
155 F. Nietzsche, op. cit. (ref. 117), Aphorism 21.

of man as the complete negation of truth. Nietzsche arrives at this conclusion because he identifies truth with logical certainty, and, therefore, when he cannot find logical certainty, he feels obliged to propose the total rejection of truth. Nevertheless, truth should not be understood merely as logical certainty, but also as a power which makes the expression of impulses more noble, more civilized.

Nietzsche seems to ignore that freedom is exercised in both extrovertive and introvertive ways. Hence, one's power should be measured not only according to the degree to which he has managed to impose the intentionality of his consciousness on others, but also according to the degree of completeness of the structure of his consciousness, according to the level of his self-awareness, and according to the extent to which he has managed to maintain and strengthen his ontological status by himself. After all, at the very moment that one feels that he is imposing his will on the natural world, through his historical action, the natural world (instinctive impulses) may be imposing its own logic on him from the inside, thus transforming him into a puppet of blind passions. In such a case, man's power becomes a shadow of itself.

In the twenty-third aphorism of *Beyond Good and Evil*, Nietzsche focuses on psychology. He describes his task as an attempt to free psychology from "moral prejudices and fears" (good-evil) and conceives psychology in a "morphological" manner, as a theory of the development of the will for power. Nietzsche argues that psychology is the victim of moral prejudices and that "a proper physio-psychology has to contend with unconscious resistance in the heart of the investigator"[156], because "a doctrine of the reciprocal dependence of the 'good' and the 'wicked' drives" and mainly "a doctrine of the derivation of good impulses from wicked ones" cause "distress and aversion in a still hale and hearty consciousness"[157]. Things change once we accept "hatred, envy, covetousness, and the lust to rule as conditions of life, as factors which fundamentally and essentially must be present in the general economy of life", if we want to strengthen the force of life, irrespective of the "seasickness" that such a view of things would cause to the 'moral' person[158]. Nietzsche argues that, if one has once lost his way in life, he must clench his

---

156 F. Nietzsche, op. cit. (ref. 117), Aphorism 23.
157 F. Nietzsche, op. cit. (ref. 117), Aphorism 23.
158 F. Nietzsche, op. cit. (ref. 117), Aphorism 23.

teeth, destroy the remains of his own morality and take risks[159]. In addition, Nietzsche, in the twelfth aphorism of his book *On the Genealogy of Morality*[160], argues that the sickness of the human being consists in the contradictory character of our impulses (the impulse of creation versus the impulse of self-destruction) and in the illusion that we are free in a world of necessities, whereas the merit of the human being consists in our psychological depth and in our wickedness (i.e., our ability of conceiving negativity).

Nietzsche develops an amoral psychology because he believes that the degree of the reality of life is equivalent to the degree of the intensity of the feeling of life. Hence, for Nietzsche, the more intensely one feels his life the more real his life is and the more fully he lives his life. Nietzsche wants to nullify such traditional European values as legal egalitarianism, democracy and social solidarity, because he believes that they are causes of mediocrity and suppression[161]. At this point, Nietzsche's analysis is extremely one-sided. He addresses the problem of how one will live his life more intensely and, hence, more fully. However, he completely ignores the problem of how life will become more viable.

The intensification of the feeling of life can lead to destructive results, like a fire, which the more intense it becomes the more destructive its consequences are. In *Timaeus*, Plato exposes the introduction of the ideas into chaos and the manner in which reason establishes a harmonious order. As we read in Plato's *Timaeus*, if feelings are not structured by reason into a harmonious order, the mind is in a corybantic[162] state as a result of an unrythm (lack of rational order) in the soul which is manifested in violent motions of the heart, then in violent body movements, and finally in generalized frenzy. Therefore, even though Sigmund Freud, like Nietzsche, accepted that humans have impulses, he proposed psychoanalysis as a method by which people can achieve a viable relationship with their impulses by bringing them to the light of consciousness and making their expression

---

159 F. Nietzsche, op. cit. (ref. 117), Aphorism 23.

160 F. Nietzsche, *On the Genealogy of Morality* (first published in 1887), trans. M. Clark and A.J. Swensen, Indianapolis: Hackett Publishing Co., 1998.

161 In psychology, suppression is one of the defence mechanisms of the ego, and it consists in an attempt to forget something that causes you anxiety.

162 Cybele was the greatest goddess in Frygia in the 5th century BC. The Corybants were Cybele's attendants and priests, and they worshiped her with an unrestrained frenzy and wildly. Thus, the adjective 'corybantic' is based on the name of Cybele's attendants and describes anything characterized by a similarly unrestrained passion.

compatible with civilization[163]. For this reason, psychoanalysis is not a morphological theory — i.e., it is not exhausted in the description of forms of behavior — but it is a therapeutic method, in the sense that its purpose is to integrate impulses into life in a creative way. Moreover, the modern civil societies of the West intensify the feeling of life — as Nietzsche wanted — through socio-economic competition, but simultaneously they recognize that the existence of society necessarily depends on a theory of justice and democracy. Thus, for instance, John Rawls defines society as a "co-operative venture for mutual advantage"[164], and he proposes the following principles for the organization of social life:

> Social and economic inequalities are to be arranged so that they are both:
>
> (a) to the greatest benefit of the least advantaged, consistent with the just savings principle and
>
> (b) attached to offices and positions open to all under conditions of fair equality of opportunity.[165]

---

163 Freud's psychological theory describes, in complex and dynamic form, a conflict between reason and passion. See: S. Freud, *Civilization and Its Discontents*, trans. J. Rivière, London: Hogarth, 1930.

164 J. Rawls, op. cit. (ref. 148), p. 4.

165 J. Rawls, op. cit. (ref. 148), p. 302.

CHAPTER 3. FROM BECOMING TO BEING: THE MEANING OF PROGRESS

3.1 Knowledge as a matter of cultural development

The term knowledge may refer to: first, the mental operation through which we know; second, the object of this operation, i.e., the object which consciousness tries to approach; third, the presence and the image of that object inside consciousness; fourth, the awareness of this presence and its identification with the given object. These four aspects of knowledge imply four partial definitions of knowledge. Thus, the term knowledge may mean: first, the mental operation through which an object is recognized as an object of consciousness; second, the mental operation through which consciousness conceives the substance of the given object; third, the object which, through its idea or image, is present inside consciousness; fourth, that content of consciousness which is considered by consciousness to be the substance of the given object. From the previous four partial definitions of knowledge, we can arrive at the following general definition of knowledge: an object of consciousness is said be an object of knowledge if and only if consciousness constantly considers that the given object corresponds to reality. This is a dynamic definition of knowledge, because it does not refer only to a given object but also to the presuppositions under which the presence of the given object inside consciousness is possible. Hence, the explanation of the genesis of an event or a phenomenon of the natural world must not be considered to be 'knowledge' unless the given event or phenomenon is simultaneously considered by one's consciousness to be a manifestation of reality.

In order to identify and evaluate consciousness's capabilities of assimilating the object of knowledge, we must first have identified and evaluated the 'critical element' of the different kinds of knowledge, i.e., that element whose presence (or absence) determines the presence (or absence) of reality inside consciousness as well as the intervention of consciousness in reality. This 'critical element' of knowledge is not necessarily inherent in objective reality, but it may be attributed to reality by the consciousness which seeks to know reality and, through this knowledge, to act upon reality.

Our attempt to identify and evaluate the different kinds of knowledge and, hence, to study the meaning of 'theory', can be substantially facilitated by the Platonic myth of the cave, which is narrated by Plato in the seventh book of his *Republic*, 514a-521b. This myth describes man's progress through different levels of knowledge as a dramatic itinerary of psychological change, as a transition from one state of existence to another state of existence, in order, finally, to exit from the 'cave', i.e., to form a free, conscious persona. Thus, Plato approaches knowledge in a dynamic way — in accordance with the general definition of knowledge which we formulated above — and not in a static way.

In the myth of the cave, Plato invites us to imagine the following:

> an underground chamber like a cave, with a long entrance open to the daylight and as wide as the cave. In this chamber are men who have been prisoners there since they were children, their legs and necks being so fastened that they can only look straight ahead of them and cannot turn their heads. Some way off, behind and higher up, a fire is burning, and between the fire and the prisoners and above them runs a road, in front of which a curtain-wall has been built, like the screen at puppet shows between the operators and their audience, above which they show their puppets... Imagine further that there are men carrying all sorts of gear along behind the curtain-wall, projecting above it and including figures of men and animals made of wood and stone and all sorts of other materials, and that some of these men, as you would expect, are talking and some are not.[166]

---

166 Plato, *Republic*, trans. D. Lee, London: Penguin Books, 1995, Book VII, 514a-c.

In this condition, the prisoners could not "see anything of themselves or their fellows except the shadows thrown by the fire on the wall of the cave opposite them"[167]. Plato continues his narration as follows:

> Then think what would naturally happen to them if they were re-leased from their bonds and cured of their delusions. Suppose one of them were let loose, and suddenly compelled to stand up and turn his head and look and walk towards the fire; all these actions would be painful and he would bee too dazzled to see properly the objects of which he used to see as shadows... he would be at a loss, and think that what he used to see was far truer than the objects now being pointed out to him... And if he were made to look directly at the light of the fire, it would hurt his eyes and he would turn back and retreat to the things which he could see properly, which he would think really clearer than the things being shown to him... And if... he were forcibly dragged up the steep and rugged ascent and not let go till he had dragged out into the sunlight, the process would be a painful one, to which he would much object, and when he emerged into the light his eyes would be so dazzled by the glare of it that he wouldn't be able to see... Because, of course, he would need to grow accus-tomed to the light before he could see things in the upper world out-side the cave. First he would find it easiest to look at shadows, next at the reflections of men and other objects in water, and later on at the objects themselves. After that he would find it easier to observe the heavenly bodies and the sky itself at night, and to look at the light of the moon and the stars rather than the sun at its light by day... The thing he would be able to do last would be to look directly at the sun itself, and gaze at it without using reflections in water or any other medium, but as it is in itself... Later on he would come to the conclusion that it is the sun that produces the changing sea-sons and years and controls everything in the visible world, and is in a sense responsible for everything that he and his fellow-prisoners used to see... And when he thought of his first home and what passed for wisdom there, and of his fellow-prisoners... he would be sorry for them.[168]

According to the Platonic myth of the cave, this released prisoner de-cides to go back to the cave in order to enlighten his fellow-prisoners, even though he knows that he would be "likely to make a fool of himself", since his fellow-prisoners "would say that his visit to the upper world had ru-ined his sight, and that the ascent was not worth even attempting" and they would be ready to kill anyone who would try to "release them and lead them up"[169].

---

167 Plato, op. cit. (ref. 166), Book VII, 515a.
168 Plato, op. cit. (ref. 166), Book VII, 515d-516c.
169 Plato, op. cit. (ref. 166), Book VII, 517a.

After the narration of the myth of the cave, Plato makes interpretive comments on it. The space of the cave corresponds to the world of senses, and, therefore, sense perception is a relationship with things which is characterized by cognitive darkness. The fire that burns corresponds to the sun of the Good (the ultimate source of goodness). The liberated prisoner's ascent towards the view of the sun corresponds to the mind's ascent form the sensible world to the intelligible world. All these correspondences have a common foundation — namely, at the edge of the sensible world, i.e., at the borderline between the sensible world and the intelligible world, the mind just starts seeing the sunlight, i.e., the mind just starts seeing the idea of the Good. When the liberated prisoner is in a condition to gaze at the 'sun' (i.e., the absolute good), he can conclude that the 'sun' is the universal cause of goodness and beauty. The sun, which is outside the cave, is the source of light, it provides the necessary condition under which things can be revealed (known) in the sensible world, and additionally it is the necessary presupposition under which we can understand which of the things we see are true and which are not true, since it allows us to conceive the intelligible reality of things. Thus, Plato argues that everyone who intends to act with discretion either in public or in private life must gaze at the sun, i.e., he must be in a position to discriminate one thing from another guided by the idea of the Good.

According to the previous interpretive comments made by Plato, and contrary to what the sophists and the empiricists maintain, knowledge is not acquired by the mind in a cumulative fashion from the external world, but it lies inside consciousness, and, therefore, the ultimate purpose of theoretical work and education is not to collect/learn new information, but to turn the mind away from darkness until it can bear to gaze at the 'sun'. Thus, in the Platonic myth of the cave, the liberated prisoner acquired knowledge not by listening to a lecture or by reading a book, but by being turned towards the most shining part of being, i.e., towards the Good. In other words, the Platonic myth of the cave urges us to put aside easy and simplistic solutions to the problems of knowledge and turn our mental vision from the wrong direction to the right direction.

If our mind is restricted in the realm of logically transmitted, or 'formal', knowledge, then this condition may prove to be harmful to our thought because our mind leads us to things that it does not control, and then our consciousness is pathetic. For instance, the rationalistic, or 'natural', theology of Thomas Aquinas ascribes a pathetic role to consciousness, since, in the Thomistic philosophical system, it is the action of external objects on the mind that provides the mind with the raw material of knowledge which (at a next stage) will be elaborated by the higher faculties of the mind into conceptual knowledge. On the other hand, the orientation of the soul towards the idea of the Good means that, under the light of a third element — the sun of the Good — which is the universal source of the meaning of being, the reality of the world is united with the reality of consciousness, and, therefore, the correspondence between reality and consciousness is not static (as in Thomism) but dynamic, and, furthermore, consciousness is not the field on which external objects act, but consciousness relates to reality according to the terms of the consciousness's intentionality.

Plato argues that the souls which are oriented towards the intelligible world do not want to descend to the sensible world, but they must descend to the sensible world in order to govern in the sensible world and objectify their knowledge in history. At this point, Plato leads us to two important conclusions. First, the freedom acquired by the knowledge of the Good does not correspond to the exercise of some 'right' (e.g., the right of enjoying the experience of this knowledge far from the darkness of the cave), but it corresponds to the undertaking of personal moral responsibility. In fact, after his enlightenment experience, the liberated prisoner decides to descend to the darkness of the cave in order to serve his fellow humans by dragging them up, even though he is aware of their reactionary behavior towards the pains of enlightenment. Second, Plato reveals a secret of good government: there must govern persons who have seen-experienced something which is qualitatively higher than political government. Only persons who have been vindicated in their lives through something which is qualitatively higher than political government, and, therefore, they do not expect to feel existentially vindicated through the exercise of political power, must assume political power.

After the previous preliminary remarks, we must mention that Plato's myth of the cave is intimately related to what Plato has described as the graph of knowledge in the sixth book of his *Republic*, 510a-511e. According to Plato, knowledge can be graphically represented by a divided line: (i) the first half of this divided line corresponds to the knowledge of the visible things, and it is further divided into two parts: the realm of shadows, and the realm of images (which are more visible than shadows); (ii) the

second half of this divided line corresponds to the knowledge of the intelligible things, and it is further divided into two parts: the ideas of logical
reasoning (the realm of logical reality), and the supersensuous reality (the
realm of the Good). The myth of the cave transforms the previous graph of
knowledge into a lively story and, thus, it explains the manner in which
the problem of knowledge is experienced by humans. In other words, by
the myth of the cave, Plato transforms the abstract diagrammatical presentation of his epistemology into an experiential presentation of the life of
a man who struggles for knowledge. Hence, by narrating the myth of the
cave, Plato's graph of knowledge becomes a symbol of man's relationship
with truth, the levels of knowledge become steps of spiritual life, and the
divided line corresponds to the human condition. Thus, truth is not merely
an object of abstract thought, but it corresponds to an existential condition,
to a way of life and to a struggle.

At this point, we must make a remark which is very useful in order to
understand Plato's epistemology. When Plato says that, in the cave, prisoners see shadows, he means that they see actual things in a totally wrong
manner as a result of a confusion of their senses. In other words, Plato does
not refer to people who actually see shadows; if people were actually seeing
shadows, i.e., if they were seeing shadows as shadows, then there would
not be a problem. The problem of shadow which is posed by Plato is that
the prisoners see actual things as if they were shadows, i.e., they suffer by
darkened perception due to the confusion of their senses. For instance, if a
person who is in such a condition saw a book about gardening, he would
regard it as a garden. Hence, darkened consciousness corresponds to a loss
in the accuracy of vision.

In the myth of the cave and in his graph of knowledge, Plato distinguishes between four different types of vision, which are four different types of
knowledge and four different states of consciousness, or existential conditions: (i) illusion, or conjecture (*eikasia*), which provides only the most
primitive and unreliable opinions, (ii) belief (*pistis*), which is an experiential
form of knowledge which allows one to distinguish between objects and
their shadows but lacks epistemological and methodological rigidity, (iii)
rule-based reasoning, or logic (*dianoia*), with which we can achieve systematic knowledge of the objects of consciousness through a disciplined application of the understanding, and (iv) intelligence (*noeisis*), which is the
comprehension of the true nature of reality.

3.2 Illusion

Illusion, or conjecture/guess, is that level of knowledge at which one perceives an object as equivalent to whatever crosses his mind at the time he sees the given object. This is a cognitive condition in which a person is sunk in a great confusion of emotions. Such a person sees things and events through the prism of his arbitrary assumptions. For instance, a child below the age of three years often lives in a condition of illusion. In the case of adult persons, illusion refers to a spiritual condition in which a person is permanently childish, in the sense that such a person lacks criteria which make the distinction between reality and pseudo-reality (illusion) possible. Hence, if a person is at the level of knowledge which Plato calls illusion, he cannot discriminate reality from that which he himself would desire to be real. Such a person cannot accurately discriminate things from their images, and, therefore, he considers that things and their images are equally true. Moreover, such a person may argue that an appellation or a characterization of an object is true while ignoring the given object. For instance, such a person may see an automobile and identify it with the image of the given automobile he saw in an advertisement.

Propaganda and advertisement are based on the function of illusion, i.e., on the identification of the image of a thing with the reality of the given thing. In general, illusion means confusion between a thing and its image, or between a thing and a characterization of it, due to lack of adequate criteria. For instance, a two-year old child being in a state of illusion may attempt to bite a plastic apple because he/she identifies the image of an apple with the reality of an apple, and, similarly, an adult person who is in the cognitive stage of illusion bites the hook that an advertiser or a propagandist has set, due to lack of discretion.

At the level of illusion, the person is a victim of his emotions, because lack of discretion implies lack of critical thinking (the concept of critical thinking will be discussed in Section 3.5), and, therefore, in the absence of critical thinking, the power of emotion is uncontested and unlimited. In other words, at the level of illusion, man's historical action is determined by his sentiments. For instance, this happens several times during historical crises. In particular, at the critical points of the business cycle, the supremacy of emotions, weakness of sound judgment, logical fallacies, and susceptibility to external influence are realized eminently.

Moreover, many 'strategic communication' and 'public relations' consultants — following the principles and the techniques of commercial advertising and the values of consumerism — advise and convince politicians to transform politics into a process in which politicians vulgarize the electorate — by appealing to the electorate's appetites and emotions in order to gain power through easy and 'cheap' words — and the electorate, in its turn, vulgarizes the politicians, since it has been vulgarized by the 'political marketing' which substitutes political slogans and images for political discourse.

There is a strong tendency among post-modern scholars to compromise with the level of knowledge which Plato calls illusion. Some of the most characteristic examples of the post-modernists' epistemological pessimism in the scholarly discipline of International Relations are the following: Richard Ashley's work in his deconstruction of Waltz[170] in James Der Derian and Michael J. Shapiro[171], R. Ashley's and R.B.J. Walker's 1990 special edition of *International Studies Quarterly*[172], in which they explained[173] their post-modern project — or, more accurately, their refusal to have a project — in International Relations, and a similarly intentioned paper by Jim George and David Campbell[174].

3.3 Belief

The level of knowledge which Plato calls 'belief' corresponds to the spiritual condition of the man who transcends his illusions by means of the

---

170 R.K. Ashley, "Living on Borderlines: Man, Poststructuralism and War", in: J. Der Derian and M. Shapiro (eds), *International/Intertextual Relations: Postmodern Readings in World Politics*, Lexington: Lexington Books, 1989, pp. 259-321.

171 J. Der Derian and M. Shapiro (eds), *International/Intertextual Relations: Postmodern Readings in World Politics*, Lexington: Lexington Books, 1989.

172 R. Ashley and R.B.J. Walker (eds), Special Issue *International Studies Quarterly*, Vol. 34, No. 3, September 1990.

173 R. Ashley and R.B.J. Walker, "Speaking the Language of Exile: Dissidence in International Studies", Special Issue *International Studies Quarterly*, Vol. 34, No. 3, September 1990, pp. 259-268. R. Ashley and R.B.J. Walker, "Reading Dissidence/Writing the Discipline: Crisis and the Question of Sovereignty in International Studies", Special Issue *International Studies Quarterly*, Vol. 34, No. 3, September 1990, pp. 367-416.

174 J. George and D. Campbell, "Patterns of Dissent and the Celebration of Difference: Critical Social Theory in International Relations", in: R. Ashley and R.B.J. Walker (eds), Special Issue *International Studies Quarterly*, Vol. 34, No. 3, September 1990, pp. 269-293.

critical examination of his sensuous data. At this stage, consciousness can act critically and thus discriminate illusion from reality. For instance, at this stage, one is aware of the difference between an apple which is to be eaten (for some reason, e.g., in order to receive nutritious elements) and an apple which is drawn in a painting. As mentioned by Plato in the seventh book of the *Republic*, 515d, at the level of belief, man can discriminate the images of things from the prototypes. Even though, at this stage, man has not yet turned towards the 'sun', he has become aware of the difference between the "shadows" and the "puppets", or, one could say, for instance, between the advertisement of a car and the car itself.

The mind of the person who has ascended to the level of belief is more logical than the mind of the person who is at the stage of illusion, and, therefore, the first can control emotion and reduce the confusion of senses. The logic of the person who has ascended to the level of belief is not spontaneous, or mechanical, like the 'logic' of instinct, but it is measurable (i.e., consciously evaluated) and allows one to make basic distinctions between things. Thus, at the level of belief, takes place a considerable distinction between emotion and logic.

The mind of the person who is at the stage of illusion is characterized by uncontrolled 'emission' of emotion, and this uncontrolled 'emission' of emotion is the spiritual chaos which transforms everything into a shadow of itself. Thus, the person who is dominated by illusions (such as absolute beliefs, absolutely idealized loves, etc.), i.e., by factors which blindfold his logic, is dominated by shadows, and, in extreme cases, such a person ends up in serious psychological sicknesses, such as psychosis. In fact, the primary purpose of psychoanalysis is to help one discriminate his shadows — which are consequences of unconscious forces — from reality[175].

Hand in hand with the development of the ability to discriminate shadows from reality go the emergence of the principle of the mean and the treatment of virtue as a kind of moderation inasmuch as it aims at the mean. Without the ability to discriminate the image of a thing from the reality of this thing, the endorsement of the principle of the mean is impossible. This explains why the principle of the mean is absent from the spiritual life of the emotional people.

---

175 See: E. Nersessian and R.G. Kopff, Jr. (eds), *Textbook of Psychoanalysis*, Washington, DC: American Psychiatric Press, 1996.

In the second book of his *Nicomachean Ethics*, Aristotle defines the principle of the mean as a condition intermediate between two other states
— namely: excess and deficiency. This principle is closely related to the
concept of critical consciousness, which we shall study in Section 3.5. In
particular, in the sixth chapter of the second book of Aristotle's *Nicomachean
Ethics*, we read:

> Virtue, then, is a state of character concerned with choice, lying
> in a mean, i.e., the mean relative to us, this being determined by a
> rational principle, and by that principle by which the man of practi-
> cal wisdom would determine it. Now it is a mean between two vices,
> that which depends on excess and that which depends on defect;
> and again it is a mean because the vices respectively fall short of or
> exceed what is right in both passions and actions, while virtue both
> finds and chooses that which is intermediate. Hence in respect of
> its substance and the definition which states its essence virtue is a
> mean, with regard to what is best and right an extreme.[176]

The principle of the mean does not abolish emotion, but it endows emotion with a concrete structure and with concrete limiting conditions, thus
making it measurable. It is due to the principle of the mean that one can
determine the limits of emotion. Without the principle of the mean, emotion is unlimited. Thus, at the level of knowledge which Plato calls belief,
a relative order is established in the spiritual life of man. At this level of
knowledge, we realize that the emotional indeterminacy which characterizes persons and peoples who are very emotional can be fought by establishing a balance between reason and emotion and thus transforming an
indeterminate emotional world into a determinate one.

For instance, let us consider an artwork. An artwork is an objectification of a determinate emotion, i.e., of an emotion which is subject to a
'mean'. This 'mean' may be extremely subjective, but its very existence determines the identity of the artwork. If something is not determinate, i.e.,
if it is not endowed with a mean, it lacks a clear purpose, and the lack of a
clear purpose leads to a disorientated mental motion and, therefore, to lack
of creativity. Indeterminate motion (chaotic behavior) is a characteristic of
persons and peoples who are fixated in a childish spiritual age.

As a conclusion, at the level of belief, the approval and the disapproval of
beliefs take place rationally, because they are based on prior criteria which
allow the discrimination of shadows from reality. Additionally, the level of

---

176 Aristotle, *The Nicomachean Ethics*, trans. D. Ross, revised by L. Brown, Oxford: Oxford University Press, 2009.

knowledge which Plato calls belief generates a continuous quest for more and more rigorous criteria of action, but the light of scientific consciousness has not shined yet.

In the scholarly discipline of International Relations, some of the most characteristic examples of theories which correspond to the level of knowledge which Plato calls belief are those developed by Hans Morgenthau, the "British School of International Relations", and Henry Kissinger.

Hans Morgenthau argued that International Relations theory must be in a position to distinguish between shadows and reality by recognizing that, in international politics, there are factors "which no government is able to control but which it can neglect only at the risk of failure"[177]. However, he did not develop a scientifically rigorous theory of international relations, and, in fact, he renounced scientific methods and positivism. Morgenthau's theory of international relations corresponds to the level of knowledge which Plato calls belief because it provides for the distinction between shadows and reality but it is not scientifically grounded. Morgenthau's theory of international relations is only a technical guide to policy based on an understanding of generalizations about human behavior, to which Morgenthau arrived by reading history without following a scientific method.

The same level of knowledge — namely, 'belief' — characterizes the so-called "British School of International Relations", whose most prominent representative is Hedley Bull:

> The main thrust of Bull's argument rests upon an unqualified rejection of scientific standards as either a realizable or even worthy goal for the humanities... Although it was only Bull who went 'public' in his condemnation of behaviouralism, it is evident that both Butterfield and Wight were increasingly aware of the differences between their classical approach and the social scientific methodology of theorists such as Deutsch and Singer.[178]

Moreover, Henry Kissinger has developed a theory of international politics (mainly of foreign policy) which corresponds to the cognitive level of 'belief', because, on the one hand, he recognizes the difference between shadow and reality — in fact, he does so to the degree that he pessimistically argues that "the problem of evolution becomes one of 'if youth but knew

---

177 H.J. Morgenthau, *Scientific Man Versus Power Politics*, Chicago: University of Chicago Press, 1946, p. 66.
178 T. Dunne, "A British School of International Relations", in: J. Hayward, B. Barry, and A. Brown (eds), *The British Study of Politics in the Twentieth Century*, Oxford: Oxford University Press, 2003, p. 417.

and age but could"'[179] — but, on the other hand, he is limited to the study of historical analogies without scientific consciousness:

> Kissinger thus recognizes that the axioms and techniques he has drawn from his historical studies must be adapted to a changed world. However, he affirms that the fundamental dilemma of history remains: how to impose some sort of temporary order on a world whose natural tendency is chaos. To Kissinger the answer is to emu-late the methods of the great statesmen of the past.[180]

It is one thing to be aware of the difference between shadows and real-ity. But it is quite another to be able to confirm the truth of the criteria by which one discriminates shadows from reality. As Morton Kaplan put it:

> There is a great demand for theories in international relations... We cannot reason without generalization and, where matters are complex, the web of reasoning logically takes the form of a theory... The very difficulties of theory building and confirmation in inter-national politics demand sincere dedication to scientific cannons of procedure.[181]

Thus, the problem of correct reasoning emerges and urges us to move to a higher level of knowledge, which is rule-based reasoning, or logic.

3.4 Rule-based reasoning, or logic

The level of knowledge which Plato calls 'rule-based reasoning', or 'logic', corresponds to the stage at which the liberated prisoner, in the Pla-tonic myth of the cave, realizes his exodus to the light. In his myth of the cave, Plato writes that, as the liberated prisoner moves towards the light, he observes the heavenly bodies and the sky. By making this remark, Plato refers to the mathematical structure (order) of the world. Now, at the stage of rule-based reasoning, man can confirm the truth of the criteria by which he discriminates shadows from reality because he becomes aware of the existence of physical entities through their material substance and math-ematical structure.

---

179 H.A. Kissinger, *The Necessity of Choice: Prospects of American Foreign Policy*, Garden City, New York: Doubleday & Co., 1962, pp. 312-315.
180 T.J. Noer, "Henry Kissinger's Philosophy of History", *Modern Age*, Spring 1975, p. 187.
181 M.A. Kaplan, "Problems of Theory Building and Theory Confirmation in Interna-tional Politics", in: K. Knorr and S. Verba (eds), *The International System*, Princeton: Princeton University Press, 1961, pp. 6, 24.

The descriptions of objects by scientific consciousness are called formal models. In general, scientific consciousness operates in the following way: It recognizes an objective reality W, which contains material objects and events. Then scientific consciousness creates models of the elements of W. These models are descriptions of elements of W which use various techniques. Furthermore, there is a universal language E which can be used by the subject in order to describe any object which belongs to W.

In a scientific theory, the subject creates objects from W by means of E. In the different scientific disciplines, consciousness can use different subsets of E which are open systems, in the sense that, as scientific research progresses, they become enriched and more complete. The models of the objects of the scientific consciousness are usually symbolized by terms of E, and phenomena are usually characterized by judgments. When the models of phenomena are concrete, they are called relations, and, as terminology becomes richer and more accurate, some relations are called operations.

Let us define the basic models–relations R: 'belongs to' (e.g., $p \supset q$ means that q belongs to p, and, hence, if p is true then q is true), 'if ...   then', (e.g., $p \rightarrow q$ means that if p is true, then q is true), 'negation' (e.g., $\neg p$ means not p, i.e., p is false), 'or' (e.g., $p \vee q$ means either p is true or q is true or both), 'and' (e.g., p&q means p and q). Moreover, let the models-relations between the elements of R be expressed by means of a given set S of judgments of formal logic. Then we define T(R,S), which is the axiomatic system of formal logic. The models which satisfy T(R,S) are called concepts. In other words, the axiomatic system of formal logic determines that type of models which is called 'concept'. Science studies objects whose models are concepts. Hence, the object of formal theories is that model which is called concept.

Formal theories are hypotheticodeductive systems. A hypotheticodeductive system is a calculus endowed with a rule for the interpretation of its terms. By the term calculus, we mean a set of symbols endowed with a set of rules for their manipulation. Questions about meaning and hence about truth or falsity cannot be posed within the framework of a calculus. A calculus is exclusively a means for the transformation of sequences of symbols according to rules set by the user of the system. When a calculus is endowed with an interpretation of its terms (i.e., with a set of rules which determine the meaning of its terms), then it becomes a hypotheticodeductive system. A hypotheticodeductive system in which the rules for the interpretation of the terms of its calculus suffice in order to assign a truth value to its consti-tutive statements is called pure, and its statements are called E-determinate, where E is the language of formalization. For instance, in the statement 'if the cat is white, then the cat is white', the relation 'if then' suffices in order to characterize this statement as true without any reference to empirical data. According to formalism, pure mathematics and symbolic logic are pure deductive systems. On the other hand, in order to assign a truth value to the statement 'the cat is white', we need a decision rule with reference to empirical data; this type of statements are said to be non-determinate in the language of formalization E, and, when they are endowed with decision rules with reference to empirical data, they are said to be statements which refer to facts. The hypotheticodeductive systems which contain statements which refer to facts are called applied deductive systems.

The use of formal methods of analysis in International Relations is based on what Michael Nicholson has called a "conceptual community":

> A 'conceptual community' is a group of people who have broadly the same mutual understanding of various concepts relevant to a particular problem... To be a part of the conceptual community does not require being a member of a common experiential community. We can imagine social states which we do not experience. Thus it is possible to describe polygamy to someone from a monogamous society and vice versa and hope to be understood. We move on by deduction and analogy to the understanding of experiences well be-yond our personal experiences. We need to do so in order to gener-ate a social science.[182]

The earliest formal models used in social science in general and in In-ternational Relations in particular are provided by Decision Theory. The purpose of Decision Theory is to analyze choices available to an actor who is uncertain about the consequences of each possible choice. Uncertain infor-mation is handled by constructing a probability distribution over the set of possibilities[183]. Additionally, according to the model, the actor must be able to measure the desirability or undesirability ('utility') of each possible out-come. Hence, one can compute the expected utility of each available choice, by multiplying the utilities of the possible outcomes by their probabilities

182 M. Nicholson, op. cit. (ref. 66), pp. 105-106.
183 Bayesian probability is used very often, because it interprets the concept of probability as "a measure of a state of knowledge", in the sense that, according to Bayesian probability theory, the researcher specifies some prior probability which is then updated in the light of new relevant data (E.T. Jaynes, *Probability Theory — The Logic of Science*, Cambridge: Cambridge University Press, 2003).

once the given choice is made. Then one criterion of rational choice is to make the choice with the greatest expected utility, thus achieving an optimal balance between potential risks and benefits. For instance, Bueno de Mesquita[184] has applied this formal method of analysis in order to study the decision to go to war as a choice maximizing an individual leader's expected utility.

However, Decision Theory is not exhausted in the maximization of a utility function, but it recognizes that the desirability of an outcome may depend on a variety of factors. In fact, in Decision Theory, there are several forms of multiple criteria analysis which allow the researcher to model the manner in which different advantages are weighted up against each other[185]. These models are very useful in decision-making, and their operational significance has been enhanced by the use of computer software which allows the rapid processing of large databases and many parameters.

Because Decision Theory deals only with a single decision-maker or a group already engaged in collective decision, Game Theory was developed in order to study decisions made separately, by independent actors, but which have an impact on each other[186]. R. Snyder has reviewed Game Theory and its application in the study of political behavior as follows:

> The purpose of game theory is two-fold: to formulate mathematically complete principles that will specify what is rational behavior in certain kinds of social situations and, on the basis of such principles, to isolate the general characteristics of such behavior. Thus it is a method of analysis and a method of selecting the best courses of action... there are five concepts of game theory that must be mentioned. Fist is the concept of *strategy*... Strategy refers to a previously decided upon set of moves that complete the game in such a way that at least a certain minimal outcome is guaranteed regardless of what an opponent does. Strategy takes into account the potential behavior of opponents... there is always an optimal strategy available for both players. If only a single strategy happens to be optimal for each player, it is called *pure strategy*. If on successive plays, a different strategy is required to minimize loss and maximize gains, the strategy is said to be *mixed*... The *pay-off* refers to the value of the game to each player as pairs of strategies clash, a value that results when each person plays his optimum strategy... In parlor games, there are well-known 'rules' that govern play... the rules are the limiting condi-

184 B.de Mesquita, *The War Trap*, New Haven: Yale University Press, 1981.

185 See for instance: D.J. White, *Decision Theory*, Chicago: Aldine, 1969.

186 The first systematic exposition of Game Theory is due to J. Von Neumann and O. Morgenstern. See: J. Von Neumann and O. Morgenstern, *Theory of Games and Economic Behavior*, Princeton: Princeton University Press, 1944.

tions under which the game takes place... Another significant build-ing block of game theory is *information*. Presumably, every game will have a structure of information... the information state is included in the rules of the game... *Coalitions* are very important in n-person games. Two or more players may gain more as a unit. The pay-off is shared by the members of a coalition and may or may not be shared equally... One important aspect of overall strategy is the discovery that the pay-off function can be measurably increased by forming a coalition and that losses can be minimized by joining forces with other players.[187]

An important development in Game Theory is hypergame analysis, which is based on the assumption that the players in a game may perceive it in quite different terms. Hence, the basic model of hypergame analysis is not a single game seen by all the players but a set of subjective games, each expressing one player's view of the situation. In fact, hypergames incorpo-rate and explain: differences in player knowledge (expertise), differences in player starting situation assessment, differences in player on-going as-sessment capability, differences in player understanding of plan projection, differences in player information, differences in robustness of each player's plans, differences in player creativity (e.g., hidden reserves, deception op-erations, etc.), and player constraints because of time[188].

Nonlinear dynamics and chaos theory have important applications in social science and allow International Relations researchers to develop sci-entifically rigorous systemic theories[189] of international politics and analyze international conflict and order while working in a management science per-spective and using formal models to improve decision making. All nonlinear feedback systems[190], such as states, systems of states, corporations, markets,

---

187 R.C. Snyder, "Game Theory and Analysis of Political Behavior", in: .J.N. Rosenau (ed.), *International Politics and Foreign Policy*, New York: The Free Press of Glencoe, 1964, pp. 383-385.

188 S. Parsons, P. Gmytrasiewicz, and M. Wooldridge (eds), *Game Theory and Decision Theory in Agent-Based Systems*, Norwell, Mass.: Kluwer Academic Publishers, 2002.

189 "Each state arrives at policies and decides on actions according to its own inter-nal processes, but its decisions are shaped by the very presence of other states as well as by interactions with them... A systems theory of international politics deals with the forces that are in play at the international, not at the national, level" (K.N. Waltz, *Theory of International Politics*, New York: McGraw-Hill, 1979, pp. 65, 71).

190 In mathematical analysis, a system is said to be nonlinear if its output is not directly proportional to its input (see for instance: N.K. Laos, *Topics in Mathematical Analysis and Differential Geometry*, London: World Scientific Publishing Co., 1998). However, the distinction between linear and nonlinear analysis is not absolute, because a considerable part of information about a nonlinear system can be ex-tracted from a local linear approximation of the nonlinear problem, and, addition-

etc., can be studied as deterministic systems. In particular, every form of human organization (e.g., states, systems of states, corporations, markets, etc.) is a deterministic nonlinear feedback system because it is characterized by decision-making rules and by predetermined relations between actors who belong to the same organization or to different organizations (this is what we mean by the term 'institutional framework'). In such a system, actors must necessarily move around nonlinear feedback loops[191] which are formed by the corresponding institutional framework, and, therefore, the system in which actors make their choices is deterministic. But every time an actor moves around such a nonlinear feedback loop is free to transform, ignore or even overturn the established institutional/structural framework of action. In fact, even though actors follow given decision-making rules and behavior patterns, these decision-making rules and behavior patterns allow freedom of choice, i.e., they are susceptible to change, and, thus, for instance, it is possible for revolutions, wars, business innovations and legal reformations to occur. Hence, actors cannot escape from the fact that their interactions have the character of a nonlinear feedback system or from the consequences of this nonlinear feedback, but they can, indeed, each time, change the established decision-making rules and the established behavior patterns.

In nonlinear dynamics, the consequences of free choice on the system are classified into the following three categories:

(i) Stable outcomes: The outcome of every free choice depends on the intervention that a given actor has decided to make (i.e., on the purpose of action) as well as on the interventions that the other actors have decided to make. Thus, when all the actors of a given system conform to a specific set of behavior rules and make choices according to these rules, the entire system will end up in a state of stable equilibrium. In such a case, the system is driven by negative feedback[192], which causes 'regular', predictable behavior.

---

ally, it is often possible to extract information about the solution of a linear system from a relative nonlinear one. The term feedback refers to a situation in which output from an event in the past will influence an occurrence or occurrences of the same event in the present or in the future.

191 The term feedback loop refers to a situation in which information about the outcome of an action is sent back to the input of the system in the form of input data.

192 Negative feedback stabilizes the system. For instance, according to the law of diminishing marginal utility, if a person increases consumption of a product, while keeping consumption of other products constant, there is a decline in the marginal utility that this person derives from consuming each additional unit of the given product.

(ii) Unstable outcomes: When all the actors of a given system continuously change the rules that govern their behavior, then none of them can depend on others and the system will be driven by positive feedback[193] to a state of predictable, explosively unstable equilibrium. In other words, as the level of confrontation (something equivalent to what natural scientists call 'entropy') increases in a human system, the system moves from a state in which it is attracted to stable equilibrium to a state in which it is attracted to unstable equilibrium.

(iii) Edge of chaos: When a nonlinear feedback system is said to be at the edge of chaos[194] (or at the edge of stability, or at the edge of instability), we mean that its behavior is simultaneously characterized by stability and instability: it is unstable in the sense that it is impossible to predict a specific behavior in the distant future (i.e., long-term forecasting is impossible), and simultaneously it is stable in the sense that there is a determinate qualitative structure in its behavior (i.e., even though the exact quantitative study of such a system's evolution is impossible, the qualitative study of such a system is possible). For instance, the ordinary, irregular behavior patterns which are exhibited by actors in financial markets which are in a state of crisis can be identified and characterized in a relatively easy manner, but it is impossible to predict each time the specific evolution path of these behavior patterns. Hence, behavior at the edge of chaos is characterized by bounded instability.

Moreover, the formal methods of analysis used in social science in general and in International Relations in particular include Artificial Intelligence (AI) methods. AI is the science of making 'intelligent' computational programmes. Within the framework of AI, 'intelligence' refers to the computational part of the ability to achieve goals in the world. However, AI has not managed to formulate a general characterization of intelligent computational procedures. Some of the most important branches of AI are: logical AI (the knowledge of a programme about the world; the programme makes decisions by inferring that certain actions are appropriate for achieving

---

193 Positive feedback leads to divergent behavior in the form of indefinite expansion/explosion (a running away towards infinity, e.g., inflation, chain reaction, etc.) or elimination of initiative and choice (a running away towards zero, e.g., bankruptcy).

194 See: D. Stacey, *Strategic Management and Organizational Dynamics*, London: Pitman, 1993, and M.M. Waldrop, *Complexity: The Emerging Science at the Edge of Order and Chaos*, London: Viking, 1992.

its goals), search (a programme examines large numbers of possibilities), pattern recognition (a programme making observations compares what it sees with a pattern), representation (facts about the world are represented by means of languages of mathematical logic), inference (from some facts others are inferred), learning from experience ('neural networks' are particularly useful), planning, etc. The applications of AI include important achievements in game playing and expert systems[195]. AI has been used in International Relations mainly in order to build systems to mimic the behavior of certain political figures and, thus, to predict the real policy-maker's response to new situations[196], and to identify patterns within large volumes of data[197].

On the other hand, the knowledge achieved at the level of rule-based reasoning, or logic, has an inherent weakness. This type of knowledge recognizes reality in its most abstract, general form, but its axes of reference are elements of the given reality, and, therefore, this type of knowledge cannot lead by itself to the ultimate heights of the mental world where Plato's idea of the Good resides. In other words, according to Plato, the knowledge achieved at the level of rule-based reasoning, or logic, is exhausted in scientific hypotheses which are related only to the logical form of reality, and, therefore, this kind of knowledge cannot lead to the first, absolute principle, i.e., the Good. The reality of the world pulls the mind down to the world of senses and does not allow the mind to ascend to the world of ideas. The limits and the inherent weakness of the knowledge which is achieved at the level of rule-based reasoning, or logic, have been exposed in a scientifically rigorous manner by the famous mathematician and logician Kurt Gödel (1906-1978).

Before dealing with Gödel's work, we must explain David Hilbert's formalism. First of all, we must mention that 'formalism' is a philosophical theory according to which mathematical statements are consequences of

---

195 "A central issue in the design of expert systems is the representation and manipulation of uncertain and incomplete knowledge" (J. Gordon and E.H. Shortliffe, "A method for Managing Evidential Reasoning in a Hierarchical Hypothesis Space: A Retrospective", in: D.G. Bobrow (ed.), *Artificial Intelligence in Perspective*, Amsterdam: MIT Press/Elsevier Science Publishers, 1994, p. 43).

196 A.L. George, "The Operational Code; a Neglected Approach to the Study of International Political Leaders and Decision-Making", *International Studies Quarterly*, Vol. 13, No. 2, 1969, pp. 190-222.

197 S.J. Cimbala (ed.), *Artificial Intelligence and National Security*, Lexington: Lexington Books, 1987.

rules for the manipulation of certain strings of symbols. Thus, according to formalism, mathematical theories, such as the Euclidean geometry, are symbolic-logical games, like chess, consisting of some strings called axioms and some rules of inference by which mathematicians create new strings from those which are already established. For instance, in the 'logical game' of Euclidean geometry, we can prove the string which is known as the Pythagorean theorem. Moreover, formalism has been articulated in the form of deductivism. According to deductivism, for instance, the Pythagorean theorem (and generally every mathematical theorem) is not an absolute truth but a relative one, in the sense that, if one assigns meaning to the strings in such a way that the rules of the game become true (i.e., if one assigns true statements to the axioms and if the rules of inference are truth preserving), then he is obliged to accept the theorem, i.e., the interpretation he has given to it must be a true statement.

One of the founders of formalism was the famous mathematician David Hilbert (1862–1943). David Hilbert developed a research programme whose purpose was to be a complete and consistent axiomatization of all mathematics. A deductive system is said to be 'complete' if it contains a finite set of axioms (original strings of symbols) which suffices in order to determine the logical validity of all the strings ('theorems') that can be deduced from these axioms. In other words, a complete deductive system contains a finite set of axioms such that it will never bring us to the position of needing to accept an additional, new axiom in order to determine the logical validity of a statement which has been deduced from the original axioms of the given system. A deductive system is said to be 'consistent' if its set of axioms neither includes nor produces contradictions. Hilbert's goal of creating a system of mathematics that is both complete and consistent is equivalent to the formalization of all logical forms of thought. The success of Hilbert's formalistic programme would render Artificial Intelligence omnipotent, because then it would be possible to create a software programme which could capture all possible logical thoughts. In a sense, the accomplishment of Hilbert's formalistic programme would coincide with the elimination of creativity, since one could know a priori all possible logical thoughts on every occasion.

Hilbert aimed to show the consistency of mathematical systems from the assumption that the "finitary arithmetic" (a subsystem of the usual arithmetic of the positive integers, whose axioms are held indubitable in some kind of Kantian sense) was consistent. In 1931, Kurt Gödel published his ground-breaking article "On Formally Undecidable Propositions of Principia Mathematica and Related Systems"[198], in which he proved that, for any computable axiomatic system that contains the finitary arithmetic[199], the following theorems hold: (i) if the system is consistent, it cannot be complete, and (ii) the consistency of the axioms cannot be proven within the system.

From the perspective of algorithmic information theory, the 'scientific method' is defined as follows:

Theory/Programme/010 → Computer → Experimental Data/Output/110100101.

In other words, a scientific theory is a computer programme which produces exactly the experimental data, and both theory and data are a finite sequence of bits (a bit string). Then the complexity of a theory is defined to be its size in bits. Within the conceptual framework of this software model of science, a programme is said to be 'elegant' if it is the smallest programme that produces the output that it does. In other words, a programme is said to be elegant if no smaller programme written in the same programming language produces the same output. David Hilbert asked if we can be sure that a programme is elegant, i.e., the best theory for its output. Gödel's incompleteness theorem proved that we cannot.

Let us suppose that we have an N-bit theory A, i.e., one having N bits of axioms (and thus the complexity of A, denoted by H(A), is equal to N), and that it is always possible to prove that individual elegant programmes are in fact elegant and that it is never possible to prove that inelegant programmes are elegant. Furthermore, let us consider the following paradoxical programme P: P runs through all possible proofs in the formal axiomatic theory A in order to find the first proof in A that an individual programme Q is elegant, where the size of Q in bits is larger than the size of P in bits. Then when P finds Q, it runs Q and then P produces as its output the output of Q, which contradicts the definition of elegance, since the output of P is the same as the output of the first provable elegant programme Q that is larger than P. P is too small to be able to prove the elegance of Q, which is larger than P. Therefore, P cannot find Q, i.e., there is no proof in the formal axi-

198 See: J.W. Dawson, Jr., "Gödel and the Limits of Logic", *Scientific American*, Vol. 280, No. 6, 1999, pp. 76-81; J.W. Dawson, Jr., *Logical Dilemmas: The Life and Work of Kurt Gödel*, Wellesley Mass.: A.K. Peters, 1997.
199 For instance, the Peano Axioms, or the Zermelo-Fraenkel Axioms.

omatic theory A that an individual programme Q is elegant. In other words, A is incomplete, which means that, in order to prove the elegance of Q in A, we need to add new axioms, i.e., to increase the complexity H(A) of our theory A.

Thus, Gödel proved that Hilbert's formalistic programme is impossible: there is no way to give an axiomatization for all of mathematics or even for the finitary arithmetic which is sufficiently strong to prove all true theorems. In fact, Gödel proved Plato's theory of logical knowledge mathematically. Gödel's theorems show that a logical statement cannot establish itself on its own, i.e., logic cannot be in control of itself.

On the one hand, as we have already argued in this book, humans can, and should, rely on logic in order to put the world in order, human reason can, in principle, evolve to higher levels, and the world is rational. On the other hand, logic cannot establish itself on its own. Logic can be established only due to a super-logical (metaphysical) principle, which Plato calls the idea of the Good. According to Gödel, who was philosophically a Platonist, human mind and thought processes are not merely algorithmic. Gödel established the following argument mathematically:

> Either... the human mind (even within the realm of pure mathematics) infinitely surpasses any finite machine, or else there exist absolutely unsolvable Diophantine problems.[200]

Thus, for Gödel, important epistemological questions require philosophical methods that transcend formal mathematical methods and bring us in the realm of metamathematics and, in fact, in the realm of metaphysics. Hao Wang, studying Gödel's theorems, points that:

> The analysis of concepts is essential to philosophy. Science only combines concepts and does not analyze concepts. It contributes to the analysis of concepts by being stimulating for real analysis... Analysis is to arrive at what thinking is based on: the inborn intuitions.[201]

Gödel's theorems and Plato's philosophy help us understand why the idea of God or the divine does not necessarily contradict scientific progress. The 'Divine Reason' is not a particular logical structure of the world, but it is the source of the significance, or ultimate purpose ('end'), of the world

---

200 K. Gödel, "Some Basic Theorems on the Foundations of Mathematics and Their Implications", in: K. Gödel, *Collected Works*, Volume III, eds S. Feferman, J.W. Dawson Jr., W. Goldfarb, C. Parsons, and R.N. Solovay, Oxford: Oxford University Press, 1995, p. 310.

201 See: Hao Wang, *A Logical Journey — From Gödel to Philosophy*, Cambridge, Mass.: MIT Press, 1996, p. 273.

and of everything that exists in it. In other words, the Divine Reason is the metaphysical ultimate source of the significance, or end, of things, and not the logical structure of the natural world itself. Thus, if we understand God as the ultimate source of the significance, or end, of things, God's existence means that the natural world is meaningful, and it does not contradict any theorem of the natural sciences. Therefore, if by the term 'God' we mean the positive void from which the significance of things stems, no theorem of the natural sciences can prove or disprove the existence of God. The basic question which guides scientific discoveries is *'how* does the world exist?', i.e., science investigates the manner in which the world evolves. The basic question which gives rise to debates about God or the divine is *'why* does the world exist?', and this question is of a purely philosophical nature, and not of a scientific one. Hence, at least to the extent that one does not identify God or the divine with the logical structure of the natural world, every transformation of theorems of the natural sciences into metaphysical/theological arguments is logically fallacious. Thus, not only was Gödel a theist but also distinguished Divine Reason from the logical structure of nature.

The proof of logic's limits by Gödel vindicated intuitionism, which was defended in mathematics by an influential Dutch mathematician and philosopher, L.E.J. Brouwer (1881-1966). In the second and the third sections of his essay *Life, Art, and Mysticism*[202], Brouwer quotes the medieval mystic Meister Eckhart[203] on how people confuse acting and knowing, living for

---

202 L.E.J. Brouwer, *Life, Art, and Mysticism*, trans. W.P. van Stigt, *Notre Dame Journal of Formal Logic*, Vol. 37, No. 3, 1996, pp. 389-429.

203 "Some people want to look upon God with their eyes, as they look upon a cow, and want to love God as they love a cow. Thus they love God for the sake of external riches and of internal solace; but these people do not love God aright... Foolish people deem that they should look upon God as though He stood there and they here. It is not thus. God and I are one in the act of knowing". This statement by Eckhart leads to a knowledge of the divine based on the experience of the inner sense, i.e., on a high form of insight: "A master says, God has become man; through this all mankind is raised and exalted. Let us rejoice that Christ our brother has ascended by his own strength above all the angelic choirs and sits on the right hand of the Father. This master has spoken well, but in truth, I do not set great store by it. What would it avail me if I had a brother who was a rich man, and for my part I were a poor man? What would it avail me if I had a brother who was a wise man, and I were a fool?... The Heavenly Father brings forth his only-begotten Son in Himself and *in me*. Why in Himself and in me? I am one with Him, and He cannot shut me out. In the same act the Holy Ghost receives its being, and it arises through me as it does through God. Why? I am in God, and if the Holy Ghost does not take its being from me it does not take it from God either. I am not shut out in any way". Eckhart reminds us of the word of Saint Paul: "Clothe yourselves in

self-made illusions while insisting on knowledge and truth, and he argues that truth is to be found within oneself. Moreover, in the seventh section of his *Life, Art, and Mysticism*, Brouwer distinguishes immanent truths, which are suggested by perception, from the transcendent truth, which is primarily approached by discriminating oneself from the sensible world and breaking the cycle of fear and desire caused by our relationship with the sensible world.

3.5 Intelligence

According to Plato, intelligence is the supreme (*ne plus ultra*) level of knowledge, and it corresponds to the knowledge of the Good, which demands a different method of knowledge. Plato calls the method which leads to the knowledge of the Good "dialectic". This is a logical as well as post-logical method of knowledge. The knowledge of the Good is logical in the sense that it presupposes that the mind has progressed from the first level of knowledge to the third level of knowledge, and, therefore, it has overcome childishness and has transcended empirical knowledge and anecdotal wisdom. Simultaneously, the knowledge of the Good is post-logical in the sense that the mind which has absorbed the knowledge of the third level is aware of the limits of logic, and, additionally, it acquires intuitive knowledge. However, we must mention that the intuitive knowledge which is acquired at the fourth level of knowledge would be impossible without the educational progress of man through the previous levels of knowledge. For instance, Albert Einstein's intuitions about relativity theory would be impossible if he had not previously studied Riemannian geometry, which allowed him to understand the concept of curvature and the geometry of curved spaces. If Einstein's logic were Euclidean — instead of Riemannian

---

Jesus Christ", in order to invite us to submerge in ourselves, plunge down into self-contemplation, and know God shining in the depths of our being: "God has become man so that I might become God". In his treatise *Über die Abgeschiedenheit*, Eckhart argues about the relationship of external to internal perception: "Here you must know that the masters say that in each man there are two kinds of men: one is called the external man, that is, sensuousness; man is served by five senses, nevertheless he acts through the force of the soul. The other man is called the inner man, that is, the interior of man. Now you must know that every man who loves God does not use the faculties of the soul in the external man any more than is required by the five senses; and the interior does not turn to the five senses except as it is the director and guide of the five senses and watches over them so that, in their strivings, they do not pander to animality". See: M. Eckhart, *Meister Eckhart: The Essential Writings*, trans. R.B. Blakney, New York: HarperCollins, 1957.

— then he could not have the intuitions which allowed him to develop his theory of relativity.

At the fourth level of knowledge — namely, intelligence — man has already accomplished the following spiritual goals:

(i) He has cured-cleansed his emotions by reason. This is necessary for two reasons. The first reason is that crude emotions, i.e., emotions which are not controlled by reason, keep the human being at the level of instinct. At the level of instinct, man's conscious operation is minimal. Instinct is a highly formalized behavioural code which reflects the logical structure of organic nature. The correctness of instinctive behavior is determined by the practice of an unlimited number of generations. In fact, the assurance which characterizes instinctive activity is based on the accumulation of an unlimited quantity of experiences by the species. At the level of instinct, adaptation takes place according to the method of 'trial and error'[204]. At this level, the creativity of the human being is minimal. Thus, the first reason for which we must cure-cleanse our emotions by reason is in order to transcend the level of instinct and, thus, become more creative. The second reason for which we must make our emotions healthy by reason — instead of merely repressing them — is because "determination and emotions play an important role" in solving problems[205].

The famous mathematician George Polya, most noted for his work in heuristics and mathematics education, adds:

> Determination fluctuates with hope and hopelessness, with satisfaction and disappointment. It is easy to keep on going when we think that the solution is just around the corner; but it is hard to persevere when we do not see any way out of the difficulty... If your purpose is set, you stick to it, but you do not make it unnecessarily difficult for yourself. You do not despise little successes, on the contrary, you seek them: *If you cannot solve the problem try to solve first some related problem.*[206]

(ii) Furthermore, a person who has arrived at the fourth level of knowledge has already managed to discriminate shadows from reality. This is initially achieved when consciousness ascends from the level of instinct to

---

204 Jean Piaget, the pre-eminent developmental psychologist of the twentieth century, has pointed out that, through trial and error experimentation by handling objects, the concept that the external world is not part of the self or an extension manifests.

205 G. Polya, *How to Solve It*, Princeton: Princeton University Press, 1973, p. 93.

206 G. Polya, op. cit. (ref. 205), pp. 93-94.

the level of experience. At the level of experience, the intentionality of consciousness is expressed through the functioning of the senses. The senses are oriented towards the external world, with which they connect existence. At the level of experience, consciousness realizes that the structure of the world is not identical with the structure of consciousness. In fact, since consciousness must try hard in order to know the world, it realizes that the knowledge of the world is not equivalent to the self-knowledge of the subject, and, therefore, consciousness understands the difference between itself and the world.

However, at the level of experience, consciousness functions in a rather pathetic manner, since, according to the empiricist philosophers, consciousness is originally a "tabula rasa", i.e., a blank slate, on which experience writes, thus filling the mind with ideas, and only at a second stage consciousness recalls those ideas which seem useful to it in order to act on various occasions. Additionally, at the level of experience, consciousness can achieve only an incomplete knowledge of its problems, either because it rashes into certain mental activities (e.g., calculations, constructions, etc.) without any plan or general idea, or because it waits clumsily for some idea to come and does practically nothing in order to accelerate the coming of an idea. In carrying out a plan for problem-solving, a conscious being which is at the level of experience tends to be careless and impatient in checking each step, and, therefore, its rational operation needs to be perfected by ascending to the level of intellect.

(iii) In addition, a person who has arrived at the level of intelligence has already developed a scientific consciousness, i.e., his consciousness has already managed to ascend from the level of experience to the level of intellect. At this level, reason plays an active role. Reason is a pre-existent (*a priori*) structure within the framework of which there exist various functions of categories, which, when they are adequately activated, can connect isolated segments of sensation (i.e., empirical data) into a whole, thus allowing the formulation of synthetic statements. Thus, reason allows consciousness to transcend the level of experience and impose its intentionality on the world. Through reason, consciousness realizes that the structure of the world is not fundamentally different from the structure of consciousness, because, otherwise, consciousness could not obtain even a partial knowledge of the world. In other words, at the level of intellect, the human being realizes that the structure of consciousness and the structure of the world are not identical, but they are united. Therefore, at this level, the human being manages to discriminate himself from the world — thus experiencing his 'royal' position in the natural world, as we read in the Bible — in order to re-integrate himself into the world under better conditions.

During this process, reason allows consciousness to operate in a 'critical' manner which consists in the following four-fold dialectical process[207]: First, consciousness conceives an ideal state of the world — namely, the idea of the Good — and aims at acting on the historical plane in order to change its existential conditions in accordance with its conception of an ideal state of the world. Second, consciousness aims at acting on the historical plane in accordance with the principle of the mean. By following the principle of the mean, consciousness avoids intervening in the world in a manner which could cause uncontrolled turbulence and thus jeopardize the continuity of existence, and also it avoids acting in a manner which would be inferior to its capabilities of improving its existential conditions. Third, when consciousness realizes that its historical action tends to cause

---

207 Throughout this book, I use the term 'critical' in order to refer to the above four-fold dialectical process. Moreover, I call every conscious being which follows the above four-fold dialectic a 'critical consciousness'. Therefore, my definition of the term 'critical' in this book is substantially different form the way this term has been defined by the 'Frankfurt School' (Max Horkheimer, Theodor Adorno, Jürgen Habermas, etc.). The definition of the term 'critical' which I follow in the present book includes the concepts of timing and kairology. One of the first intuitive ways of understanding timing can be found in the Bible, where Solomon King of Israel writes in Ecclesiastes 3:1-8: "To every thing there is a season, and a time to every purpose under the heaven: A time to be born, and a time to die; a time to plant, and a time to pluck up that which is planted; A time to kill, and a time to heal; a time to break down, and a time to build up; A time to weep, and a time to laugh; a time to mourn, and a time to dance; A time to cast away stones, and a time to gather stones together; A time to embrace, and a time to refrain from embracing; A time to get, and a time to lose; a time to keep, and a time to cast away; A time to rend, and a time to sew; a time to keep silence, and a time to speak; A time to love, and a time to hate; a time of war, and a time of peace". The concept of kairology is derived from the ancient Greek god Kairos, who was assumed to be in control of the right moment, i.e., Kairos was the god of the contemporary notion of timing. See: H. Kelman, "Kairos — The Auspicious Moment", *American Journal of Psychoanalysis*, Vol. 29, 1969; M. Bakhtin, *The Dialogic Imagination*, Austin: University of Texas Press, 1981; E. Moutsopoulos, *Kairos et alternance: d' Empédocle à Platon*, Athènes: Académie d' Athènes, 1989; and R.B. Onians, *The Origins of European Thought about the Body, the Mind, the Soul, the World, Time, and Fate*, New York: Arno Press, 1973. Ian A. Williams, in his *Kairology — A Time for Personal Development* (New Zealand: Phantom Publishing, 2008), explains that 'kairos' is an ancient Greek term for non-chronological time, or the "intersection of timing and opportunity". The human behavior which I call 'critical' throughout this book has been characterized as "kairic" by E. Moutsopoulos (ibid).

uncontrolled turbulence and thus jeopardize the continuity of existence, it undertakes new action which balances its previous action, and, when consciousness realizes that its historical action is inferior to its capabilities of improving its existential conditions, it intensifies its intervention in the world. Fourth, during its action upon the reality of the world, consciousness aims at forming the necessary conditions which will allow consciousness to continue acting upon the reality of the world in the future.

Thus, from the above critical perspective, history is an expression of humans' potential. Humanity is in a process of more and more intense confirmation of its presence in the world, by becoming more and more aware of its presence in the world. However, due to the critical activity of humanity, the continuity of the historical becoming is not completely substituted by the discontinuity which is caused by the action of consciousness upon the world; instead, the continuity of the historical becoming is reconstructed by the imposition of the intentionality of consciousness on time. As a conclusion, instead of being defeated in his battle against a necessary historical becoming, man overcomes natural necessity due to his freedom which allows him, through critical action, to reconstruct the world.

As the ancient Greek geometrician Pappus of Alexandria has pointed out, reason is based on a dual mental tool: analysis and synthesis[208]. In analysis, we start from what is required, i.e., we take it for granted, and we draw more and more consequences from it until we reach a point that we can use as starting point in synthesis; thus, analysis is also known as regressive reasoning. In synthesis, we reverse the process by starting from the point which we reached last of all in synthesis and we derive from it the things that preceded it in the analysis, and continue making derivations until we finally arrive at what is required.

As I have already mentioned, at the level of 'intelligence', the idea of the Good which is conceived by consciousness and guides the historical action of consciousness is the outcome of a process which is simultaneously logical and post-logical. At the fourth level of knowledge, the mental sensitivity of the person has been increased dramatically, through the spiritual itinerary he has followed until then, and thus he feels subtle signs of spiritual progress or notices their absence where the persons who belong to a lower level of knowledge are unable to perceive the difference.

---

208 See: T.L. Heath, *The Thirteen Books of Euclid's Elements*, Cambridge: Cambridge University Press, 1908, Vol. 1, p. 138.

In order to understand the level of knowledge which corresponds to intelligence, we must bear in mind that, according to Plato and Aristotle, knowledge does not consist in abstraction, but it is a relationship with an idea which can be known by human consciousness and simultaneously it transcends human consciousness. On the other hand, many modern philosophers dissociate 'truth' from 'reality' and identify truth with a logical abstraction of reality. Contrary to what many scholars argue, this idealistic attitude of modern philosophy is not compatible with Aristotle's conception of the abstract character of general concepts. For, even though Aristotle substitutes immaterial species (kinds), or forms, for the transcendental Platonic ideas and, thus, he articulates a philosophy of the 'immanent' (since 'form' is the universal aspect of a sensuous thing, i.e., the highest level of abstraction of a sensuous thing), he argues that the knowledge of the abstract is a task of the soul in its intellectual operations and that reason — which is, potentially, whatever the soul can conceive or think — can be distinguished into creative reason and passive reason.

In passive reason, concepts are merely potential, and passive reason operates in the medium of sensuous images. On the other hand, active reason is pure actuality, and, in it, the intellectual activity of the soul and its object are united. Therefore, because, in Aristotle's philosophy, creative reason is not trained by the senses, but it transcends the body and the sensuous faculty of the soul, Aristotle's conception of 'theory'[209] is in agreement with Plato's philosophy, and Aristotle understands 'substantial truth' as a transition from potentiality to actuality, i.e., as the natural or spiritual perfection of a being, and not as an abstraction of a particular being. Therefore, both the rationalist interpreters of Aristotle's philosophy — such as Thomas Aquinas — who thought that Aristotle's theory of concepts provided grounds for the justification of natural theology (a logo-centric approach to God), and the nominalists, who thought that Aristotle's approach to concepts provided grounds for cognitive relativism, have failed to grasp important aspects of Aristotle's philosophy, which prove the fundamental agreement between Platonism and Aristotelianism on the suprarational character of

---

209 For instance, K. Knight, in his *Aristotelian Philosophy — Ethics and Politics from Aristotle to MacIntyre* (London: Polity Press, 2007), has methodically shown that Aristotle's practical philosophy — namely, his ethics and politics — is decisively connected to and shaped by his metaphysics, and he has emphasized that, for Aristotle, theory (*theoria*), the noblest human activity, is the contemplation of the pure being.

the ultimate source of knowledge. Moreover, many modern philosophers, radically departing from Platonism and Aristotelianism, argue that truth is only an outcome of logical deductions, because they consider that truth is a logical abstraction separated from the reality of the idea. However, I have already mentioned that it has been logico-mathematically proved by Gödel that truth cannot be fully formalized by any logical/mathematical method. Hence, it becomes useful to look more carefully into Plato's dialectic.

There is an important difference between the type of universalism which is based on 'concepts' and the type of universalism which is based on Platonic 'ideas'. The type of universalism which is based on concepts implies that the degree of reality of an object is equivalent to its degree of generality. Thus, from the viewpoint of the type of universalism which is based on concepts, the individual is not real, and therefore we can ignore it, oppress it, or even send it to concentration and extermination camps, such as those of the Nazis and the Soviet Gulag, so long as we serve the universal, which may be the 'whole', the 'society', the 'people', the 'proletariat', the 'nation', the 'race', the 'state', etc., according to the ideology of the elite which has the monopoly of knowing the universal exactly because it occupies the apex of the social pyramid. The nominalists attempted to safeguard the value of the individual by arguing that general concepts are only names and that the individual is real. However, in this way, the nominalists opened a path to nihilism. If only the individual is real, truth does not have any universal value. If there is not a universal truth by which and in which individuals can be related to each other and structured in an ordered world ('cosmos'), or society, then, ultimately, the chaos of nihilism is the only alternative.

On the other hand, the universality of the Platonic idea does not imply a suppressive generality — such as the generality of a concept — in which the value of the individual is nullified. Instead, the Platonic idea is universal due to its ontological autonomy, and simultaneously the individual can partake of the reality of the idea. In other words, the Platonic idea is not a general concept which suppresses every entity which has a lower degree of generality than the given concept, but it is the ultimate meaning of existence, which transforms history into an itinerary towards a potential perfection. Thus, the Platonic idea, far from nullifying the value of the individual, ascribes infinite value to the individual which partakes of the reality of the idea, because, by partaking of the reality of the idea, the individual's life is an itinerary towards the Absolute. Through its participation in the Platonic idea, the individual consciousness is intensified because it is in a personal relationship with the Absolute. Hence, within the framework of the Platonic theory of ideas, universalism does not contradict individualism. Within the framework of the Platonic theory of ideas, we, as individual human beings, are not victims of the generality of a concept, but we are partakers of the Absolute on the basis of our free, personal decision to recognize the Absolute as the end of our life and to experience the Absolute mystically in our consciousness.

Contrary to what the German idealist Eduard Zeller[210] has argued, in Platonic philosophy, the 'individual' is not absorbed or nullified by the 'universal', since Platonic 'ideas' are not 'concepts'. It is because Thomas Aquinas and other scholastic philosophers identified the term 'idea' with the term 'concept' that many scholars interpret Platonic philosophy as if it were a totalitarian formula. Totalitarianism is the outcome of the thesis that the degree of generality is equivalent to the degree of reality. The argument that the degree of generality is equivalent to the degree of reality has been defended by Thomas Aquinas and other rationalist interpreters of the Greek philosophy. However, this is not the case with Plato.

The sixth book of Plato's *Republic* makes amply clear that, in Plato's philosophy, the term 'idea' should not be identified with the term 'concept' for two reasons. First, in Plato's *Republic*, the Good itself is not determined by its essence — namely, it is free from every essential determination — since it is beyond and above the world of ideas and it is the ultimate, absolutely transcendental, cause of the existence of ideas and of man's cognitive capacity. Second, because in Plato's *Republic*, 508d, the Good is synonymous to the terms truth and idea. Under the light of the Good, truth is the revelation of the being in its perfection (in its 'idea'), as opposed to its imperfect empirical reality ('phenomenon'). The Good is absolutely transcendental, and, therefore, external to human consciousness, but it embraces the human being from the inside, i.e., it is available to be known by the psyche which decides to turn towards the Good. As we read in Plato's *Republic*, 476b, as well as in the entire Platonic dialogue *Phaedro*, the relationship between the philosopher and the Good is not only a cognitive one but also an erotic one. Within the framework of Plato's philosophy, the human being becomes in-

---

210 E. Zeller, *A History of Greek Philosophy*, trans. S.F. Alleyne, London: Longmans, Green and Co., 1881.

dividuated through its *personal* — namely, free from every rational necessity — relationship with the Good[211].

In Plato's philosophy, the 'idea' is not a historical entity, but it is a transhistorical, metaphysical entity (irreducible to practice) which is the end and the guide of historical action. Therefore, Plato's *Republic* is not an exposition of a coercive cornucopia, but it is an exposition of the metaphysical idea which should inspire and guide an actual republic, and, exactly because Plato's *Republic* is not a practical political platform itself, but it is the transcendental end of practice, it rules out totalitarianism. Totalitarianism is based on the doctrine that the end of practice, i.e., of historical action, is a necessary practical, historical, goal. On the other hand, when the end of historical action is not a historical goal, but a metaphysical one of purely qualitative character — such as the idea of the Good — then historical action is based on freedom, because it is a matter of personal choice. Thus, Plato's *Republic* should not be interpreted as a political-legal institution, but as an archetype, or symbol, of political-legal institutions. Plato's *Republic* teaches that the 'idea' is a principle which guides practice, but the 'idea' itself is irreducible to practice. Thus, Plato's metaphysics saves history from both totalitarianism and nihilism. For, totalitarianism is based on the transformation of an absolute principle into a political-legal institution, and nihilism is based on the transformation of every goal into a means for the pursuit of another goal. But, as Thomas Jefferson wrote to John Adams in 1816, "true wisdom does not lie in mere practice without principle"[212].

According to Plato, ideas are the life of God's essence and, thus, the partaker of the world of ideas is a partaker of divinity. From the perspective of man's perfection through his participation in the world of ideas, the reduction of the 'mind' to the 'intellect' (i.e., to logic) is equivalent to the "ancestral sin", because it implies that a person is self-restricted in his logical structures and refuses to receive the light of the metaphysical 'sun' of the Good. Hence, the 'mind' must be distinguished from the 'intellect', because, in Plato's philosophy, the mind is receptive to the light of the metaphysical 'sun' of the Good and connects the person with what Carl Gustav Jung[213] has called the archetypes of the collective unconscious. In other words,

---

211 See also: M.M. McCabe, *Plato's Individuals*, Princeton: Princeton University Press, 1994.

212 T. Jefferson, "Thomas Jefferson to John Adams", 1816, Memorial Edition, Vol. 15, p. 75.

213 A. Casement, *Carl Gustav Jung*, London: Sage, 2001, pp. 40-41

within the framework of Plato's philosophy, the mind is a spiritual entity in the image of God[214], and, therefore, it transcends consciousness, it is 'unconscious' (or one could also say 'superconscious'), which, for Jung, means that it is equivalent to the undiscovered area of the psyche. Thus, the mind knows through its participation in the Good (the divine), which is the ultimate meaning of existence. On the other hand, if the mind is reduced to the intellect, i.e., to the rational operation of consciousness, then reason loses its link with the ultimate meaning of existence (which is post-logical, i.e., suprarational), and, under the painful experience of this spiritual loss, the mind looks for the meaning of existence in the practical use and utility of sensuous things. Then, within the human mind, the position of the trans-temporal ultimate meaning of existence is taken by a temporal meaning of existence which reflects a utilitarian approach to existence. Whereas the intellect perceives things as objects without any metaphysical significance, the mind extends the knowledge of things in order to capture their ultimate significance and it affirms that things are not merely material realities, but primarily they are spiritual realities. Therefore, Plato's theory of ideas achieves a spiritual unity of the world without ruling out the diversity of the world.

Plato extended his dialectical method far beyond Socrates' method of 'maieutics'[215]. In Plato's dialogue *Sophist*, 253c-d and 264c-265, it is shown

---

214 The spiritual progress of the human being through its participation in the Good, which has been described in a rigorous philosophical language by Plato in his theory of ideas, plays a central role in the Judeo-Christian religious scriptures: "God said, 'Let us make man in our image, after our likeness.'" (Genesis 1:26). "You, therefore, must be perfect, as your heavenly Father is perfect." (Matthew 5:48). "Do you not know that you are God's temple and that God's Spirit dwells in you?... For God's temple is holy, and that temple you are." (1 Corinthians 3:16-17). "I have been crucified with Christ; it is no longer I who live, but Christ who lives in me." (Galatians 2:20). "As God is called merciful and gracious, so you be merciful and gracious, offering gifts gratis to all; as the Lord is called righteous and loving, so you be righteous and loving." (Midrash, Sifre Deuteronomy). "Beloved is man, for he was created in the image of God. But it was by a special love that it was made known to him that he was created in the image of God." (Mishnah, Abot 3:18). "Let a man always consider himself as if the Holy One dwells within him." (Talmud, Ta'anit 11b).

215 Maieutics means midwifery, and it is a pedagogical method according to which the idea of truth is latent in the mind of every human being due to his innate reason, but it has to be 'given birth' through a form of inquiry and debate between individuals with opposing viewpoints based on asking and answering questions in order to stimulate critical thinking and thus illuminate ideas. See: Liddell, Scott and Jones, *Greek-English Lexicon*, 9th Edition, and *Webster's New World College Dictionary*, 4th Edition.

---

that Plato developed dialectic as a taxonomic method by which beings can be classified into genera[216] and species in order to become objects of rational inquiry. Before Plato, dialectic was a method of seeking truth through oppositional discussion and a negative method of hypothesis elimination in order to convince the opponent. In Plato's dialogue *Phaedo*, 90a-b and 100d-e, it becomes clear that Plato transformed dialectic into an art of reconciliation with one's spiritual self, and, in Plato's dialogues *Theaetetus*, 154d-e, *Charmides*, 166c-e, *Philebus*, 38c-e, *Sophist*, 263e, and *Laws*, 893a, we realize that Plato understood dialectic as a form of inner dialogue which presupposes that the philosopher's soul seeks truth in order to achieve existential perfection. Moreover, in his *Phaedo*, 89d-90d, Plato argues that, without a method of correct reasoning ("belief without art"), every argument becomes an idol, an illusion, and undermines every attempt to develop a conceptual study of phenomena. In his *Philebus*, 57-58, Plato shows that his method of classifying things into genera and species leads from one concept to another until the philosopher's mind conceives the ultimate causes of things, and, therefore, the philosopher manages to know the truth of phenomena through their reduction to ideas.

According to Plato's philosophy, reducing a collection of phenomena to an idea is equivalent to understanding their unity into a 'whole' which is a universal significance and value (idea). In other words, the purpose of the mind's movement from impressions to truth and from phenomena to ideas is a value. Hence, within the framework of Plato's philosophy, ideas are neither our own concepts of things nor images of things, but they are the fundamental values of things, which hold universally, irrespective of whether some persons, like, for instance, the prisoners in the Platonic myth of the cave, want to know them or not. Ideas hold universally because, within them, life acquires an intrinsic value (i.e., a value beyond ephemeral conventions), whereas every other existential condition lacks intrinsic value, since it is conventional, and, hence, it is perilous because it is self-overcoming and, thus, potentially self-destructive. For instance, the prisoners in the Platonic myth of the cave can establish an order of things based on their illusions, but this order will be threatened with collapse immediately after the first expression of doubt about its merits, and the expression of doubt

---

216 In biology, the term genus (plural: genera) is a taxonomic category above a species, since it consists of a group of species exhibiting similar characteristics. By analogy, in logic, the term genus refers to a class of objects divided into subordinate species having common attributes.

about its merits will be only a matter of time, since illusions rule out the knowledge of truth as universal value, which could underpin a real peace.

The difference between a conventional order and a real peace has been emphasized by Henry Kissinger as follows:

> [T]he attainment of peace is not as easy as the desire for it. Not for nothing is history associated with the figure of Nemesis, which defeats man by fulfilling his wishes in a different form or by answering his prayers too completely. Those ages which in retrospect seem most peaceful were least in search of peace. Those whose quest for it seems unending appear least able to achieve tranquillity. Whenever peace — conceived as the avoidance of war — has been the primary objective of a power or a group of powers, the international system has been at the mercy of the most ruthless member of the international community. Whenever the international order has acknowledged that certain principles could not be compromised even for the sake of peace, stability based on an equilibrium of forces was at least conceivable.
>
> Stability, then, has commonly resulted not from a quest for peace but from a generally accepted legitimacy. Legitimacy as here used should not be confused with justice. It means no more than an international agreement about the nature of workable arrangements and about the permissible aims and methods of foreign policy. It implies the acceptance of the framework of the international order by all major powers, at least to the extent that no state is so dissatisfied that, like Germany after the Treaty of Versailles, it expresses its dissatisfaction in a revolutionary foreign policy. A legitimate order does not make conflicts impossible, but it limits their scope. Wars may occur, but they will be fought *in the name of* the existing structure and the peace which follows will be justified as a better expression of the legitimate, general consensus. Diplomacy in the classic sense, the adjustment of differences through negotiation, is possible only in legitimate international orders.
>
> Whenever there exists a power which considers the international order or the manner of legitimizing it oppressive, relations between it and other powers will be revolutionary. In such cases, it is not the adjustment of differences within a given system which will be at issue, but the system itself. Adjustments are possible, but they will be conceived as tactical manoeuvres to consolidate positions for the inevitable showdown, or as tools to undermine the morale of the antagonist. To be sure, the motivation of the revolutionary power may well be defensive; it may well be sincere in its protestations of feeling threatened. But the distinguishing feature of a revolutionary power is not that it feels threatened — such feeling is inherent in the nature of international relations based on sovereign states — *but that nothing can reassure it.* Only absolute security — the neutralization of the opponent — is considered a sufficient guarantee, and thus the

desire of one power for absolute security means absolute insecurity for all the others...

> The characteristic of a stable order is its spontaneity; the essence of a revolutionary situation is its self-consciousness. Principles of obligation in a period of legitimacy are taken so much for granted that they are never talked about, and such periods therefore appear to posterity as shallow and self-righteous. Principles in a revolutionary situation are so central that they are constantly talked about. The very sterility of the effort soon drains them of all meaning, and it is not unusual to find both sides invoking their version of the true nature of legitimacy in identical terms. And because in revolutionary situations the contending systems are less concerned with the adjustment of differences than with the subversion of loyalties, diplomacy is replaced either by war or by an armaments race.[217]

Kissinger's conception of international order is equivalent to a plan to nullify the spirit; in this case, by the term 'spirit', we mean that part of the human being which transcends biological and historical necessities, and, thus, spirituality signifies the deepest values and meanings by which consciousness evaluates and modifies its existential conditions. For, as I have already shown, meaning-giving is an essential human function and the presence of sensible data within the human consciousness is always related to the meaning that consciousness gives to them. By arguing that a legitimate international order is spontaneous and by treating self-consciousness as a cause of international disorder, Kissinger exhibits an extreme form of mistrust to the spiritual potential of the human being and additionally he proposes the elimination of freedom and moral responsibility from human life as a necessary presupposition of order. But then what is the value of such an order?

Kissinger endorses a pessimistic, in fact nihilistic, attitude towards the idea of peace, because his political theory corresponds to the level of knowledge which Plato calls belief, and, therefore, he refuses to think beyond a conventional order of things based on impressions. On the other hand, truth as universal value — something ignored by Kissinger and the British political legacy which Kissinger praises — enters deeply into the mind of agents and thus it has a deeply transformative cultural impact. Kissinger exposed his departure from the humanistic ethos of Thomas Jefferson and his self-imprisonment in the darkness of the intellectual 'cave' of the 'British

---

217 H.A. Kissinger, *A World Restored — Europe after Napoleon: The Politics of Conservatism in a Revolutionary Age*, New York: Grosset and Dunlap, 1964, pp. 1-3.

School' of international politics in a speech he delivered on 10 May 1982 at the Royal Institute of International Affairs under the title "Reflections on a Partnership: British and American Attitudes to Postwar Foreign Policy". In particular, Kissinger said in that speech:

> The British undoubtedly saw the Americans as naïve, moralistic, and evading responsibility for helping secure the global equilibrium. The dispute was resolved according to American preferences — in my view, to the detriment of postwar security. Fortunately, Britain had a decisive influence over America's rapid awakening to maturity in the years following. In the 1940s and '50s our two countries responded together to the geopolitical challenge of the Soviet Union and took the lead in creating the structures of Western cooperation for the postwar era which brought a generation of security and prosperity... Where Americans have tended to believe that wars were caused by the moral failure of leaders, the British view is that aggression has thrived on opportunity as much as on moral propensity, and must be restrained by some kind of balance of power. Where Americans treated diplomacy as episodic — a series of isolated problems to be solved on their merits — the British have always understood it as an organic historical process requiring constant manipulation to keep it moving in the right direction. Britain has rarely proclaimed moral absolutes... In moral matters Britain has traditionally practiced a convenient form of ethical egoism, believing that what was good for Britain was best for the rest.[218]

Kissinger argues that the British ideological influence helped Americans mature by compromising, or even abandoning, the moral visions and goals of the Founding Fathers of the American Republic. However, the British ideological influence which Kissinger praises had exactly the opposite impact on the American psyche than the one which Kissinger contends. Far from helping Americans mature, the British ideological influence methodically undermined the maturity and the spiritual autonomy of the United States of America.

In a balance-of-power system of international politics, like the one which Henry Kissinger espouses, the behaviours of the states are not co-ordinated by any universal moral code. On the contrary, the states' behaviours serve the logic of selfish historical goals and particularly are based on the calculation of necessities of policy which arise from the unregulated competition among them. The calculation of necessities of policy can only temporarily balance the explosiveness of the expansionism of the state and harmonize

---

218 H.A. Kissinger, "Reflections on a Partnership: British and American Attitudes to Postwar Foreign Policy", *Executive Intelligence Review*, 11 January 2002.

it with a form of social consciousness which is necessary in order to create anti-hegemonic alliances and thus sustain equilibrium. The calculation of necessities of policy can only temporarily balance the explosiveness of the expansionism of the state because, according to the system of balance of power, the state — with its selfish goals and requests — is the ultimate criterion of balance-of-power politics. When the individual state — with its selfish goals and requests — is the ultimate criterion of an international order, and when this international order is not guided by any universal values which could transcend the sovereignty of the state (due to their universality), then this international order is self-destructive and ends to war, not because states stop calculating their interests, but exactly because they calculate the maximization of their interests independently of any moral code and culture as the source of that moral code. In other words, since the state — with its selfish goals and requests — is the ultimate criterion of balance-of-power politics, an international order based on balance of power makes states more and more ego-centric and hence less and less social, and this means that states become less and less capable of creating viable alliances among them in order to keep the international system in equilibrium.

A balance of power is not a self-sufficient ideal. Power is sought for certain ends, which reflect the value systems of different societies. The first Europeans who talked of redressing the balance and formed coalitions were fighting for concrete values against concrete threats. In particular, they were protecting their political and religious liberties. For instance, when William of Orange (1650-1702) taught the British to think in terms of the balance of power, it was because Britain was threatened with an invasion which would end up in the restoration of a despotic king. Moreover, when The Right Hon. William Pitt (1759-1806) revived the principle of balance of power against Napoleon, he was representing a nation which was fighting for hearts and homes. Neither William of Orange nor William Pitt aspired to a balance as a principle good and necessary in itself, or as a necessary condition for Europe.

When a statesman — such as Cardinal Richelieu (1585-1642) or Henry Kissinger — talks of a balance as an end in itself, he usually means a balance favourable to himself. Without any agreement on common values and institutions, the balance-of-power system means that all negotiation is carried on according to power calculations. Therefore, this system urges the states to negotiate in order to maintain the status quo, and at the same time it urges them to continuously increase their power, since their arguments are weighed by the power of each player. Hence, the balance-of-power system ends up in catastrophic results, as great powers become more and more concerned with the maximization of their power, since they do not share a common set of moral and institutional commitments, or as all great powers are regimented — as they were before World War I — in one coalition or another and thus they lose the advantage of open-mindedness in political problem-solving.

The balance-of-power system recognizes the significance of collective action for the maintenance of international order (what Kissinger calls "legitimacy"), but the absence of common values and institutions and the obsession with power calculations implant mutual hatred and suspicion and they make states split into factions, at feud with one another and incapable of undertaking effective initiatives of joint action. The effect of the spiritual poverty of the balance-of-power system is, apparently, to make united action impossible because of factions and quarrels and also to set every member of the international society at enmity with any opponent and with the powers which want to maintain the established international order. As a conclusion, by eroding the social consciousness of the members of the international society, the balance-of-power system incubates phenomena that it is supposed to deter — namely, nationalism and/or rigid coalitions.

At this point, we need to stress that, when truth is understood as logical certainty, then it can lead to naïve behaviours, because it is chimerical and cultivates arbitrary idealistic mentalities. From this perspective, the aim of the British empiricism-skepticism and of the British conservatism to show the uncertainty of knowledge seems to be vindicated. However, the Platonic myth of the cave shows an alternative way of understanding truth. In particular, instead of understanding truth as logical certainty, we can understand truth as value and ultimate cause. Plato and Aristotle started philosophizing by seeking the ultimate cause, the ultimate meaning, of beings, and this quest led them to a notion of truth whose value consists in its universality and, therefore, in its ability to lead humanity to the principles of legal egalitarianism and justice which transcend every conventional political and legal order, and, exactly because they transcend every conventional political and legal order, they are the deontological underpinnings of all positive law. On the other hand, many modern philosophers have a different starting point. In particular, many modern philosophers' starting point is a radical departure from the Platonic idea of truth and the declaration that individual consciousness is an ontologically sufficient foundation of truth. For instance, Cartesianism identified truth with the certainty of thinking, empiricism identified truth with feelings and impressions, voluntarism identified truth with will, Hegelianism identified truth with the certainty of the self-awareness of the nation, etc. Thus, even though these modern philosophers exposed the dynamic character of human consciousness and promoted the individuation of man through self-awareness, they cultivated a feeling of existential tragedy, because the modern individual had to live in a world without universal values. This existential tragedy gave birth to the tragic nihilism of Nietzsche and of the post-modernists.

On the other hand, Plato's philosophical legacy rejects the reasoning of every kind of tragedy and does not compromise with any form of fear because it is focused on the unity between the individual soul and the universal truth. In fact, this unity underpins Aristotle's conception of man as a political animal[219], i.e., as a *naturally* social being. Thomas Jefferson was intuitively following the spiritual legacy of Plato and Aristotle when he was arguing that "truth is the first object"[220] and that "truth is certainly a branch of morality, and a very important one to society"[221].

Plato — contrary to modern monistic philosophies of the idealistic type — did not reject the reality of the sensible world. Plato's aim was not to separate our mental life from the sensible world and phenomena; instead, his aim was to provide a firm foundation for the sensible world and phenomena. Thus, Plato proposed his theory of ideas because he wanted to expose the reality of the sensible world and not out of some negative feeling towards the sensible world. Moreover, in Plato's ideal world, unity includes plurality. For instance, Plato's argument that, in any particular horse, he sees 'horseness' (i.e., the general property of being a horse) does not mean that he wants to nullify the reality of the sensuous horse; instead, it means that his knowledge of the sensuous horse is related to the unity of horses' substance ('horseness'), a unity which cannot be founded on the senses, but

---

219 According to Aristotle's *Politics*, 1253a2, we are by nature "political animals" exactly because we participate in a universal spiritual reality, and, for this reason, Aristotle — in his *Politics*, 1280a25ff — explicitly rejects the view that the state's authority rests on any 'social contract'.

220 T. Jefferson, "Thomas Jefferson to Dr Maese", 1809, Memorial Edition, Vol. 12, p. 232.

221 T. Jefferson, "Thomas Jefferson to Thomas Law", 1814, Memorial Edition, Vol. 14, p. 139.

on the idea of a horse, i.e., on that level of existence which is not exhausted in biological operations. By asking the question 'what is it?' — namely, by asking for the substance of a being — Plato endows the transient and uncertain form of the term 'horse' with a firm foundation — namely, its idea ('horseness').

From the perspective of Plato's theory of ideas, words signify that being is united with becoming, i.e., being is united with the image of a mode of existence which is circumstantial and diversified. Thus, we can say "E pluribus unum": out of many, one (the idea). Due to the 'idea', words do not merely signify phenomena (becoming) but also they signify being, and, thus, due to the 'idea', human reason can lead to knowledge. Idea is the answer to the question 'what is it?', and, therefore, it is neither a formal reproduction of a phenomenon nor a copy of the sensible world, but it integrates otherwise unrelated sensuous elements into a unified whole, and, thus, it proves to be the purpose and the structure of sensuous phenomena, and not merely an abstraction. At the level of the senses, life is dominated by transient and unrelated experiences of the present, and, thus, knowledge is necessarily local and uncertain, whereas, at the level of the idea, one achieves a unified, global knowledge of the sensuous elements.

As we have already mentioned, Plato does not nullify the reality of the material world, because his philosophy is based on a hierarchical understanding of the world and not on abstraction. Abstraction leads to a transcendental world which is dominated by the logical identity relation[222], and, therefore, whatever deviates from the established truth is abolished. On the other hand, according to Plato's hierarchical perspective of the world, there is no reason to nullify the reality of the sensible world, and simultaneously the circumstances of the sensible world cannot, and should not, be the foundation of knowledge. Thus, Plato created the hierarchical system of the four levels of knowledge — namely, illusion, belief, logic, and intelligence — which we studied in the previous sections of this chapter.

In Plato's philosophy, 'existence' is the area between being and becoming. These two poles of existence are very different from each other. Being corresponds to the eternal and the infinite. Becoming corresponds to that whose genesis has taken place in time and to the finite. The unity between these two poles of existence gives birth to particular beings which are not

---

222 In logic, the identity relation is defined to be the binary relation that holds only between a thing and itself.

eternal, like the ideas, but they are mixed (combinations of being and be-coming) and born in time. Thus, Plato, in *Timaeus*, 37a-38b, argues that being as being corresponds to the trans-temporal, becoming corresponds to the temporal, i.e., to that which takes place in time, and particular beings, e.g., the human being, exist in time because they are the outcome of the unity between being and becoming.

Plato's hierarchical conception of the world endows sensible events with a moral end and leads to the conclusion that all things have a meaning which transcends the logic of the sensible world. This is emphasized by Plato in *Timaeus*, where we read that the sensible world participates in the harmony and the perfection of the ideal world. The idea of the participation of the sensible world in the harmony and the perfection of the ideal world led Aristotle to argue, in his *Metaphysics*, 1080a19, that the qualities of the sensible world are compatible with the qualities of the ideal world, because the difference between the mental world and the sensible world does not imply that the first is a distinct species (kind) from the second, but it im-plies that the sensible world is characterized by necessity[223] whereas the ideal (intelligible) world is characterized by freedom. However, there is a unity between the sensible world (becoming) and the ideal world (being) in the same way that there is a dialectical relationship between necessity and freedom.

If we approach and seek to know things only in terms of their becoming, then we cannot have a theory of justice, but only theories of governance. A.T. Williams has pointed out the inability of the modern world to develop a theory of justice for so long as it continues to see things only in terms of their becoming:

> values, the most fundamental of which appear in Article 6(1) of the Treaty of European Union, have been applied in a haphazard fashion and without an understanding of normative content. The European Court of Justice has instead adopted a largely pragmatic approach that has focused on principles or virtues of governance rather than attempting to offer a way of satisfactorily defining values or ensur-ing their realization. The underlying philosophy thus appears to be

---

223 Physical time is, more or less, uniform. On the other hand, historical time is sub-ject to structural changes. Moreover, as it has been shown by I. Prigogine and I. Stengers, in their book *Order Out of Chaos — Man's New Dialogue with Nature*, New York: Bentam, 1984, physical time obeys its own entropy, which means that it flows in a precise and unalterable (irreversible) direction towards a precise but unknown aim. On the other hand, historical time is a free outcome of human consciousness.

based on a theory of interpretation (of original political will) rather than a theory of justice.[224]

Only if we approach and seek to know things from the perspective of being can we talk meaningfully about justice.

3.6 The psychological presuppositions of intelligence, and justice

In order to understand Plato's philosophy, we must always keep in mind that the absolute good is not a concept, and, therefore, man's relationship with it is based not only on logic but also on intuitive reason. In other words, humans can attain a personal experience of the absolute good, but they cannot logically deduce the absolute good from a necessary chain of syllogisms; for, as we have shown in Section 3.5, logic is limited, whereas the absolute good is unlimited. Furthermore, the absolute good is the absolute being, whereas the human is a 'mixed' being (partaking of being and becoming).

The absolute good is subjectively experienced by humans within the framework of a personal relationship, but the absolute good itself is not subjective, and, therefore, the subjectivity of the states of human consciousness do not undermine the objectivity of the absolute good, and the objectivity of the absolute good does not contradict the subjective aspects of human life. Only if the absolute good were a concept would it contradict the subjective aspects of human life and would impose itself on humans in a totalitarian manner. It is because the absolute good is the absolute being that it is free from every logical determination (by contrast with concepts) and that it can be known by the human being only if the latter decides to turn its mental eyes towards the absolute good. Hence, the knowledge of the absolute good by the human being is a dynamic process which signifies a progressive itinerary of the human being towards perfection. In other words, the knowledge of the absolute being by the human being is equivalent to one's transition from becoming to being. Thus, Plato emphasizes that the knowledge of the absolute good presupposes not only the ability to give an account but also a psychic cleansing or cure.

According to Plato's *Meno* and *Gorgias*, the knowledge of something presupposes the ability to give an account. In *Meno*, 97e-98a, Plato distinguishes the level of knowledge which corresponds to intelligence from belief as

---

224 A.T. Williams, "Taking Values Seriously: Towards a Philosophy of EU Law", *Oxford Journal of Legal Studies*, Vol. 29, 2009, p. 549.

something which requires us to "work on the reason" before it becomes "stable", and he argues that a belief that is not examined rationally will "run away from a man's mind" as the statues of Daedalus escape when they are not tied down. In *Gorgias*, 454e and 465a, Plato distinguishes flattery from crafts because it cannot provide a rational account of itself, and he argues that, in cases where rhetoric is a form of flattery, it can only produce belief without knowledge. Moreover, according to Plato, the 'elenchos' is the means through which one seeks such an account, and, in the seventh book of the *Republic*, he argues that the ability to give an account characterizes the followers of his dialectical method, who investigate the beautiful and the good.

However, as we explained in Section 3.5, the knowledge which corresponds to the level of intelligence does not consist merely in the ability to give an account, but it is the result of the soul's participation in the pure being, so that, for Plato, the power of reason has two different aspects: the contemplative or intuitive, which corresponds to intelligence, and the logical, most often denoted by the term 'dianoia'. The metaphysical type of knowledge which corresponds to intelligence is what Plato has in his mind in *Phaedro*, 247c-e, where he describes the soul journeying in "that place beyond the heavens":

> It is there that true being dwells, without color or shape, that cannot be touched; reason alone, the soul's pilot, can behold it, and all true knowledge is knowledge thereof. Now even as the mind of a god is nourished by reason and knowledge, so also is it with every soul that has a care to receive her proper food; wherefore when at last she has beheld being she is well content, and contemplating truth she is nourished and prospers, until the heaven's revolution brings her back full circle. And while she is borne around she discerns justice, its very self, and likewise temperance, and knowledge, not the knowledge that is neighbour to becoming, and varies with the various objects to which we commonly ascribe being, but the veritable knowledge of being that veritably is. And when she has contemplated likewise and feasted upon all else that has true being, she descends again within the heavens and comes back home. And having so come, her charioteer sets his steeds at their manger, and puts ambrosia and draught of nectar to drink withal.

Thus, as we have already mentioned, ideas, being the life of the Good's essence and the teleological structures of things, can only be contemplated by man when he is in a certain state, i.e., when he is has cleansed, or cured his soul. In his *Republic*, 443d-e, Plato argues that one has cured his soul if he has

> attained to self-mastery and beautiful order within himself, and... harmonized these three principles [the three parts of the soul: reason, the emotions, and the appetites], the notes or intervals of these three terms quite literally the lowest, the highest, and the mean, and all the others there may be between them, and... linked and bound all three together and made himself a unit, one man instead of many, self-controlled and in unison.

According to Plato, this harmony is attained when each part of the human soul fulfils its proper role, which, as we read in Plato's *Republic*, 441d-e, means that the rational part of the soul, aided by the thymos (emotions, or spiritedness), must rule over the entire soul "being wise and exercising forethought in behalf" of it. In other words, the cure of the soul is equivalent to the introduction of order in the soul.

The cure of the soul, for Plato, does not imply that reason should repress appetites or emotions. Instead, in Plato's *Republic*, 572a, we read that the necessary condition for psychic harmony is that appetites and emotions are "neither starved nor indulged to repletion". Hence, the three parts of the soul must be organized in harmonious rule, and each part should fulfil its own function.

Combining knowledge with psychic cleansing or cure, Plato shows the nature of truth, which, as we have already mentioned, is not equivalent to an abstract concept, but it holds as a reality which is identical with the transcendental divine essence and is experienced by humans as an inner psychic harmony and through an inner psychic harmony. It is exactly because truth exists outside us, i.e., transcends us, that the knowledge of truth is connected with psychic cleansing or cure. This transcendental truth is in Plato's mind when, in *Republic*, 520e, he refers to the world outside the cave where the philosopher lives in a state of psychic cleansing, and when, in *Phaedo*, 109b, he articulates a mythological cosmography ("the earth itself is pure and is situated in the pure heaven in which the stars are"). Furthermore, Plato exposes his theory of truth in the sixth book of the *Republic*, where he refers to the illumination of the material bodies by the sunlight by analogy with the illumination of the intelligible objects by the Good.

In order to understand the Good, Plato, in the *Republic*, 507a-508d, invites us to imagine that the Good is like the sun, which, by casting its light, makes the objects of the sensible world visible. By analogy, as we read in

Plato's *Republic*, 508c-d, the Good sheds truth on the objects of the intelligible world and makes them accessible to our understanding, so long as they are illuminated by the truth. The presence of the sunlight as a third factor between our eyes and the objects of our vision implies that the function of vision is not representational, but it is formative, in the sense that the cause of our understanding of all things is the Good, which makes all knowledge hung together, and, thus, our vision represents that special significance which constitutes the spiritual substance of the object of our vision. Without this significance which illuminates the object of vision and makes it accessible to our mind, vision is blurred and darkened. Thus, the sunlight reveals not only the corporeal substance of beings, i.e., their individuality, but also their spiritual substance, so that individuality is endowed with a moral quality — namely, 'society', since, as I mentioned before, all things are teleologically united in the Good. In fact, this is, for Plato, the ultimate foundation and source of 'society': the teleological unity of all things in the Good.

Sine, as we read in Plato's *Republic*, 585b, the purpose of our existence is our participation in the pure being (the Good) and our unification with the Good, psychic cleansing is a necessary presupposition for our transformation into the corresponding absolute principle; for, as Plato argues in *Phaedo*, 67b, "it cannot be that the impure attain the pure". Plato emphasizes purification, i.e., psychic cleansing and cure, because he understands vision as witnessing of the sunlight. Without this third factor, the sunlight, our vision becomes essentially subjective and the significances of the objects of our vision reduce to abstract concepts. On the other hand, as I have already explained, in the sunlight, all things are teleologically united in the Good and our vision corresponds to our understanding of the teleological way of existence of the objects of our vision. Hence, Plato's approach to psychic cleansing consists in the liberation of the spirit from the relativity of subjective existential criteria, and this liberation allows humans to partake of the pure being, transcending their material self, as much as possible.

The prisoners in the Platonic myth of the cave symbolize that soul which, being imprisoned in the bodily senses and suffering by the senses' inability to create a cosmos (i.e., a harmonious whole), gives priority to appetites and emotions over reason. In fact, in Plato's *Republic*, 517b, we read: "And if you assume that the ascent and the contemplation of the things above is the soul's ascension to the intelligible region, you will not miss my surmise, since that is what you desire to hear". It is exactly because the Platonic myth of the cave symbolizes the itinerary of the soul towards the light that it is a dramatic narration of the human being's existential itinerary, and not merely a theory of knowledge. Plato understands the knowledge of truth not only as a form of accurate perception but also as a therapeutic training of the soul, i.e., as *paideia*, and therefore he symbolizes the soul by a man and articulates the myth of the cave.

Therefore, Plato develops a theory of justice which is centred on quality instead of quantity. In fact, in *Crito*, 48a, Plato argues that where justice is concerned,

> what we ought to consider is not so much what people in general will say about us, but how we stand with the expert in right and wrong, the one authority who represents the actual truth. So in the first place, your proposition is not correct when you say that we should consider popular opinion in questions of what is right, honourable and good, or the opposite.

This amounts to Plato's refusal to substitute the quantitative for the qualitative, and it is a clear rejection of *ad populum* inferences.

The most common form of ad populum argument is "the mob-appeal subtype", which "occurs where a speaker whips up the emotions and enthusiasms of a mass audience", i.e., he arouses a "mob mentality"[225]. Adolf Hitler is a characteristic example of a master of this technique. Additionally, in "the bandwagon type of ad populum argument, a whole group of people are involved, and presumably, they are unanimous or all agree that proposition A is true"[226]. This moral justification type of ad populum argument can be used in different ways — for instance: in some cases, "it is used to argue for an action or policy by using the premise 'Everybody (who is good) is doing it'"[227], and, in other cases, the ad populum argument "is used as an excuse. When somebody is accused of doing something bad, their reply is, 'Well, everybody else is doing it, so it couldn't be so bad after all — or at least it is excusable'"[228]. Many crimes against humanity and many phenomena of economic corruption are based on ad populum inferences. Plato is aware of that, and, therefore, Crito, if he is to convince the Platonic Socrates, he must appeal to valid arguments, instead of following the practice of ad populum arguments.

225 D. Walton, *Appeal to Popular Opinion*, Pennsylvania: The Pennsylvania University Press, 1999, p. 196.
226 D. Walton, op. cit. (ref. 225), p. 204.
227 D. Walton, op. cit. (ref. 225), p. 208
228 D. Walton, op. cit. (ref. 225), p. 208

Moreover, Socrates, in his *Apology*, emphasizes that justice presupposes a cultivation of the soul which will allow people to ascend to the same level of knowledge and, thus, they will be able to understand the meaning of *being* just; for, otherwise, those people who are at a lower spiritual level, like the prisoners in the Platonic myth of the cave, react against those who are at a higher spiritual level. In fact, Socrates said in his *Apology*, according to Plato:

> O men of Athens, that if I had engaged in politics, I should have perished long ago and done no good either to you or to myself. And don't be offended at my telling you the truth: for the truth is that no man who goes to war with you or any other multitude, honestly struggling against the commission of unrighteousness and wrong in the state, will save his life; he who will really fight for the right, if he would live even for a little while, must have a private station and not a public one.

Socrates makes clear that the Athenians are not fit to govern themselves in a just manner, and, therefore, if the Athenian mob has any authority, it will prevent anyone from imposing justice in the city of Athens. Hence, if democracy is dissociated from training in dialectic, there can be no such thing as just democracy. Thus, for Plato, psychic cleansing or cure is the essence of justice, and the Platonic dialectic is the proper method for attaining it.

The soul/city analogy is explicitly proposed by Plato in the *Republic*, 435b, where he argues that "a just man will not differ at all from a just city in respect of the very form of justice, but will be like it". The soul, like the city, will be just because "three natural kinds existing in it performed each its own function" (ibid).

Plato's philosophy helps us understand that the present is the point where the outcome of the past meets the potential of the future (ontological perfection). Justice in the individual is the harmony of the individual's soul, a harmony that makes the individual a partaker of the absolute being, the Good. From this perspective, justice in society is a state in which political life helps the human soul experience and deploy its potential towards perfection. Thus, justice in society is a form of social harmony which implies that the destiny of humanity is to work collectively as a societal mediator and bridge-maker between the intelligible realm of the pure being and the sensible realm of becoming.

In Plato's philosophy, justice, injustice, and punishment are the three reference axes for the articulation of his psychological thought. According to Plato's *Phaedro*, 271, the term 'psychological' refers to the training of the soul in order to attain virtue, and not to the modern concept of psychology, which refers to the subjective, inner world of the individual. In other words, justice, injustice, and punishment underpin Plato's pedagogical humanism, which can be summarized in the following four principles:

First, as we read in Plato's *Alcibiades*, 130c, *Phaedo*, 115c, and *Republic*, 469d, the value of the human being is not an abstract concept, but it is re-ducible to the honour which belongs to the human soul (i.e., the person-hood of the human being) due to its participation in the absolute being (the Divine Reason) and requires a specific way of life, a way of life whose aim is continuous self-improvement through the practice of virtue. In *Gorgias*, Plato argues that the human who has false priorities, and, thus, appetites and emotions take precedence over reason in his soul, harms his soul, and this happens whenever he refuses to undertake his personal responsibility for unjust acts committed by him, when he is pathetically guided by his ap-petites against the law, and when he believes that life itself is the ultimate value and fails to acknowledge that the ultimate meaning of life — namely, the idea of 'good life' — transcends life itself.

In the history of Greek thought, the earliest evidence for the doctrine of human imitation of the divine shows the notion's importance for Py-thagorean thought, which influenced Plato. One of the most thoroughgo-ing sources for Pythagorean doctrine, Iamblichus' biography of Pythagoras, places the imitation of God at the centre of Pythagorean ethics:

> All their decisions with regard to actions to be performed and to be avoided are directed towards agreement with the Divine: this is the first principle and their entire life is directed to following God. The meaning of this philosophy is that a person acts in a ridiculous fashion when seeking the good elsewhere than with the gods: just as if a person in a country ruled by a king were to honour one of the citizens as a governor, neglecting the ruler of the country as a whole. This is how they think that people in fact behave.[229]

Second, at every level of human life — namely, at the individual, the moral, the social, and the political levels — Plato gives priority to the idea of organization, or harmony, since the Good safeguards the teleological unity of all things. In *Timaeus*, 44e-44d, Plato emphasizes that the human being will have no rest until it brings the irrational forces of its soul (appetites and

---

229 Iamblichus, *Vita Pythagorica*, 86-87. See: L. Deubner, *Iamblichi de vita Pythagorica*, Leipzig: Teubner, 1937.

emotions) into conformity with the uniform motion of reason, and, in the *Laws*, 713e-714a, Plato, following *Timaeus* and the *Republic*, treats reason as the divine or immortal element within us.

Third, intimately related to the previous principle is the emphasis Plato places on the unity between true knowledge, justice and virtue, as we see, for instance, in the dialogues *Menexenus*, 274a, and *Laws*, 864a. At this point, it is useful to make an important remark about 'Platonic psychotherapy'. The love which characterizes 'Platonic man' and which is based on the lovable nature of the Good or the divine and on the teleological unity of all humans in the Good, obviates the emotional forms of religiousness/spirituality in which each believer has his own private, and thus selfish, relationship with God or the divine. This fact has immense significance for the loneliness and existential abandonment which often accompany psychological impairment. Given that, in the Platonic philosophy, all humans are teleologically united in the Good, the 'I' contains the 'You', since the subject is a morally responsible person. Thus, from this standpoint, the individual will does not necessarily undermine the cohesion of the society or the moral stability of the individual.

Fourth, in *Gorgias*, Plato proposes a model of reformative punishment which involves a complex system of conditioning, encouragement and education, and which is described as therapy. Additionally, in the *Republic* (409a ff, 445a), the medical metaphor remains unchanged, and it is emphasized that the criminal is to be completely converted (445b3). According to the *Republic*, conditioning is suitable treatment for the appetitive part of the soul (554a7), encouragement is appropriate for the emotional part (468a ff), and education refers to reason (444d8 ff). Furthermore, in the fifth book of the *Laws*, Plato introduces the question of punishment again by the prudential argument: a man's soul is his most divine possession, but people tend, giving in to the blandishments of pleasure, to harm their souls instead of honouring them. Hence, as we read in the *Laws*, 725b ff, one may deny responsibility for his misdeeds, considering wrongdoing to be beneficial, whereas it is harmful. The criminal is an unfortunate person, whose mind must be fully converted in order to understand his true benefit. However, in the *Laws*, Plato adds that there must exist a subordinate system of more severe punishments for the penal treatment of incurable criminals.

Chapter 4. Moral Consciousness, Humanity, and Normative Issues

4.1 Values and moral consciousness

From a broad perspective, the concept of civilization includes the concept of culture, but, from a narrower perspective, 'civilization' can be differentiated from 'culture' on the basis of the argument that 'civilization' is simultaneously the means and the result of the collective consciousness's attempt to achieve better terms for its adaptation to the world, whereas 'culture' is the result of man's reflection on his life. The word civilization is derived from the Latin word 'civis', which means citizen of a city, and thus it is etymologically indicated that civilization refers to the means and the consequences of civil life. Civilization is a structure which consists of technology and institutions. On the other hand, culture is a reflective attitude towards institutions and an attempt to transcend institutions through ideas.

The primary pursuit of civilization is to impose human reason on the world and thus control the forces of the world. In other words, civilization means the transformation of the natural world into the dominion of human reason and will. Human reason, under its different manifestations — namely, technical, scientific, and moral ones — superintends the successive phases of civilization and evaluates them according to its own criteria, i.e., according to the criteria of the collective consciousness, whose highest expression is human reason itself. These criteria are subject to change according to the manner in which a society conceives its needs, i.e., according to the manner in which a society conceives the problem of scarcity of resources[230]. Irrespective of the particular mix of material and spiritual goals towards which a civilization is oriented, the material element is, generally speaking, more striking in civilizations rather than in the corresponding cultural structures. In other words, from a rather narrow perspective, civilizations tend to be "mechanical"[231], in the sense that they give priority to the satisfaction of needs over the acquisition of spiritual goods.

However, civilization and culture are neither contradictory nor incompatible to each other. There is a fundamental and substantial difference between them due to the fact that civilization corresponds to 'technical construction', whereas culture corresponds to 'spiritual creation'. Nevertheless, civilization not only includes culture, but also it underpins the historical subsistence of culture.

Hence, there is a dialectical relationship between civilization and culture, both at the level of their essence and at the level of their expressions. Civilization primarily refers to institutions and technology, whereas culture is primarily associated with the inner life of the human being, i.e., with the ideas which guide the human being in creating institutions and technology. Thus, from the perspective of civilization, the progress of man's historical itinerary is evaluated according to the degree to which he continuously invents and utilizes new means by which the conscious mind can act on the external world. On the other hand, from the perspective of culture, the progress of man's historical itinerary is evaluated according to the degree to which the objects of consciousness persist and are qualitatively enriched over time, as it happens with philosophy, religion, science, and art. The dialectical relationship between civilization and culture indicates a strong connection between these two manifestations of the intentionality of consciousness, so that we cannot talk about a sharp 'distinction' between civilization and culture but rather about a 'differentiation' between them.

---

230 In an influential 1932 essay, Lionel Robbins defined economics as "the science which studies human behavior as a relationship between ends and scarce means which have alternative uses" (L. Robbins, *An Essay on the Nature and Significance of Economic Science*, 2nd edn, London: Macmillan, 1935, p. 16).

231 This argument has been discussed extensively by the French philosopher Émile-Auguste Chartier, commonly known as Alain (1868-1951). See: A. Maurois, *Alain*, Paris: Gallimard, 1963.

The research work of Claude Lévi-Strauss[232] in structural anthropology has shown that a form of culture was present even during the most primitive stages of the development of spiritual life and that culture consists in a reflection and a transcendence of the material civilization. The structures of culture correspond almost completely to the structures of civilization, even though the structures of culture act 'correctively', and this makes them more harmonious and more complex than the structures of civilization. Intimately related to the concept of culture is the concept of value. As Raymond Polin[233] has put it, value is the "centre of interest" of consciousness when the latter is engaged in practice. Hence, value transcends practice by being the guide of practice and simultaneously dwells in practice by being the structure of practice, which, in its turn, confirms the existence of value. Practice is a specific expression of two things: (i) the turn of consciousness towards a value and consciousness's quest for that value; (ii) the incorporation of value in the object of practical action.

With respect to its nature, moral consciousness is not a different entity than consciousness in general. In general, 'consciousness' is an ontological synopsis of the human being as well as the means by which the human being confirms its autonomy and its quest for other beings, which it meets at the level of their own conscious minds[234]. Moral consciousness is consciousness itself when it expresses approval or disapproval of the structure and the style of an action whose aim is to change the relationship between a being and the world or the relationship between a being and other beings. Moral consciousness, as a special function of the consciousness of existence, can be differentiated from psychological consciousness. Psychological consciousness is a consciousness which conceives itself as an alive being, and,

---

232 C. Lévi-Strauss, *Structural Anthropology*, trans. C. Jacobson, New York: Basic Books, 1963.

233 See: C. Smith, *Contemporary French Philosophy*, London: Methuen & Co., 1964, ch. 11.

234 This meeting is accomplished by the intentionality of consciousness which is expressed by establishing a critical relationship between its individual quests and the field of the mutual interaction between the different conscious beings. The means by which conscious beings communicate with each other are called symbols. Symbols derive from activities which express the tendency of different conscious beings to meet and understand each other. In other words, symbols are objects which express commonly accepted intentions and activities and are organized in sets which are called codes. When conscious beings act and behave according to common codes, then a society of conscious beings is an inter-subjective and conscious continuum, since there are things which have the same meaning for all conscious beings.

thus, it operates as a witness. Moral consciousness is a consciousness which makes evaluative judgments, and, thus, it operates as a judge.

Moral consciousness is a structurally and functionally unified entity, but it is not a homogeneous entity. As a functional existential reality, it is a function of three variables which are emotion, reason, and volition. The significance of the emotional elements of moral consciousness is determined by our experience of them, because a value about which we think that it should be respected by all conscious beings is affirmed or rejected by us according to whether our actions conform to it or violate it, respectively. Such emotional elements are respect, guilt, pride, etc. According to what I have already argued in Chapters 1 and 3, reason refers, first, to positivist knowledge, which consists in concepts to which the various forms of existence are logically reducible, and, second, to the knowledge of substances. Finally, the volitional elements of moral consciousness refer to a firm decision of moral consciousness to accomplish a deontological programme, e.g., to do its duty, to defend its rights, etc.

The above three variables of the function of moral consciousness are inextricably linked to each other. Both the logo-centric character of Kant's deontological morality and the emotional character of the utilitarians' consequentialist morality are over-simplifications of moral consciousness. In fact, William David Ross explains the manner in which the logo-centric character of Kant's deontological morality "over-simplifies the moral life"[235]. In particular, Ross argues that Kant's request that "the rightness or wrongness of an individual act can be inferred with certainty from its falling or not falling under a rule capable of being universalized"[236] is an over-simplification. For instance, how could you give a sincere answer to a person who asks where is another person whom the first person wants to assassinate? The goal of eliminating sensitivity from moral life in order to make the latter more consistent and logically rigorous deprives moral consciousness from motives which play important role in its full development. For instance, in Kant's morality, love plays only a secondary role, being treated simply as a factor which encourages and underpins the expression of respect. Hence, in opposition to Kant, Ross has emphasized that it is wrong to think that there is only one moral motive that has value[237]. For instance, a concept may

---

235 W.D. Ross, *Foundations of Ethics*, Oxford: Oxford University Press, 1939, p. 189.
236 W.D. Ross, op. cit. (ref. 235), p. 189.
237 W.D. Ross, op. cit. (ref. 235), p. 206.

be blurred, but moral consciousness itself may be in the position to evaluate a situation correctly and accurately due to its correct emotional orientation. Furthermore, Ross argues that Kant is wrong to think that moral rules have "absolute authority admitting of no exception"[238]. However, Ross is equally critical towards the ideal utilitarianism of both G.E. Moore[239] and Hastings Rashdall[240]. In particular, Ross argues that utilitarianism wrongly assumes that there is a "general character which makes right acts right" — namely, that of maximizing a set of intrinsic goods[241]. Additionally, he points out that, due to its single-minded commitment to the utility-maximization doctrine, ideal utilitarianism distorts our understanding of moral deliberation[242]. For instance, when deciding whether to fulfil a promise, our thought is focused more on the fact that, in the past, we have made a promise than on the consequences of the fulfilment of the given promise. Finally, Ross argues that ideal utilitarianism is wrong to contend that the only morally significant relation "in which my neighbours stand to me is that of being possible beneficiaries by my action"[243].

With respect to its value, moral consciousness is the object of evaluative judgments on the basis of the stability or the instability of its manifestations. When we study the functions of moral consciousness, we realize that, from some aspects, moral consciousness is stable, and, from some other aspects, it exhibits change. In fact, the negative evaluations of moral consciousness by skeptics, such as Gorgias and Montaigne, are due to the fact that moral consciousness exhibits change.

However, it can be argued that changes in moral consciousness are structured into series of progress. The progress of moral consciousness is manifested by the following processes: (i) Specialization: moral rules are continuously differentiated from other rules; (ii) Internalization: morality is internalized, since, as Kant showed, moral consciousness does not evaluate only the consequences of an action but also the intentions of the agent; (iii) Individuation: moral consciousness does not emphasize only the rights of the community but also the rights of the individual; (iv) Expansion: moral consciousness broadens its consideration of moral issues beyond the rights

---

238 W.D. Ross, op. cit. (ref. 235), p. 313.
239 G.E. Moore, *Principia Ethica*, Cambridge: Cambridge University Press, 1903.
240 H. Rashdall, *Ethics*, London: T.C. & E.C. Jack, 1913.
241 W.D. Ross, *The Right and the Good*, Oxford: Oxford University Press, 1930, p. 16.
242 W.D. Ross, op. cit. (ref. 241), p. 17.
243 W.D. Ross, op. cit. (ref. 241), p. 19.

of the individual and a particular community in order to cover the rights of the human kind in general.

Moreover, the progress of human consciousness is manifested by progresses in the field of social institutions. For instance, the abolition of slavery was a significant step towards further social integration, and, even though the United Nations has not the status of a global government and, in many cases, its interventions have been unsuccessful, the Universal Declaration of Human Rights, which was approved and proclaimed on 10 December 1948 by the UN General Assembly, exerts global authority.

Finally, progress takes place in the sensitivity of moral consciousness. For instance, some conditions which, in previous historical periods, were regarded as normal, such as the slaughter of political opponents and ethnic minorities in absolutist political systems and the violation of women's rights by authoritarian and theocratic regimes are unacceptable to modern moral persons and cause reactions.

The previous series of the progress of moral consciousness provide important counter-arguments to the skeptics' approach to moral consciousness, but, of course, they do not suffice in order to eliminate skepticism completely. Indeed, apart from cases of moral progress, history provides cases of moral regression. Stalinism and Nazism are characteristic examples of historical periods in which the evil was dominant among people. As Zbigniew Brzezinski put it in his book *Out of Control*, "both the Nazis and the Communists deliberately abetted the moral deformation of the human being"[244].

However, beyond the analyses which emphasize the progress of moral consciousness and those that emphasize the instability of moral consciousness, we can identify certain stable structural elements of moral consciousness. Apart from the temporary taxonomies of values in each historical period, we can identify a kernel moral consciousness which is prior to every partial, culturally-dependent form of moral consciousness.

As I have already mentioned, moral consciousness is a special manifestation of the consciousness of existence. Within the framework of the consciousness of existence, the human being internalizes a sense of responsibility towards itself and towards God. In fact, human consciousness internalizes a sense of responsibility towards itself. This sense of responsibil-

---

244 Z. Brzezinski, *Out of Control — Global Turmoil on the Eve of the 21st Century*, New York: Macmillan, 1993, p. 36.

ity consists in an attempt to protect the continuity of its existence and to improve its existential conditions. Furthermore, in its attempt to impose its intentionality on the reality of the world, and, thus, to survive and improve its existential conditions, human consciousness seeks the reason of things, since the knowledge of the reason of things can endow the human being with a royal position in the world. Thus, human consciousness internalizes a sense of responsibility towards the universal reason. This sense of responsibility towards the universal reason takes the form of a sense of responsibility towards God, or the Divine Logos. This primordial internalization of a sense of responsibility towards itself and towards God by the consciousness of existence constitutes the kernel moral consciousness which, in its historical itinerary, is manifested in various culturally-dependent manners. Therefore, even though moral consciousness is structurally conditioned by society, it is not created by society, but it is innate (a priori).

Moral consciousness as moral responsibility transcends every conventional legal relationship, because, within the framework of positive law, the concept of responsibility is inextricably linked to the concept of liability, whereas, within the framework of moral responsibility, one assumes responsibility for something without having previously been held liable for it by the legal system. For instance, when people in the Western world feel responsible for the impact of their car emissions on the global ecosystem and on humanity's life in general, they feel this way without having previously been held legally liable for a specific behavior; they just feel morally responsible towards 'humanity' (i.e., towards all the people on earth and even towards future generations). In fact, without this a priori sense of moral responsibility, no trustworthy agreement between social partners is possible.

In classical Greek philosophy, truth and virtue constitute, broadly speaking, the manner in which the individual soul is harmoniously integrated into the cosmos in general and into the political community in particular. In other words, truth and virtue constitute a quasi-natural morality, and the transgression of this morality by man is the cause of tragedy in human life. Therefore, Plato emphasizes that there are different levels of knowledge: starting from the formation of an opinion, we move, through conceptual knowledge, to the 'epopteia' of the ideas, and, we end up in the theory of the Good (which is symbolized by the sun in the Platonic myth of the cave).

In *Symposium*, 210e, Plato argues that the Good is conceived in a manner which "suddenly" unites the theorizer with the object of theorizing, and, in *Symposium*, 211a, he adds that this knowledge cannot be expressed in rational language. Thus, the Platonic idea is neither simply a vision nor an abstraction, but it is the ideal of the philosophical way of life.

According to Plato, 'theoretical life' (*theoretikos bios*) has two aspects: the first aspect refers to the object of theorizing, and the second aspect refers to necessary presuppositions which make theory possible. The objects of theorizing are the perfect being, the absolute, immovable intelligible principle, which is contrasted to the continuously changing sensible objects, and the source of the intelligible. The source of the intelligible is called 'Good' in Plato's *Republic* and 'Beauty' in Plato's *Symposium*. In fact, we read in Plato's *Symposium*, 210a-211b:

> For he who would proceed aright in this matter should begin in youth to visit beautiful forms; and first, if he be guided by his instructor aright, to love one such form only — out of that he should create fair thoughts; and soon he will of himself perceive that the beauty of one form is akin to the beauty of another; and then if beauty of form in general is his pursuit, how foolish would he be not to recognize that the beauty in every form is one and the same! And when he perceives this he will abate his violent love of the one, which he will despise and deem a small thing, and will become a lover of all beautiful forms; in the next stage he will consider that the beauty of the mind is more honourable than the beauty of the outward form... drawing towards and contemplating the vast sea of beauty, he will create many fair and noble thoughts and notions in boundless love of wisdom; until on that shore he grows and waxes strong, and at last the vision is revealed to him of a single science, which is the science of beauty everywhere. To this I will proceed... He who has been instructed thus far in the things of love, and who has learned to see the beautiful in due order and succession, when he comes towards the end will suddenly perceive a nature of wondrous beauty (and this, Socrates, is the final cause of all our former toils) — a nature which in the first place is everlasting, not growing and decaying, or waxing and waning; secondly, not fair in one point of view and foul in another, or at one time or in one relation or at one place fair, at another time or in another relation or at another place foul, as if fair to some and foul to others, or in the likeness of a face or hands or any other part of the bodily frame, or in any form of speech or knowledge, or existing in any other being, as for example, in an animal, or in heaven, or in earth, or in any other place; but beauty absolute, separate, simple, and everlasting, which without diminution and without increase, or any change, is imparted to the ever-growing and perishing beauties of all other things.

The dual character of theory (as theory of the perfect being and as theory of the source of the intelligible) corresponds to a dual action of the mind.

When the mind is oriented towards the species (kinds) of things, then, as we read in Plato's *Theaetetus*, theory is equivalent to the science of the divine and of the human affairs. When the mind is focused on the absolute good, then it ceases to be merely a means of knowledge, and it becomes an organ of spiritual liberty, since, as we read in Plato's *Phaedo*, 65b, and *Symposium*, 212a, the mind, having transcended the love for particular sensible and intelligible things, through the knowledge of the pure form (idea) of beauty-good, attains the comprehension of the absolute beauty-good. Thus, theoretical life is an expansion and transformation of philosophical knowledge ('epopteia') into a form of mystical experience, which, in modern philosophy, has been emphasized by he intuitionism of L.E.J. Brouwer (to whom I referred in Section 3.4) as well as by Henri-Louis Bergson.

According to Bergson, there are two ways in which an object can be known: absolutely and relatively. The method of knowing an object relatively is called analysis, and the method of knowing an object absolutely is called intuition[245]. Bergson calls intuition "sympathy"[246], which consists in putting ourselves in the place of others. In other words, Bergsonian intuition consists in entering into the object of consciousness, and thus it differs from the analytical method, which consists in dividing the object of consciousness into different parts, according to a chosen viewpoint, and translating these parts into symbols in order to reconstruct an image of the original object. This 'entering into', which reveals the object's meaning, for Bergson, gives us absolute knowledge.

Within the framework of the Platonic philosophy, intuition transcends Bergson's concept of intuition. From the perspective of Plato's philosophy, intuition is that synthetic understanding which can be achieved by the soul when the latter turns towards the absolute good and thus the personality of the human being is coordinated with the absolute good and atoned. Hence, from this perspective, intuition is a comprehensive grip of the principle of universality, because, at this level, the human being is aware of the teleological unity of all beings and experiences that universal love which is not an emotion or an affectionate reaction, but it is a mode of existence. In fact, universal love is that mode of existence which consists in one's spiritual unification with all beings, since all beings are conceived as outcomes of the

245 H. Bergson, *The Creative Mind*, tr. M.L. Andison, New York: The Citadel Press, 1992.
246 H. Bergson, op. cit. (ref. 245), p. 159.

creative action of the absolute good. Then is true compassion and charity known, because, at this level of existence, one loves because this is the way he exists, and not because he has an emotion of love. If love is understood as an emotion, then it is a function of the emotional satisfaction one receives from the object of his love, and, thus, the energy of love, ultimately, returns to the person who loves. On the other hand, love as a mode of existence implies that one loves because he experiences the teleological unity of all beings due to the absolute good and within the absolute good, and not in order to satisfy selfish emotional expediencies.

Plato's conception of 'theory' transcends modern intuitionism, because, according to Plato, theory is a continuous mental energy, a way of life, and not simply the acquisition of a specific type of knowledge. In other words, for Plato, 'theorizing' is not equivalent with 'learning' or 'knowing', because it is an active, mystical view of the truth. Hence, 'idea' is the act of viewing as well as the object of viewing. The knowledge of the idea is based on both reason and the senses, since it consists in the view of a visible form as well as of the ultimate (supersensuous) reality of the given form. As I have already mentioned, according to Plato, the human soul is a 'mixed entity', since it exists between being and becoming. Therefore, since the act of viewing takes place by this mixed entity — namely, the human soul — it includes the view of the becoming (i.e., the changeable material reality) of an object as well as the view of the firm and absolute being of the same object.

The knowledge of the idea of a certain thing does not correspond to a conceptual definition of that thing, but it consists in the understanding of that thing's teleological significance. Every entity is not merely itself here and now, as we perceive it by our senses, but, simultaneously, it bears its idea, which consists in its potentially perfect being. In other words, every entity is itself plus something more: it is united with a meaning which transcends its sensible form (its becoming) and reveals its potentiality, i.e., its potential existence in a state of perfection, its being. For instance, when Plato asks 'what is bravery?', he wants to know the relationship between a particular manifestation of bravery and the absolute truth of bravery, and not to describe an empirical manifestation of bravery in abstract terms. Therefore, in *Laches*, 192b, Plato answers that bravery is the soul's courage, and not the boldness of a soldier in a war, because his aim is to reduce an empirical object to its end — namely, to its spiritual content and meaning — instead of showing the empirical, practical aspect of bravery.

In Plato's philosophy, human existence is given an ontological foundation, manifesting those qualities bestowed on it by the Divine Archetype, the Absolute Being. Hence, the human exists in a unity of person and substance. The human being attains to genuine ontology by its participation and sharing in divine existence ('divine' in the sense of absolute-eternal), taking on an absolute-eternal dimension for itself. The awareness of the genuine ontology attained by the human being due to its participation and sharing in the Absolute Being — which has been formulated in a philosophically rigorous language by Plato — is the essence of religion. According to M.S. Jaffee's definition:

> Religion is an intense and sustained cultivation of a style of life that heightens human awareness of morally binding connections between the self, the human community, and the most essential structures of reality. Religions posit various orders of reality and help individuals and groups to negotiate their relations with these orders.[247]

Religion, manipulating the mythological content of the collective consciousness, teaches the human's participation and sharing in the divine. For instance, in the Bible we read that God said: "Let us make man in our image, after our likeness." (Genesis 1:26). In the Qur'an, we read that God said: "I have breathed into man of My spirit." (Qur'an 15.29). In Hinduism, we read: "That which is the finest essence — this the whole world has as its soul. That is Reality. That is the Self. That art thou." (Chandogya Upanishad 6.8.7). In Buddhism, we read: "Every being has the Buddha Nature. This is the self." (Mahaparinirvana Sutra 214). In Confucianism and Taoism, we read: "Fire blazing from the earth. The Superior man reflects in his person [Heaven's] virtue." (I Ching 35: Progress).

Myth, on which religion and generally culture are based, translates experienced reality into a symbolic language, and in this way it leads towards the experiential participation of the collective consciousness in the same experience of reality[248], since myth allows the participation of all areas of

---

247 M.S. Jaffee, *Early Judaism*, Upper Saddle River, NJ: Prentice Hall, 1997, p. 5.
248 Lévi-Strauss has pointed out that, on the one hand, mythical stories are fantastic and unpredictable: the content of myth seems completely arbitrary, but, on the other hand, the myths of different cultures are surprisingly similar: "On the one hand it would seem that in the course of a myth anything is likely to happen... But on the other hand, this apparent arbitrariness is belied by the astounding similarity between myths collected in widely different regions. Therefore the problem: If the content of myth is contingent, how are we to explain the fact that myths throughout the world are so similar?" (C. Lévi-Strauss, op. cit., ref. 232, p.

the conscious and the unconscious mind in the same experience of reality[249]. The mythological ideal is the symbolic point which gives a historical position to the collective consciousness and determines the point from which the collective consciousness becomes visible. Thus, through myth, consciousness transcends historical institutions.

Furthermore, myth itself can be transcended by philosophy, because the rise of philosophical discourse unchained the human brain. Let us look at the first history of philosophy — namely, the opening book of Aristotle's *Metaphysics*. Here Aristotle is setting out the basic results of his philosophical itinerary: The first result has to do with intensifying human awareness and its ability, first, to detach itself from the world of necessity (a world that its creative instinct had responded to) and, second, to relate thereafter to other objects which awake the wonder and puzzlement of human consciousness, and which are independent of all endurance and also independent of all exigency. Thus, meaning-giving is the essential human function.

---

208). Thus, he proposed that universal laws must govern mythical thought and resolve this seeming paradox, producing similar myths in different cultures. In other words, according to Lévi-Strauss, even though each myth may seem unique, it is just one particular instance of a universal law of human thought. In studying myth, Lévi-Strauss tries "to reduce apparently arbitrary data to some kind of order, and to attain a level at which a kind of necessity becomes apparent, underlying the illusions of liberty" (C. Lévi-Strauss, *The Raw and the Cooked*, trans. John and Doreen Weightman, Chicago: The University of Chicago Press, 1969, p. 10). According to Lévi-Strauss, "mythical thought always progresses from the awareness of oppositions towards their resolution" (C. Lévi-Strauss, op. cit., ref. 232, p. 224). In other words, myths consist of: (i) elements that oppose or contradict each other, and (ii) other elements that "mediate", or resolve, those oppositions. Moreover, see: Alain (pseudonym of Émile-August Chartier), *Préliminaires à la mythologie* (originally written in 1932-1933), Paris: Paul Hartmann, Éditeur, 1943.

249 This process has been analyzed extensively by Carl Gustav Jung, the founder of analytical psychology. Apart from their differences, both Lévi-Strauss and Jung assert meaning-giving as the essential human function, and they both use mythology to illustrate the unconscious operation of this function within the psyche. According to Jung, "to the degree that human brains are uniformly differentiated, the mental functioning thereby made possible is also collective and universal. This explains, for example, the interesting fact that the unconscious processes of the most widely separated peoples and races show a quite remarkable correspondence, which displays itself among other things, in the extraordinary but well-authenticated analogies between the forms and motifs of autochthonous myths. The universal similarity of human brains leads to the universal possibility of a uniform mental functioning. This functioning is the *collective psyche*" (C.G. Jung, "The Relations Between the Ego and the Unconscious", in: J. Campbell (ed.), *The Portable Jung*, New York: Penguin Books, 1971, p. 93).

Giving meaning to things means that one endows everyday action with a clear purpose and with criteria. Human life consists of rational actions — namely, actions which have a reason, i.e., an end — and logical criteria on the basis of which one can judge the extent to which and the manner in which an act serves one's goal. The acknowledgement of a specific purpose of life necessarily depends upon the level of knowledge one has attained, according to the hierarchy of knowledge which we studied in Chapter 3 (i.e., illusion, belief, logic, and intelligence). For instance, at the level of knowledge which Plato calls intelligence, people understand that the ultimate cause of existence is a transcendental Reason which structures reality into a cosmos — namely, into a harmonious and ordered whole — and that the truth of this Reason — namely, its continuous presence in consciousness — corresponds to the manner of existence of the phenomenal natural cosmos. Then, for such people, the purpose of human life is a teleological consequence of the ultimate Reason of existence, and, thus, human life is true to the extent that it imitates the way of life of this ultimate Reason. In case people have such a mentality, politics is not a technique of managing utilitarian expediencies, but it is an art which reveals the reason of universal social cohesion, thus signifying humans' creative participation in the true way of life. In such a case, the 'city' (*polis*), i.e., a politically organized human community, has a holy character, not because it serves a narrowly defined religious expediency (as was the case, for instance, with ancient Israel), but because it realizes and manifests the most authentic form of holiness, which is the true way of life, i.e., human's existence in relation to the Absolute Being.

On the other hand, a human community which endorses an agnostic or nihilistic attitude towards ontological issues and believes that the only truth we know is the phenomenology of things, necessarily infers the purpose of human life from the previous agnostic attitude. Thus, for such people, whose philosophical starting point consists in ignorance and in an ontological gap (lack of an ultimate reason of existence), the presence of the human being in the world does not have any special existential reason-purpose, and truth reduces to utilitarian expediencies dictated by the phenomenal needs of the natural human being. In such a case, the phenomenology of human needs is the only theoretical and practical foundation of social norms, i.e., the purposes and the criteria of normative political thought reduce to the survival and the hedonistic calculus of the natural human being.

Thus, from this perspective, the meaning of one's integration into society is his struggle to deny and postpone death[250].

4.2 A universal theory of human rights

Human rights are rights possessed by human beings a priori. The idea of a human right is that of a right which is 'natural', in the sense that, according to Aristotle's *Nicomachean Ethics*, 189, "the natural is that which has the same validity everywhere and does not depend upon acceptance".

According to the United Nations Declaration of Human Rights of 1948, human rights fall roughly into the following six categories:

(i) Security of existence:
- Protection of life, liberty, and security of person (Article 3).
- No torture or cruel punishments (Article 5).

(ii) Freedom:
- No slavery or servitude (Article 4).
- No arbitrary interference with one's privacy, family, home, or correspondence (Article 12).
- Freedom of movement and residence (Article 13).
- Freedom to leave and return to one's country (Article 13).
- Freedom to seek and enjoy in other countries asylum from persecution (Article 14).
- No marriage without full and free consent of the intending spouses (Article 16.2).
- Freedom to own property individually and collectively (Article 17.1).
- Freedom of thought, consciousness, and religion (Article 18).
- Freedom of opinion and expression (Article 19).
- Freedom of peaceful assembly and association (Article 20).
- Freedom to form and join trade unions (Article 23.4).
- Freedom of parents to choose the kind of education that shall be given to their children (Article 26).
- Freedom to participate in cultural life (Article 27).

(iii) Rule of law and correct administration of justice:

---

250 M. Foucault, *Les Mots et les Choses*, Paris: Gallimard, 1996.

- Right to an effective remedy for violations of rights (Article 8) and to a social and international order in which human rights can be enjoyed (Article 28).
- Legal personality (Article 6) and equality before the law (Article 7).
- No arbitrary arrest, detention, or exile (Article 9).
- Right to a trial in criminal cases (Article 10).
- Presumption of innocence in criminal cases (Article 11).
- No retroactive criminal laws or penalties (Article 11).
- No arbitrary deprivation of nationality (Article 15).
- No arbitrary deprivation of property (Article 17.2).
- Protection of moral and material interests resulting from any scientific, literary, or artistic production of which one is author (Article 27.2).

(iv) Rights concerning the individual's status as citizen:
- Freedom to participate in government, directly or through freely chosen representatives (Article 21.1).
- Equal access to public service (Article 21.2).
- Opportunities to vote in periodic and genuine elections (Article 21.3).

(v) Equality rights:
- Equality of fundamental rights and freedoms (Article 2).
- Freedom from discrimination (Articles 2 and 7).
- Equal rights in marriage and family (Article 16).
- Equal pay for equal work (Article 22).
- Equal social protection for children born out of wedlock (Article 25.2).

(vi) Economic and Social rights:
- Social security (Article 22).
- Just and favourable remuneration for workers (Article 23.3).
- Rest and leisure (Article 24).
- Adequate standard of living for health and well-being (Article 25).
- Health care (Article 25).
- Special care during motherhood and childhood (Article 25.1).
- Educational opportunities (Article 26).

Furthermore, two characteristic events which show that the international community becomes increasingly aware of the emergence of a new understanding of the moral autonomy and responsibility of the human person are the Vienna Declaration and Programme of Action (VDPA), which was adopted by the World Conference on Human Rights in Vienna on 25 June 1993, and the UN Millennium Declaration, which was adopted by the UN General Assembly on 8 September 2000. P. Kathrani has made the following remarks with respect to the previous two documents:

> this new global morality, or greater desire to work together, can now provide an effective basis for states to enforce international human rights... One recent example is the growing movement behind 'responsibility to protect', which recognises that it is no longer right, in an interconnected world, for states to hide behind the shield of sovereignty and territorial integrity in order to commit gross human rights violations against their people; and that other states should also have a moral responsibility to protect the nationals of another country if there are justifiable and legitimate grounds to do so, albeit that this remains in the developmental stage. There was recently a session in the United Nations General Assembly on this and while a concerted policy on the responsibility to protect is some way off, the drive towards it provides some evidence of a greater desire to work together on issues which would once have sharply divided the international community. Another issue that can potentially be addressed by this new global accord is international poverty. While states may once have been content with ensuring the welfare of their own people, it is arguable that they should now, in a globalising world, work together in alleviating the suffering of people in other parts of the world, something that has been recognised, for example, by the UN Global Compact.[251]

The VDPA: emphasizes that all human rights are of equal importance, seeking to end the qualitative division between civil and political rights and economic, social and cultural rights[252] (Part I, paragraph 5), draws a direct connection between respect for human rights, democracy and international development[253] (Part I, paragraph 8), makes a direct link between

---

251 P. Kathrani, "A Decade of Change: A Case for Global Morality, Dialogue and Transnational Trust-Building", *Jurisprudence*, Vol. 4, 2009, p. 102.

252 "All human rights are universal, indivisible and interdependent and interrelated. The international community must treat human rights globally in a fair and equal manner, on the same footing, and with the same emphasis. While the significance of national and regional particularities and various historical, cultural and religious backgrounds must be borne in mind, it is the duty of States, regardless of their political, economic and cultural systems, to promote and protect all human rights and fundamental freedoms".

253 "Democracy, development and respect for human rights and fundamental freedoms are interdependent and mutually reinforcing. Democracy is based on the freely expressed will of the people to determine their own political, economic, social and cultural systems and their full participation in all aspects of their lives.

poverty and the realization of human rights[254] (Part I, paragraph 14), and reaffirms the right to development in connection with human rights[255] (Part I, paragraph 10) and the responsibility of the state as well as of non-state actors (e.g., non-governmental organizations) to protect and promote human rights[256] (Part I, paragraph 1, and Part I, paragraph 13). In the same spirit, the UN Millennium Declaration promotes international co-operation based on humanistic values and principles.

As human consciousness expands, it takes in ever widening arcs of awareness. Fortunately — as former UN Secretary-General Kofi Annan stated in 2000 — the UN

> is more than a mere tool... As its Charter makes clear, the United Nations was intended to introduce new principles into international

In the context of the above, the promotion and protection of human rights and fundamental freedoms at the national and international levels should be universal and conducted without conditions attached. The international community should support the strengthening and promoting of democracy, development and respect for human rights and fundamental freedoms in the entire world".

254 "The existence of widespread extreme poverty inhibits the full and effective enjoyment of human rights; its immediate alleviation and eventual elimination must remain a high priority for the international community".

255 "The World Conference on Human Rights reaffirms the right to development, as established in the Declaration on the Right to Development, as a universal and inalienable right and an integral part of fundamental human rights. As stated in the Declaration on the Right to Development, the human person is the central subject of development. While development facilitates the enjoyment of all human rights, the lack of development may not be invoked to justify the abridgement of internationally recognized human rights. States should cooperate with each other in ensuring development and eliminating obstacles to development. The international community should promote an effective international cooperation for the realization of the right to development and the elimination of obstacles to development. Lasting progress towards the implementation of the right to development requires effective development policies at the national level, as well as equitable economic relations and a favourable economic environment at the international level".

256 "The World Conference on Human Rights reaffirms the solemn commitment of all States to fulfil their obligations to promote universal respect for, and observance and protection of, all human rights and fundamental freedoms for all in accordance with the Charter of the United Nations, other instruments relating to human rights, and international law. The universal nature of these rights and freedoms is beyond question. In this framework, enhancement of international cooperation in the field of human rights is essential for the full achievement of the purposes of the United Nations. Human rights and fundamental freedoms are the birthright of all human beings; their protection and promotion is the first responsibility of Governments". "There is a need for States and international organizations, in cooperation with non-governmental organizations, to create favourable conditions at the national, regional and international levels to ensure the full and effective enjoyment of human rights. States should eliminate all violations of human rights and their causes, as well as obstacles to the enjoyment of these rights".

relations, making qualitative difference to their day-to-day conduct... In other words, quite apart from whatever practical tasks the UN is asked to perform, it has the avowed purpose of transforming relations among states, and the methods by which the world's affairs are managed.[257]

Given that human rights are universal in scope and, additionally, have an essentially egalitarian character and categorical validity, the following question emerges: how are human rights to be justified? Before we attempt to answer this question, we must clarify why this question is important. Postmodernists, following a nihilistic epistemological research programme, have questioned the very sense of a philosophical foundation of human rights. For instance, Richard Rorty argues that, instead of asking ourselves 'why' we have rights, we should pragmatically restrain ourselves to find solutions for the implementation of a 'human rights culture'[258]. In particular, Rorty argues that we just need to learn to put ourselves in the position of the victims of human rights violations in order to 'feel' the inhuman character of such practices. According to Rorty, this can be achieved by the manipulation of emotion through the narration of sad and touching stories. Rorty insists that "no useful work seems to be done by insisting on a purportedly ahistorical human nature" and that "there probably is no such nature, or at least nothing in that nature that is relevant to our moral choices"[259]. First of all, it must be mentioned that I have already shown the fallacies of nihilism and of the emotive approaches to morality, and additionally I have shown the a priori character of moral consciousness. Second, in the light of my previous arguments, Rorty's approach to human rights is not only fallacious but also it fails even to explain why we should prefer a human rights respective culture to any other culture if we cannot ask 'why' we have rights and, hence, 'why' it should be better.

Moreover, various pragmatist scholars — even though they do not explicitly adhere to the postmodernists' epistemological nihilism — attempt to evade the question of the philosophical justification of human rights by perceiving them as empirical facts, i.e., as self-evident data, of the contemporary world. However, morality is fundamentally concerned with what

---

257 K. Annan, *We the Peoples: the Role of the United Nations in the 21ˢᵗ Century* — Report of the Secretary-General, New York: UN General Assembly Edition, March 2000, p.3.
258 R. Rorty, "Human Rights, Rationality and Sentimentality", in: *Truth and Progress*, Cambridge: Cambridge University Press, 1998, pp. 167-185.
259 R. Rorty, op. cit. (ref. 258), p. 172.

'ought to be' the case, and, therefore, one cannot manage moral affairs by appeals to what 'is' the case, or to how the case 'is perceived'. Hence, the question of the validity of human rights cannot be settled by appealing to empirical data.

In the 20th century, two particular approaches to the question of the validity of human rights predominated: the 'interests theory approach' and the 'will theory approach'. According to John Finnis[260], a characteristic representative of the 'interests theory approach', the validity of human rights is determined by their instrumental value for securing the necessary conditions of human well-being. In particular, Finnis argues that the following five "basic forms of good" (fundamental interests) are the essential prerequisites for human well-being, and, as such, they serve to justify our claims to the corresponding rights, i.e., they provide the basis for human rights: (i) life and its capacity for development, (ii) the acquisition of knowledge as an end in itself, (iii) play as a capacity for reaction, (iv) sociability and friendship, and (v) religion, or the capacity for spiritual experience.

Other philosophers who have defended human rights from an interests-based approach attempt to provide what James Nickel has termed "prudential reasons" in support of human rights:

> [A] prudential argument from fundamental interests attempts to show that it would be reasonable to accept and comply with human rights, in circumstances where most others are likely to do so, because these norms are part of the best means for protecting one's fundamental interests against actions and omissions that endanger them.[261]

According to this argument, all human beings possess some fundamental interests, and the protection of one's own fundamental interests requires that others are willing to recognize and respect those interests, which, in turn, requires that the fundamental interests of others are reciprocally recognized and respected. The roots of the interests theory approach can be found in the political thought of Thomas Hobbes. In particular, in the fourteenth chapter of his *Leviathan*, Hobbes argues that there is one fundamental right of nature and one fundamental law: the right is "the liberty each man has to use his own power, as he will himself, for the preservation of his own nature", and the law is "every man ought to endeavour peace, as far as he has

---

260 J. Finnis, *Natural Law and Natural Rights*, Oxford: Clarendon Press, 1980.
261 J. Nickel, *Making Sense of Human Rights — Philosophical Reflections on the Universal Declaration of Human Rights*, Berkeley: University of California Press, 1987, p. 84.

hope of obtaining it; and when he cannot obtain it... he may seek, and use, all helps and advantages of war"[262].

It is easily seen that the interests theory approach to human rights can be criticized in a manner similar to the one in which I have criticized utilitarianism, and therefore it is not successful in its attempt to lead us to a universal theory of human rights. Moreover, the interests theory approach has been criticized for subordinating the exercise of freedom as a principal moral idea, since the defenders of the interests-based approach argue that fundamental interests are pre-determinants of human moral agency. According to the interests theory approach, freedom can be included in the set of fundamental interests, but freedom is not constitutive of our interests, and, therefore, this approach rules out the freedom of moral consciousness. This type of criticism has been followed by the defenders of the will theory approach to human rights.

The focal point of the defenders of the will theory approach is the ideal of personal autonomy. For instance, H.L.A. Hart, argues that all rights are reducible to a single, fundamental right: the "equal right of all men to be free"[263]. According to Hart, this right implies both negative freedom from coercion or restraint — except if used to hinder coercion or restraint — and positive freedom to act freely — except if one's free action causes coercion, restraint or injury to others. In fact, these two exceptions are implicit in the term 'equal' right. Moreover, Hart argues that the "equal right of all men to be free" is a natural right because all individuals have it independent of their membership to a particular society and it is not created by the voluntary actions of others. However, Henry Shue[264] argues that Hart's "equal right of all men to be free" is not ultimately sufficient for grounding all human rights, because many of these rights include security from violence and the necessary material conditions for survival. Thus, according to Shue, human rights should be grounded on freedom, security, and subsistence (instead of just freedom). Shue argues that freedom, security, and subsistence are "genuinely basic" rights because any attempt to enjoy another right by sacrificing any of these basic rights would be self-defeating.

---

262 T. Hobbes, *Leviathan*, ed. C.B. Macpherson, Harmondsworth: Penguin, 1968, Chapter 14.

263 H.L.A. Hart, "Are There Any Natural Rights?", *Philosophical Review*, Vol. 64, 1955, pp. 175-191.

264 H. Shue, *Basic Rights — Subsistence, Affluence, and U.S. Foreign Policy*, second edition, Princeton: Princeton University Press, 1996.

The will theory approach has an apparent logical force: indeed, to talk meaningfully about the universal validity of human rights, one must place emphasis on the autonomy of the human being. However, the defenders of the will theory approach, such as Hart and Shue, have defined the autonomy of the human being in a manner which is narrow and, therefore, leads to contradictions. In particular, inherent in Hart's and Shue's theories is the assumption that human autonomy is equivalent to a specific understanding of rationality. If we assume that human autonomy is equivalent to rationality, and particularly to the way in which Hart and Shue understand rationality, then it logically follows that persons who do not behave according to the established rational norms are not bearers of human rights, and, therefore, human rights cease to be universal and a priori and become socially determined. Shue, in particular, ignores not only the case of persons who suffer from psychological problems and, therefore, they do not behave according to the rational calculations of his theory of "genuinely basic" rights, but also all those persons — such as religious heroes ('saints'), national heroes, social revolutionaries, etc. — who voluntarily sacrifice rights which, according to Shue, are "genuinely basic". Therefore, if the ultimate foundation of human rights is rationality, and if the ultimate source of value of the human being is its rationality, then people with psychological problems as well as various forms of 'heroes' and, generally, people who do not conform to the established rational norms of their societies should have neither inherent value nor human rights. In other words, the rationalistic character of the will theory approach implies that one's autonomy reduces to his conformity to a socially constructed criterion of 'normality', and, hence, it opens more debates than the ones it is supposed to settle. Although Hart's and Shue's theories correctly recognize the need to address the issue of the autonomy of the human being, they deal with this issue in a manner which contradicts the attempt to develop a universal theory of human rights.

The ultimate cause of the weaknesses of the will theory approach is that, due to its rationalistic reasoning, it attempts to justify rights in terms of other rights by calling the latter more basic than the first and transforming them into a measure of 'normal' behavior. In other words, the will theory approach attempts to transform the realm of human rights into an ontologically sufficient, closed logical structure. However, the universal value of human rights cannot be proved within the closed system of human rights for the same reason that — as Gödel has proved — the validity of no logico-mathematical structure can be proved within itself.

As a conclusion, neither the interests theory approach nor the will theory approach can justify the universalistic character of human rights. The weaknesses of the previous theories can be overcome if we follow Plato's theory of ideas in the way that I have explained it in previous sections. For, in Plato's thought, society is founded on a universal truth and not on the rights of its constituent parts. Rights as such are individual claims and, therefore, at a fundamental level, they divide people, and they lead to a social cohesion which is based only on legal conventions. Thus, a society of rights is an assemblage of individual claims which can be compromised with each other but they cannot be united, since such a society lacks that truth which would spiritually unite all people within itself. Plato's theory of ideas has shown that the truth which is identified with the absolute good unites all people within itself, and this unity is not a formal relationship, but it is an experience of participation in the same spirit, and, thus, since everyone participates in the same spirit (i.e., in the absolute being or the Good/divine), everyone *participates in* (not merely relates to) everyone else. Hence, the idea of humanity emerges.

In the light of what I have argued in previous sections, the Platonic theory of ideas does not negate the empirical substance of things, but it considers them to be always united with a spiritual end, which consists in the actualization of the potential perfection of their substance. In fact, as I have argued in Chapter 3, the *raison d'être*, the very being or existence of events, is neither in their happening itself, i.e., it is not in their becoming, nor in their own essence. The *raison d'être*, the very being or existence of events, is in the end, the ultimate purpose, for which they happen, i.e., in their participation in a significance which transcends them, the Idea. Thus, from the viewpoint of Plato's theory of ideas, when we see a human being, we must not see only the temporary empirical reality of the given human being — i.e., what this human being is (or seems to be) here and now — but we must also see the potential perfection of the given human being, beyond this being's actual, transient characteristics, e.g., friend/foe, ally/enemy, compatriot/foreigner, law-abiding citizen/criminal, employer/employee, partner/competitor, psychologically balanced/psychologically imbalanced, etc. From this teleological perspective, all humans are equal not because of what they actually are at each segment of space-time but because of what they are potentially

— namely, because they are partakers of the absolute being, i.e., because they are beings-in-the-process-of-perfection, irrespective of whether they succeed or fail to move towards perfection at each segment of space-time. Hence, as I mentioned in Chapter 3, Plato placed great emphasis on the distinction between different levels of knowledge, and his theory of morality was inextricably linked to his theory of knowledge.

Human beings, like the prisoners in the Platonic myth of the cave, can actualize their spiritual potential or they can refuse to do so. Their attitude towards their spiritual potential determines their actual qualities and the actual state of human civilization in general. But, apart from the actual condition of human life and human civilization, the human being is capable of progress and can be considered as the historical manifestation of a potential perfection. It is because human beings bear a trans-historical significance or end (i.e., their potential unification with the perfection of the idea) that they bear a value independent of every historical condition and institution, and, therefore, human rights — rights possessed by human beings exactly because they are human beings — are justified. Only if we see the human being from the perspective of Plato's theory of ideas, i.e., if we see the human being dynamically (as potentiality), and not statically (as actuality), can we justify the universalistic character of human rights.

If we acknowledge that a human being is not only its actual, transient self at each segment of space-time, but also it bears an absolute (trans-historical) meaning (its potential perfection), then we can create a society which is characterized by absolute individualism and absolute universalism. Due to its participation in the perfection of the idea, the individual human being acquires an absolute, inherent value. Simultaneously, because all human beings participate in the perfection of the idea, all human beings equally acquire an absolute, inherent value. From this perspective, the foundation of an authentic 'society' — namely, the essence of social unity — is not a 'politically correct' freedom which simply recognizes and legitimizes the existence of all the agents which constitute a given society, but it is the humans' relationship with a truth which transcends every social agent and, therefore, it cannot be manipulated by any social agent. This universal truth is the spiritual substance of the human being, since the spiritual substance of the human being transcends — and, hence is free from — every historical/social necessity. That is why, according to Aristotle's *Politics*, 1253a 20-21, the term 'catastrophy' can be defined as the separation of the part from the whole.

4.3 Justice and international relations

The idea of justice draws our attention to the notion of efficient social organization, in the sense that individuals receive the treatment that is proper or fitting to them. In particular, Plato, in his *Republic*, argues that justice is a harmonious relationship between the warring parts of the person and of the city. Hence, in an ideally just city, every citizen is just at the right place, doing his best and giving the precise equivalent of what he has received.

As I have already mentioned, according to Plato, human existence is between being (idea-perfection-firmness) and becoming (history-imperfection-change), partaking of both, and, therefore, Plato calls the human being a 'mixed' being. Given this 'mixed' character of human existence, human justice is, in a sense, 'mixed', too. Human justice is firmly oriented towards its goal — which is the Good, corresponding to being — and it is 'critical' in its application. In other words, from the perspective of being, human justice is stable, i.e., firmly oriented towards the Good, but, from the perspective of becoming, human justice is critical, i.e., it is characterized by discretion. By the term 'critical', I mean just the four-fold dialectical process which I analyzed in Section 3.5 — namely: First, consciousness is firmly oriented towards the idea of the Good and aims at acting on the historical plane in order to change its existential conditions in accordance with the idea of the Good. Second, consciousness avoids intervening in the world in a manner which could cause uncontrolled turbulence and thus jeopardize the continuity of existence, and acting in a manner which would be inferior to its capabilities of improving its existential conditions. Third, when consciousness realizes that its historical action tends to cause uncontrolled turbulence and thus jeopardize the continuity of existence, it undertakes new action which balances its previous action, and, when consciousness realizes that its historical action is inferior to its capabilities of improving its existential conditions, it intensifies its intervention in the world. Fourth, during its action upon the reality of the world, consciousness aims at forming the necessary conditions which will allow consciousness to continue acting upon the reality of the world in the future.

In the light of what I have argued in Chapters 3 and 4, the 'mixed' character of justice means that the firm goal of justice should be the safeguarding and protection of human rights; for, human rights are the supreme legal good, since they are founded on the 'being' pole of the human existence, i.e., on the human being as an idea. Given that the existence of the human being is between the pole of being and the pole of becoming, human rights must be based on the pole of being, if we want them to be absolute and universal principles. However, since the human being does not exist in the world of pure being, but it partakes of the imperfect world of becoming, the firm orientation of justice towards the world of pure being (idea) is objectified in the world of becoming (history) in a manner which reflects the level of spiritual development of each society. Thus, even though justice is, and should be, absolute in its orientation towards the idea of the Good, it is relative in its historical application because history and man are imperfect and subject to change.

As human beings progress through the different levels of knowledge which I analyzed in Chapter 3, they move from the state of becoming towards the state of being, thus reducing the distance which separates them as historical entities from the perfection of the idea, and, hence, the objectification of the idea of justice in each historical segment reflects the corresponding spiritual progress which has been achieved by human beings (of course, as I have already mentioned, regression is also possible, since the itinerary of the human consciousness is not deterministic).

At this point, I must mention that, in normative international relations theory, communitarians emphatically point to the tremendous political, cultural, ideological and religious differences within the modern political system. In fact, communitarians emphasize that these differences cause competing and irreconcilable 'local' — e.g., African[265], Asian[266], Islamic[267], etc. — conceptions of the self, society and rights, ruling out the concept of a global community. The communitarian thesis reflects cognitive and moral relativism. However, I have shown in this book that this cognitive

---

265 See for instance: R.E. Howard, *Human Rights in Commonwealth Africa*, Totowa: Rowman and Littlefield, 1986, and K. M'Baye, "Human Rights in Africa", in: K. Vasak and P. Alston (eds), *The International Dimensions of Human Rights*, Westport: Greenwood Press, 1982, pp. 583-600.

266 See for instance: J.C. Hsiung (ed.), *Human Rights in East Asia — A Cultural Perspective*, New York: Paragon, 1985.

267 See for instance: A. A'la Mawdudi, *Human Rights in Islam*, Leicester: The Islamic Foundation, 1980.

and moral relativism is theoretically fallacious and practically dangerous. Cognitive and moral relativism is theoretically fallacious because, as I have argued, diversity is not a value in itself. In some cases, diversity reflects the different ways in which persons experience the idea of the Good, and, in some other cases, diversity reflects the different levels of humanity's spiritual development. Additionally, cognitive and moral relativism is practically dangerous because it is contradictory to designate the state as the guarantor of human rights and to allow it to espouse the moral claims of 'community' when states are the most frequent violators of human rights.

The communitarian approach to international justice encourages a particular attitude towards the ethics of intervention. This attitude consists in the argument that the norm of non-intervention should be a fundamental principle of the world order, because intervention contradicts the moral autonomy of the state and, generally, the conception of the international system as a moral arena of communities[268], and, thus, intervention threatens international (as well as domestic) order. J.S. Mill[269] has defended the communitarian norm of non-intervention on the grounds that, no matter how strong may be the case for intervention, freedom is not something that can be given to a certain community from people who are not members of the given community, but the members of the given community must gain freedom for themselves as an expression of their community's self-identification. However, J.S. Mill adds that one country is justified in helping the people of another in a struggle against their government for free institutions in case the yoke which the people are attempting to throw off is a foreign government or in case we are dealing with members of an equal community of nations, like Christian Europe.

In the light of what I have argued until now in this book, the problem with the communitarians' norm of non-intervention is not its supposed prudence in the management of international affairs, but the cognitive and moral relativism which is hidden behind the communitarians' prudent rhetoric about international politics. As I argued earlier in this Section, justice is, and should be, firm and absolute in its orientation towards the Good, but it is, and should be, 'critical' in its application in history, in the sense

---

268 See: C. Navari, "Intervention, Nonintervention and the Construction of the State", in: I. Forbes and M. Hoffman (eds), *Political Theory, International Relations and the Ethics of Intervention*, London: Macmillan, 1993, pp. 43-60.

269 J.S. Mill, "A Few Words on Nonintervention", *Dissertations and Discussions*, Vol. 3, London: Longmans, 1873.

that the historical application of justice must be characterized by a deep sense of the appropriate moment (timing), the right occasion to act, and the correct evaluation of the situation and conditions, so that the agent can respond to events successfully. As Thomas Jefferson wrote to Elbridge Gerry in 1801, "Unequivocal in principle, reasonable in manner, we shall be able I hope to do a great deal of good to the cause of freedom and harmony"[270]. Hence, intervention against unjust states is morally legitimate and a necessary presupposition for the transformation of the international system along the lines of humanism, but the manner in which this intervention will take place in each case must be characterized by a critical attitude. This mentality is implicit in the 2010 United Nations Approach to Transitional Justice Guidance Note.

In fact, in March 2010, the United Nations published a "Guidance Note of the Secretary-General" which exposes the "United Nations Approach to Transitional Justice"[271]. In this Note, it is mentioned that:

> The UN should consistently promote the compliance of transitional justice processes and mechanisms with international norms and standards. The normative foundation for the work of UN in advancing transitional justice is the Charter of the United Nations, along with four of the pillars of the modern international legal system: international human rights law, international humanitarian law, international criminal law, and international refugee law... These international standards further set the normative boundaries of UN engagement, for example: the UN will neither establish nor provide assistance to any tribunal that allows for capital punishment, nor endorse provisions in peace agreements that include amnesties for genocide, war crimes, crimes against humanity, and gross violations of human rights.[272]

Simultaneously, the same Note mentions that the UN should "take account of the political context when designing and implementing transitional justice processes and mechanisms"[273]. In particular, we read in this Note:

---

270 T. Jefferson, "Thomas Jefferson to Elbridge Gerry", 1801, Memorial Edition, Vol. 10, p. 255.

271 United Nations, *Guidance Note of the Secretary-General — United Nations Approach to Transitional Justice*, New York, 2010. In page 2 of the previous Note, we read: "For the United Nations, transitional justice is the full range of processes and mechanisms associated with a society's attempt to come to terms with a legacy of large-scale of past abuses, in order to ensure accountability, serve justice and achieve reconciliation".

272 United Nations, op. cit. (ref. 271), pp. 3-4.

273 United Nations, op. cit. (ref. 271), pp. 4.

Transitional justice processes and mechanisms do not operate in a political vacuum, but are often designed and implemented in fragile post-conflict and transitional environments. The UN must be fully aware of the political context and the potential implications of transitional justice mechanisms. In line with the Charter, the UN supports accountability, justice and reconciliation at all times. Peace and justice should be promoted as mutually reinforcing imperatives and the perception that they are at odds should be countered. The question for the UN is never whether to pursue accountability and justice, but rather when and how.[274]

Furthermore, when we study the problem of intervention, we must bear in mind that the humanistic tradition of the European civilization is a series of answers to a series of questions posed by persons who had progressed to high levels of spiritual development. In order for a society to really assimilate the essence of humanism — namely, the human being as a bearer of intrinsic, ontologically grounded, value — its collective consciousness must, first of all, pose the adequate existential and moral questions, and, in order to do so, it must have previously progressed to the corresponding level of knowledge. Hence, intervention against unjust states is inextricably linked to the accomplishment of cultural operations whose purpose should be to promote and accelerate the spiritual progress of humanity. In other words, intervention against unjust states is inextricably linked to the conduct of cultural diplomacy, which is intimately related to operations which aim at influencing and shaping the value system of decision makers[275].

---

274 United Nations, op. cit. (ref. 271), pp. 4.

275 As P. van Ham notes, "globalization and the media revolution have made each state more aware of itself, its image, its reputation, and its attitude — in short, its brand" (P. van Ham, "The Rise of the Brand State: The Postmodern Politics of Image and Reputation", *Foreign Affairs*, Vol. 80, 2001, p. 3). Within this value-centred framework of analysis, the politics of identity construction becomes the main focus of activity for policy-makers and nations in general. Moreover, G. Wiseman notes that "in the Westphalian sense, only states are thought to conduct diplomacy", and he argues that sub-national polities, even though they lack the diplomatic status and privileges of national governments, do conduct diplomacy, especially if we accept Wiseman's notion that diplomacy consists of "certain norms and values (the desirability of continuous dialogue through mutual recognition and representation); certain institutions (foreign ministries, embassies); certain processes (accreditation, a written code of diplomatic communications); and certain individuals (foreign ministry officials, ambassadors, and other diplomats)"; see: G. Wiseman, "Pax Americana: Bumping into Diplomatic Culture", *International Studies Perspectives*, Vol. 6, 2005, pp. 409-430.

4.4 Sustainable development

Intimately related to the idea of justice as harmony is the issue of sustainable development. The concept of sustainable development encompasses the following principles: environmental limits and efficiency, demand management, welfare efficiency, and equality[276]. The *London Sustainability Exchange* (founded in 2001 by the City of London and a group of influential partners) use the definition of *sustainable development developed by the Forum for the Future*, their founding consortium partner, which is:

> A dynamic process which enables all people to realise their potential and improve their quality of life in ways which simultaneously protect and enhance the Earth's life support systems...

However, the most well-known definition of sustainable development is due to the Brundtland Commission[277], which published a report entitled "Our Common Future" in 1987. In this report, the following definition of sustainable development is proposed:

> Sustainable development is development that meets the needs of the present without compromising the ability of future generations to meet their own needs. It contains within it two key concepts: the concept of 'needs', in particular the essential needs of the world's poor, to which overriding priority should be given; and the idea of 'limitations' imposed by the state of technology and social organization on the environment's ability to meet present and future needs.

The duration of the existence of the human consciousness and the improvement of the existential conditions of the human consciousness depend on the continuing ability of the environment to provide resources, absorb wastes, and provide basic life support services, such as temperature maintenance and protection against radiation. The environment can impose thresholds for certain human activities and urges the human consciousness to act critically. The critical attitude of consciousness implies that it abandons every kind of arbitrary idealistic activity, which breaks, or risks breaking, some important environmental threshold, and simultaneously directs the activity of the human mind, through its own intentionality, to the accomplishment of practical goals, which entail the profitability of situations

---

276 European Commission, *European Sustainable Cities*, Report by the Expert Group on Urban Environment, Brussels, 1996.

277 The Brundtland Commission, formally the World Commission on Environment and Development, known by the name of its Chair Gro Harlem Brundtland, was convened by the United Nations in 1983.

and the establishment of new relations by means of which the human being becomes aware of the applicability of its critical models to the objective situations it intends to take advantage of. As a result of the critical operation of the human consciousness, environmental thresholds do not call for a transition from an anthropo-centric to a bio-centric approach to existence, which would signal the human being's defeat by natural necessities, but they necessitate a more active operation of the critical factor of the human consciousness within objective conditions in order to avoid both exaggeration, or overacting, and defection, or omission. In other words, environmental thresholds call for a concern for rightness and measure. Thus, sustainable development calls for managing demands, instead of 'meeting' them. Demand management means that human activities must be carried out 'critically', and, therefore, policy processes are needed which are designed in order to reduce or redirect certain demands, rather than to meet them.

The critical operation of the human consciousness underpins the principle of environmental efficiency, which means the achievement of the maximum benefit for each unit of resources used. The following factors have an important positive contribution to environmental efficiency: increasing durability, increasing the technical efficiency of resource conversion, closing resource loops (by increasing reuse, recycling and salvage and avoiding pollution), and avoiding the consumption of renewable resources (e.g., water and energy) faster than the natural system can replenish them.

Environmental concerns compel us to think in 'cosmopolitan' terms and, thus, connect environmental concerns with human rights and equity issues. In fact, environmental concerns emphasize the responsibility of the present people towards one another for the continued viability of 'global commons' and towards future generations[278]. Additionally, environmental issues are connected to the issue of the equitable distribution of wealth, because the poor are worst affected by environmental problems and least able to provide adequate solutions to them, and, on the other hand, wealth encourages over-consumption of natural resources and energy and over-production of waste. Hence, inequitable distribution of wealth encourages the expression of unsustainable behavior and inhibits behavior change.

Furthermore, the inequalities of income across the globe are exceeded by the inequalities of scientific output and technological innovation. If the

---

278 See for instance: J.E. Lovelock, *Gaia — A New Look at Life on Earth*, Oxford: Oxford University Press, 1979.

poor countries have a higher access to the science and technology resources of the rich countries, then the need for the destruction of sensitive ecological areas in order to provide food for growing populations diminishes. For instance, the G8 ministers and European Commissioner responsible for science and technology met for the first time in Okinawa on 15 June 2008 together with ministers and senior officials from Brazil, China, India, Mexico, Philippines, the Republic of Korea, and South Africa, and they highlighted that "science and technology is an important key to sustainable development all over the world", and they reaffirmed "the importance of promoting science and technology cooperation based on international collaboration".

The social equivalent to the principle of environmental efficiency is the principle of welfare efficiency, which means the maximization of human benefit from each unit of economic activity. The following factors have an important positive contribution to welfare efficiency: maximizing the social utility of economic assets, increasing social inclusiveness in order to maximize the possible range of activities and means of exploiting economic assets through their life cycles, and promoting democratic decision-making in order to, first, develop efficient feedback systems and, second, promote the social control of economic processes. As it has been argued by Alan Atkinson, "the solo voice of economics must be joined by the strong voices of social and natural science, principled political leadership, idealistic citizen activism, cultural questioning of consumerist habits and values, and much more"[279].

The principle of welfare efficiency calls for a new way of understanding development. From the perspective of welfare efficiency, development can be considered as a social process of qualitative change, and, therefore, the 'economic growth', the 'value system', and the 'power relationships' which characterize the society under investigation must all explicitly find their position in every cognitively significant theory of development. Development programming is the outcome of the interplay between knowledge and action. Moreover, development presupposes a transition form a quantitative way of thinking to a qualitative way of thinking whose aim is to achieve a sustainable rate of socio-cultural and economic growth, which otherwise would be impossible.

---

279 A. Atkinson, *Pushing 'Reset' on Sustainable Development*, Sustainable Development Insights, The Frederick S. Pardee Center for the Study of the Long Range Future, October 2009, p. 7.

Positivist economists tend to construe programming in a static manner within the framework of neoclassical economics — i.e., in a manner related to the economic thought of Léon Walras (equilibrium-optimization) — whereas a normative approach to political economy calls for an understanding of programming as a transition from a quantitative way of thinking to a qualitative way of thinking, and, therefore, as 'qualitative programming'. Qualitative programming implies that programming is not a passive application of economic generalizations, but the manifestation of the spiritual autonomy and the intentionality of human consciousness in political economy.

4.5 The cultural presuppositions of economic development and justice

The aim of this section is to analyze the manner in which international inequality can be addressed within the framework of international relations. The problem of international inequality calls for the analysis of the responsibilities of the rich countries/peoples as well as of the responsibilities of the poor countries/peoples.

First of all, we must mention that there are many defective formulations of the argument that the rich countries/peoples are responsible for the underdevelopment of the poor countries/peoples. These arguments point simply to "the record of imperial rule over the last four centuries, and the exploitation in this period of those countries that are poor today by many of those that are today rich"[280]. All these arguments are defective because, by identifying development with economic growth, they become self-overcoming, because, as C. Brown has pointed out:

> The full balance sheet of empire is less one-sided. This is not simply a matter of listing the crimes of empire on one side of the balance and its alleged benefits on the other; such attempts to find a moral calculus which allows one to measure, say, the destruction of a local economy against the introduction of an effective transport system are distasteful and unsuccessful. More to the point is the fact that the successor states of imperialism are themselves the product of empire.[281]

Indeed, Chris Brown is right in asserting that the "there is a remarkable consensus around the view that" the new societies created by imperialism "are superior [to their predecessors], encompassing liberal defenders of

---

280 C. Brown, op. cit. (ref. 1), p. 159.
281 C. Brown, op. cit. (ref. 1), p. 160.

capitalism, Marxist opponents and, more to the point, for the time being at least, most of the postcolonial elites"[282]. Hence, the "the continuity required by the 'reparations' argument is difficult to establish"[283].

Another, more promising, formulation of the argument that the rich countries/peoples are responsible for the underdevelopment of the poor countries/peoples is that international trade between rich and poor countries necessarily involves the exploitation of the latter. C. Brown has shown the weakness of many of these arguments as follows:

> It is easy to see that manifestly unfair bargains sometimes follow from the exploitation of political inequalities, but, as Marx argues in *Capital*, it is not possible to base a systematic theory of exploitation on acts of plunder and piracy, which is why he assumes in his political economy that commodities exchange at their average values. Some structuralists simply dodge this point... The best, indeed only, attempt to come up with a theoretically sophisticated account of unequal exchange — that of Arrighi Emmanuel — suggests that wages are the key independent variable. In the process of exchange high-wage countries exploit low-wage countries... Even if this were a widely accepted argument, which it is not, it could hardly explain how the structure of exploitation came into being in a period *before* wide differentials in wages.[284]

However, the pictures of the world drawn by the previous arguments as well as by Brown's counter-arguments change once we extricate ourselves from the intellectual cuffs of a materialistic, narrow-minded definition of development, which, in fact, underpins the above debates. As I mentioned in Section 4.4, 'development' should not be identified with 'economic growth', but it should be understood as programmed qualitative change whose aim is to achieve a sustainable rate of socio-cultural and economic growth which otherwise would be impossible. Therefore, development should be inextricably linked with human rights.

We cannot talk meaningfully about development if we do not address the purpose and the methodology of a development programme. A development programme is morally legitimate if its purpose is the safeguarding and protection of human rights, if its methodology complies with the criteria of science, and if its application reflects the social consensus.

Therefore, in order to address the problem of international inequality correctly, we must investigate the purpose and the methodology of the pro-

---

282 C. Brown, op. cit. (ref. 1), p. 160.
283 C. Brown, op. cit. (ref. 1), p.160.
284 C. Brown, op. cit. (ref. 1), p. 161.

grammes of economic development. The responsibility of imperial powers for the underdevelopment of many countries/peoples primarily consists in the following facts: (i) the programmes of economic development followed by many underdeveloped countries/peoples primarily reflect the selfish interests of the imperial powers, and not the real needs of the local societies; (ii) the imperial powers, traditionally, approached the underdeveloped countries/peoples as lands and societies from which they could extract resources and not as societies which should be adequately guided in order to participate in a higher civilization. Thus, colonialism collapsed under the weight of its moral nihilism and cynic opportunism and was often succeeded by political and economic mayhem and poverty. No empire can survive for a long time if it is unable to conquer the spirit of the peoples which it has managed to integrate into its political, economic and military structures.

On the other hand, Alexander the Great (356–323 BC), who conquered the Persian Empire, including Anatolia, Syria, Phoenicia, Judea, Gaza, Egypt, Bactria and Mesopotamia and extended the boundaries of his own empire as far as the Punjab, set a different example of imperialism: he was methodically trying to convince the nations that he was conquering that he was neither a barbarian conqueror nor an avenger, but an agent of a superior civilization. Thus, he spread the Greek culture over the Middle East and far into Asia so that, after his death in 323 BC, the influence of Greek civilization continued to expand over the Mediterranean world, Greek became the common language of the East Mediterranean lands and thus Greek literature became known by all those who learned this language, a new literature sprang from Alexandria, Egypt (the town founded in 331 BC by Alexander), and arose a new interest in science. Alexander the Great founded his empire upon a cosmopolitan cultural ideal, which was underpinning unity and order throughout his vast empire, and not on opportunism or selfish materialistic goals[285]. Thus, Alexander the Great, bearing an attractive and

---

285 Alexander the Great, instead of building up an empire merely by establishing regimes based only on physical-spatial unity, was founding new cities which were loci of the Greek *paideia*. See: W. *Jaeger, Paideia — The Ideals of Greek Culture*, Oxford: Oxford University Press, 1945. In this famous research work, Jaeger explains that 'paideia' is a word we translate as "education", but which, according to ancient Greeks, means not only the rearing and education of children (*pais* is the simple Greek for child) but also "mental culture, civilization", and then "objectively, the literature and accomplishments of an age or people". It was rendered in Latin as *humanitas*. As Jaeger put it in the much quoted Introduction of his book *Paideia*, "other nations made gods, kings, spirits; the Greeks alone made men". Men must

convincing spiritual proposal for life, managed to conquer not only territories but also the minds of the people who were living in the territories of his vast empire. The history of the Greek empires of Alexander the Great and of Byzantium shows that the ultimate cause of the success of an empire is its ability to unite its people spiritually. In fact, the Byzantine Empire, by convincing its people that the Byzantine ideal of life was the best, managed to survive for more than one thousand years.

Moreover, the Romans like Alexander the Great and by contrast with modern colonialism, used their colonies as models of the genius of the Roman system of public administration, which could inspire and attract foreign peoples. In fact, the Roman law was the cultural-institutional glue that bound the Roman Empire together. Thus, inhabitants from the farthest reaches of the empire wanted to be — and became — "Roman"[286]. During the zenith of the empire, being 'Roman' was a cultural identity "that allowed citizens from savage and barbarous nations to participate in the political process and share in the power and prestige of the empire"[287]. Hence, the Roman Empire had a powerful attraction: conquered subjects from Britannia to Arabia wanted to be 'Roman'.

Therefore, the ultimate goals and the culture of the most privileged members of the international system must always find their position in every cognitively significant analysis of the problem of international inequality. Let us consider, for instance, the financial/currency crises in Asia in 1997-1998, in Brazil in 1998-1999, and in Russia in 1998. How did the International Monetary Fund (IMF) and the World Bank handle these situations? First of all, they demanded that the emerging economies open their domestic capital markets to international speculative funds on the grounds that the emerging economies needed the inflow of international capital in order to finance their development. The opening of the emerging economies' capital markets was combined with the elimination of all barriers to the direct and fast repatriation of the invested capitals, but it was not combined with the application of development programmes which complied with the criteria of welfare efficiency which I mentioned above. Therefore, Western and Japanese funds flowed massively into emerging economies and created

---

see, in the traditional heroes Pindar glorified, "their true selves raised to a higher plane".

286 A. Chua, *Day of Empire — How Hyperpowers Rise to Global Dominance and Why They Fall*, New York: Doubleday, 2007, p. 29.

287 A. Chua, op. cit. (ref. 286), p. 41.

economic bubbles — namely, in these cases, 'development' became equivalent to trade in high volumes at prices that are considerably at variance with intrinsic values[288].

The outbreak of a crisis in an emerging economy — which was usually triggered by a negative political or economic event — signaled massive outflow of capital from this country. During such phases, the IMF's response was to demand that the given emerging economy maintain 'hard' currency policies at any cost. The protection of the stability of exchange rates implied that the central bank of an emerging economy which was undergoing a financial crisis had to use its reserves in order to purchase its national currency[289] and increase interest rates[290], thus making its financial crisis even worse and, ultimately, leading to the collapse of its national currency, since it was unable to continue supporting it in the global foreign exchange market, and to the waste of its foreign currency reserves. Hence, the attempt of an emerging economy to protect the stability of its national currency's exchange rates implied that — due to the pressures exercised on its national currency by speculative funds — it had to waste the international financial assistance it was receiving as well as its central bank's foreign currency reserves in order for foreign investors to enjoy a satisfactory exchange

288 J. Lahart, "Bernanke's Bubble Laboratory — A Princeton Protégés of Fed Chief, Study the Economics of Manias", *The Wall Street Journal*, 16 May 2008, p. A1.

289 Central banks can influence exchange rates by intervening in the foreign exchange market. However, if the underlying forces in the market are strong, then central banks cannot resist them in the long-run. In fact, the power of a central bank to buy its own currency (in order to pursue a policy of 'hard currency' in the FOREX market) is limited by its reserves; the power of a central bank to increase the supply of money is limited by the risk of inflation. There is a large literature on international currency crises. One strand of this literature seeks to develop early warning signals of exchange rate crises. In 1998, G. Kaminsky, S. Lizondo and C.M. Reinhart reviewed the results of 25 selected studies on currency crisis and identified several crises indicators (G. Kaminsky, S. Lizondo and C.M. Reinhart, "Leading Indicators of Currency Crises", IMF Staff Papers, Vol. 45, 1998). A second strand of the currency literature examines the issue of currency contagion. For instance, in 1996, J. Sachs, A. Tornell and A. Velasco showed that countries with weak fundamentals are more susceptible to contagion (J. Sachs, A. Tornell and A. Velasco, "Financial Crises in Emerging Markets: The Lessons from 1995", *Brookings Papers on Economic Activity*, New York: The Brookings Institution, Vol. 27, 1996, pp. 147-216). Moreover, in 1996, B. Eichengreen, A.K. Rose and C. Wyplosz showed that "speculative attacks tend to be temporarily correlated; that is, currency crises appear to pass 'contagiously' from one country to another" (B. Eichengreen, A.K. Rose and C. Wyplosz, "Contagious Currency Crises", *Scandinavian Journal of Economics*, Vol. 98, 1996).

290 Differences between the levels of interest rates in two countries will influence the flow of funds from the one to the other for investment purposes.

rate for the repatriation of their capitals before the final collapse of the local currency.

After the monetary collapse of an emerging economy, the IMF's directives were emphasizing that, in order for such an economy to continue having access to international credit, it had to stabilize its domestic economic system and sell state assets. The IMF was expecting that economic growth would automatically follow as a consequence of market liberalization, privatizations and low inflation. The IMF's economic recipe implied increases in taxation and interest rates and reductions in the social expenses of the state budget. However, these measures and the waste of huge national resources for the sake of the protection of the interests of foreign investors brought about the opposite results. The increases in taxation and interest rates reduced demand and the local economy's productive capacity, and the indiscriminate policy of privatizations led to the acquisition of state assets by business elites without adequate provisions having been made by the government for the reinforcement of economic competitiveness and social cohesion through efficient private investments.

The analysis of the 1990s currency crises in several emerging economies shows that the major international financial institutions — namely, the International Monetary Fund and the World Bank — were primarily oriented towards the establishment and safeguarding of an irrational economic system, which was based on what Max Webber has classified as "greedy adventurism", and which operated as an incubator of economic bubbles, and not towards the formulation and application of rational and morally sensitive development programmes.

On the other hand, the underdeveloped countries/peoples have their own responsibilities for their conditions. The essence of their responsibilities is their resistance to creative change, i.e., their failure to assimilate the best qualities of the most privileged members of the international system (e.g., rational management of political and economic affairs, rule of law, science, human rights, etc.), as well as their 'quantitative' — as opposed to 'qualitative' — approach to the issue of progress, which makes the underdeveloped countries/peoples reproduce the developed countries'/peoples' bad self.

In the modern theory of economic development, J.A. Ryan has attempted to promote a qualitative — as opposed to quantitative — way of thinking about economic development through the canon of human welfare. The canon of human welfare can be summarized as follows:

> Human welfare means the well-being of persons, considered individually as well as collectively. It includes but is not identical with public welfare or even social welfare. Not infrequently the latter phrase is synonymous with the welfare of the dominant social group... The canon of human welfare... requires that all human beings be treated as persons, as possessed of natural rights: this is equality. It demands that all industrial persons receive at least that amount of income which is necessary for decent living and reasonable self-development: this is a recognition of need. The canon of human welfare declares that some consideration must be accorded to manifestations of good will by those who take part in the process of industry: this is recognition of efforts and sacrifices. And it gives reasonable recognition to the canons of productivity and scarcity.[291]

Moreover, in 1993, Gerald Barney, a physicist, policy analyst and executive director of the Millennium Institute, addressing the Parliament of the World Religions, held in Chicago, acknowledged the growing urgency for a new global orientation, saying that:

> [W]e can no longer guide our countries and our corporations because we no longer know what 'development' is. We no longer know how to distinguish 'progress' from 'failure'... we are now a species without a vision. We cannot act together because we no longer know our goal.

That is why we find that the Commission on Global Governance[292], in its report entitled *Our Global Neighbourhood*, affirms the need for "neighbourhood ethics" and "neighbourhood values" as the cornerstone of future global governance. The report favourably quotes Barbara Ward as suggesting that "people have to see with new eyes and understand with new minds before they can truly turn to new ways of living"[293], and this quotation continues:

> The most important change that people can make is to change their way of looking at the world. We can change studies, jobs, neighbourhoods, even countries and continents and still remain much as we always were. But change our fundamental angle of vision and everything changes — our priorities, our values, our judgments, our pursuits. Again and again, in the history of religion, this

---

291 J.A. Ryan, *Economic Justice — Selections from Distributive Justice and a Living Wage*, ed. H.R. Beckley, Louisville, Kentucky: Westminister John Knox Press, 1996, p. 74.

292 The Commission on Global Governance was an organization co-chaired by Ingvar Carlsson, then Prime Minister of Sweden, and Guyana Shridath Ramphal, Commonwealth Secretary-General from 1975 to 1990, which produced the report *Our Global Neighbourhood*, Oxford: Oxford University Press, 1995.

293 Commission on Global Governance, op. cit. (ref. 292), p.47.

total upheaval in the imagination has marked the beginning of a new life... a turning of the heart, a 'metanoia', by which men see with new eyes and understand with new minds and turn their energies to new ways of living.

In his book *A Contribution to the Critique of Political Economy*[294], Karl Marx correctly pointed out that the primary formation of capital was not due to the ownership of land or to the medieval trade-unions, but it was due to the wealth which was accumulated through usury and commerce. The accumulation of such wealth became possible in the 15th century when the Papal Church adopted the view of the scholastic theologians that money bears a secret, innate virtue on the basis of which it can multiply by itself. This new 'theological' view — which, departing from the Platonic humanism, introduced the concept of money as an end in itself and offered moral legitimacy to the profession of usury — created the necessary spiritual presuppositions of capitalism, and these spiritual underpinnings of capitalism were enhanced by the Puritan movement[295]. Capitalism appeared in the historical foreground as a peculiar form of trade organized by the Fugger family in Germany. The Fugger family was a historically prominent group of European bankers who were members of the fifteenth- and sixteenth-century mercantile patriciate of Augsburg.

Money existed in the ancient and the medieval societies of Europe, but it could not be transformed into 'capital' because financial wealth as such had no value in the conscious minds of those people, who were creating personal relationships with the land and with their trades. In order for such an economic regime to change, the landowner had to give priority to the exchange-value of his revenue over the use-value of his revenue, and thus to transform his revenue — which until then was a kind of wealth shared by the landowner and his serfs, since all of them were subsisting on the same resources — into an instrument of 'individual' power. This became possible as a consequence of the spiritual value which was ascribed to the financial wealth in the 15th century, and, thus, the landowner transformed his serfs into a free labour force which he could employ ad hoc as a capitalist, i.e., using the capital he owned. As a conclusion, the genesis of capitalism was due to the acknowledgement of a new dimension of money — namely, the exchange-value of money, next to the traditional use-value of money —

---

294 K. Marx, op. cit. (ref. 112).
295 M. Weber, *The Protestant Ethic and the Spirit of Capitalism*, London: Allen & Unwin, 1930.

which, in turn, was due to the scholastic theologians' departure from the Platonic humanistic economic legacy. The Platonic humanistic economic legacy was refusing to acknowledge money, or financial wealth, as an end in itself, i.e., as a bearer of an intrinsic value, and was treating money only as a use-value for the sake of the human well-being.

At this point, I must emphasize that there is a substantial difference between 'ownership' and 'capital'. Ownership is a legal relationship, which exists in both pre-capitalistic and capitalistic societies. On the other hand, 'capital' — irrespective of whether it is private or public — is not the outcome of a specific type of ownership, but it is the outcome of the speculative employment of labour force by the owners of capital (irrespective of whether the owners of capital are private entrepreneurs or the state). At the bottom line, capitalism signifies a spiritual attitude: the treatment of financial wealth as a bearer of an intrinsic value and thus as an end in itself. This explains, for instance, why capitalist speculators trade in capital markets and money markets, through various speculative schemes and tools, instead of using money in order to acquire other assets, such as real estate, or build ship-vessels, factories, etc.

Furthermore, the treatment of financial wealth as a bearer of an intrinsic value and as an end in itself is the spiritual foundation and the most important determining factor of the character and the social impact of globalization in the 21st century, and particularly of the following events: (i) the predominance of financial capital and speculation over productive capital and human labour; (ii) the liberalization of exchange and the over-exploitation of natural resources, causing social dislocation and ecological damages; (iii) the development and implementation of new technologies whose ultimate goal is profit maximization and not the amelioration of the labour force's quality of life; (iv) growing military control over natural resources.

The social and humanitarian crisis of the 21st century global economy is intimately related to the following factors[296]: (i) the hike in food prices caused by speculation and the destruction of peasant agriculture as a result of such factors as the promotion of monoculture, the destruction of bio-diversity, water pollution, etc.; (ii) the hike in oil prices caused by speculation and the blackmailing of the global economy by the OPEC oil cartel; (iii) the increasing concentration of wealth as a result of a profit oriented mental-

---

296 F. Houtart, "The Multiple Crisis and Beyond", *Globalizations*, Vol. 7, 2010, pp. 17-22.

ity according to which it is more profitable (and therefore preferable) for capitalism, to invest in the production of goods with added value that are purchased by the top 20% of the world population rather than cater to the needs of the poor (housing, food, education, etc.).

On the other hand, the Soviet economists who were criticizing the capitalist system of the West during the 20th century were doing so without refuting the dominant logic of the capitalist system — namely, the views that capital accumulation is the foundation of the economy and that many externalities (e.g., environmental, social etc.) should be ignored for the sake of capital accumulation. The supporters of state capitalism, which is often called 'socialism', focus only on the debate about the ownership of capital and ignore the spiritual foundations and the spiritual problems of capitalism. Thus, socialism as state capitalism is nothing else but a coercive utopia.

Therefore, in order to talk meaningfully about justice, one must focus on the core of the mentality which underpins an economic system, instead of restricting the debate to economic institutions and statistics. For instance, when Chris Brown argues that "the economic failures of eastern Europe and the former Soviet Union must cast considerable doubt upon the ability of any kind of planned economy to replace capitalist market relations as a route to a stable economic system capable of removing basic poverty"[297], he completely ignores that the Soviet socialism was nothing else but a form of state capitalism, and, thus, it had common spiritual roots with the market capitalism of the West. But, as I mentioned before, we cannot understand the spiritual problem of capitalism if we restrict our analysis to the issue of the ownership of capital. The fundamental characteristic of the capitalist mentality — which pervades both market capitalism and state capitalism — is the autonomy of the accumulation of capital, i.e., growth for the sake of growth, which goes back to the decision of 15th century scholastics and 16th and 17th century Puritans to treat capital as a ticket to paradise.

On the other hand, Plato's theory of ideas leads to a humanistic approach to economic development. In the *Laws*, 729a, and in the *Apology of Socrates*, 41e and 29d-e, Plato inveighs against excessive commercialism which puts money before the human interest (well-being), thereby causing injustice, degenerate luxury, vicious extremes of wealth and poverty, and wars. Plato does not teach an ascetic attitude which fails to acknowledge the value of economic wealth. Plato emphasizes that the human being

---

297 C. Brown, op. cit. (ref. 1), p. 185.

must be the master of economic wealth, and that economic wealth must not spiritually enslave the human being. Moreover, for Plato, economic wealth is good when it serves the well-being of the people. Hence, in the *Laws*, 743e and 870b, Plato emphasizes that it is not business that should be curbed, but bad business.

Plato condemns excessive wealth and commercialism on the following grounds: (i) excessive private wealth is practically impossible without corresponding extremes of poverty, and this condition is a most fruitful cause of dissension; (ii) extremes of wealth or poverty cause industrial inefficiency; (iii) no man can accumulate great wealth by just acquisition, because, even though he may have done no conscious injustice, his excessive accumulation has been due to unjust social conditions; (iv) expenditures of great private fortunes are too liable to be marked by foolish luxury and waste and, therefore, are not likely to be helpful either to individual or to community; (v) the national demand for unlimited wealth is a fruitful cause of international differences; (vi) the purpose of economic science must be the well-being of humanity and not finance for its own sake; (vii) a true definition of economic wealth must be based on the innate quality of an object for good or harm.

According to the arguments which I have already put forward in the present book, the core of the issue of development is the manner in which people understand freedom. By the term freedom, I mean an impulse of one's will towards 'infinity'. In other words, freedom signifies action, and not a condition of life. However, there is a substantial difference between something which is quantitatively infinite and something which is qualitatively infinite. If freedom is an impulse of our will towards something which is qualitatively infinite (e.g., towards that which Plato calls the Good), then freedom becomes a force of the Good. If, on the other hand, we perceive something which is quantitatively infinite (e.g., the accumulation of capital) as an absolute principle, and if such a quantitatively infinite principle guides the exercise of our freedom, then we cause tragic consequences.

A quantitative — as opposed to qualitative — approach to the concept of infinity underpins the foundations of every desperate consciousness's decision to use evil means in order to pursue good goals, e.g., to use crime in order to give rise to a better world. If 'infinity' is understood in qualitative terms, then time is motion in relation to a firm trans-historical purpose, or meaning of existence — that which Plato calls the idea of the Good. If 'infinity' is understood in quantitative terms, then time is deprived of the spiritual unity which it acquires when it is an itinerary towards a trans-temporal end. If time has not a trans-temporal end, and if history is exhausted in the pursuit of historical purposes, then the human being has no 'sun' towards which to turn its consciousness, and it is sunk in the darkness of its psychological 'cave'. And then, every evil can be justified in the name of historical necessity.

The temporal life of the human being is characterized by a dialectical relationship between will and being, i.e., between the intentionality of consciousness and reality. This dialectical relationship creates an expectation for a new beginning, for whose sake one may undertake risks: he may fight for the good by uniting his will with the veritable being (trans-historical idea), or he may decide to sacrifice his humanity in order to pursue a quantitative satisfaction of his will. 'Evil' is born when one believes that his present self is inferior to a quantitatively infinite principle which guides him in the exercise of his freedom. When one internalizes his present situation negatively, then, in his psychological world, he penalizes the 'other' and he refuses to acknowledge that the 'other' bears any intrinsic value. Thus, evil is not an outcome of social conditions, but it is an outcome of one's decision to commit himself to a quantitatively infinite principle, as opposed to a qualitatively infinite one.

Moreover, it is not the Enlightenment's quest for progress as such that generates evil, but it is the quantitative, as opposed to qualitative, approach to progress that generates evil, since it cultivates the mentality that a good end can justify evil means. For instance, a freedom fighter who resorts to terrorism is not less evil than a ruthless colonial ruler, an anti-globalization activist who defends economic nationalism because the maximization of his income depends on economic nationalism is not less evil than a cynic multinational corporation which pursues the maximization of its profits by transgressing national borders, a Marxist proletariat who wants to seize control of a capitalist structure in order to maximize his materialistic utility function is not less evil than a harsh capitalist who wants to maintain his control over a capitalist structure in order to maximize his own materialistic utility function, because all of them understand progress in quantitative terms.

As a conclusion, behind the problems of inequality and underdevelopment, lies a more fundamental problem, which has to do with the manner in which one understands time. If we understand time as an itinerary towards a trans-temporal and trans-historical end — namely, the Idea — then we can take distance from all historical things (while we are still alive and historically active) and, thus, we can safeguard our spiritual autonomy from them and our ability to evaluate and manage them rationally.

4.6 The cultural underpinnings of terrorism

The Convention for the Prevention and Punishment of Terrorism of 1937 — known also as the Geneva Convention of 1937 — and the European Convention on the Suppression of Terrorism of 1977, as amended by its Protocol of 15 May 2003, may be treated as the milestones on the road of long-lasting efforts of the world society to create an effective legal response to terrorism. However, the concept of terrorism is blurred, and it causes disagreements among states when they have to take common legal measures to counter terrorism.

For instance, in the British Prevention of Terrorism Act, s. 20, terrorism is defined as follows:

> the use of violence for political ends and includes any use of violence for the purpose of putting the public or any section of the public in fear.

And according to US Law 100-204 of 1987, s. 901,

> The term terrorist activity means the organizing or participating in a wanton or indiscriminate act of violence with extreme indifference to the risk of causing death or serious bodily harm to individuals not taking part in armed hostilities.

Additionally, according to US Law 104-302 of 1996, a "federal crime of terrorism" is a crime "calculated to influence or affect the conduct of government by intimidation or coercion, or to retaliate against government conduct" and to other crimes mentioned in US law, such as unlawful acts against the safety of civil aviation, crimes against internationally protected persons, etc. According to the French Law of 1986, 'terrorism' refers to individual or collective acts which aim at causing social intimidation by terror.

At this point, I must mention that there is a conceptual relationship between 'terrorism' and 'political offence' since most often political motives govern terrorist activities. Hence, given that many bilateral and multilateral international conventions exclude political offences from the list of crimes that justify extradition, several terrorist activities could become unpunishable if certain states decided to characterize them as political offences and terrorists as political offenders. The right of political asylum was originally an expression of sympathy on behalf of liberal states towards similarly minded people who fight in other states for liberal values. The French Revolution played a crucial role in this. Article 120 of the French Constitution of 1793 offered political asylum. Additionally, the scholarly works of wellknown experts in international law, such as Louis Renault, F.P.G. Guizot and H.P. Kluit, opposed the extradition of political offenders.

In general, there are two main reasons that can justify the non-extradition of political offenders: (a) the relativity of the concept of political offence and (b) the lack of trust in the impartial administration of justice in a state requiring the extradition of an offender. However, assassination and the creation of a state of terror as means to a political end are detestable crimes against human goods. Martin Rudner, Director of the Canadian Centre of Intelligence and Security Studies at Ottawa's Carleton University, has argued that:

> There is the famous statement: 'One man's terrorist is another man's freedom fighter'. But that is grossly misleading. It assesses the validity of the cause when terrorism is an act. One can have a perfectly beautiful cause and yet if one commits terrorist acts, it is terrorism regardless.[298]

The Geneva Conventions[299] and their Protocols are focused on the requirement to distinguish between civilians and combatants, and the prohibition of attacks on civilians or indiscriminate attacks. In addition to an express prohibition of all acts aimed at spreading terror among the civilian population (Article 51, paragraph 2, Protocol I; and Article 13, paragraph 2, Protocol II), International Humanitarian Law also proscribes the following acts, which could be considered as terrorist attacks:

---

298 Quoted in A. Humphreys, "One Official's 'Refugee' Is Another's 'Terrorist'", *National Post*, 17 January 2006.

299 The four Geneva Conventions are the following: (i) First Geneva Convention for the Amelioration of the Condition of the Wounded and Sick in Armed Forces in the Field, 1864; (ii) Second Geneva Convention for the Amelioration of the Condition of Wounded, Sick and Shipwrecked Members of Armed Forces at Sea, 1906; (iii) Third Geneva Convention relative to the Treatment of Prisoners of War, 1929; (iv) Fourth Geneva Convention relative to the Protection of Civilian Persons in Time of War, 1949. The 1949 conventions have been modified with three amendment protocols: (i) Protocol I (1977) relating to the Protection of Victims of International Armed Conflicts; (ii) Protocol II (1977) relating to the Protection of Victims of Non-International Armed Conflicts; (iii) Protocol III (2005) relating to the Adoption of an Additional Distinctive Emblem (for medical).

(i) attacks on civilians and civilian objects (Article 51, paragraphs 2 and 52, Protocol I; and Article 13, Protocol II);

(ii) indiscriminate attacks (Article 51, paragraph 4, Protocol I);

(iii) attacks on places of worship (Article 53, Protocol I; and Article 16, Protocol II);

(iv) attacks on works and installations containing dangerous forces (Article 56, Protocol I; and Article 15, Protocol II);

(v) the taking of hostages (Article 75, Protocol I; Article 3 common to the four Conventions; and Article 4, paragraph 2b, Protocol II);

(vi) murder of persons not or no longer taking part in hostilities (Article 75, Protocol I; Article 3 common to the four Conventions; and Article 4, paragraph 2a, Protocol II).

Additionally, humanitarian law contains stipulations to repress violations of these prohibitions and mechanisms for implementing these obligations[300].

On 27 September 2010, the UN Secretary-General Ban Ki-moon submitted the following remarks to a Security Council's open debate on countering terrorism:

> Terrorism may be a gathering storm, but the international response is gathering steam. Over the past five years, the United Nations has expanded its counter-terrorism activities, increased inter-agency coordination and enhanced partnerships with a wide range of international and regional organizations. Joint initiatives with Member States in many regions — including the Sahel, the Horn of Africa, the Middle East and South and Central Asia — have shown that there is much we can do. Countering terrorism demands a broad approach: First, we must continue our efforts in the fields of security and law enforcement. That includes measures to further deprive terrorists of financial resources and mobility, and to prevent them from acquiring and using weapons of mass destruction. Second, other areas deserve more attention. Education, development, intercultural dialogue and conflict prevention all have growing relevance in addressing conditions conducive to the spread of terrorism. Third, we must do more to understand the reasons people are drawn to violence, so that we can do more to prevent others from following that path. Fourth, we need to continue strengthening the legal regime, building on existing international counter-terrorism instruments and relevant resolutions of the Security Council. The value of these measures, and of the United Nations Global Counter-Terrorism Strategy, lies in their consistent and equal implementation. Fifth, we must improve the way we share information and best practices. That means estab-

---

300 See: D. Fleck (ed.), *The Handbook of International Humanitarian Law*, Oxford: Oxford University Press, 2008.

lishing national focal points and regional networks, and mobilizing civil society, the private sector, and the media. No counter-terrorism approach would be complete without a full commitment to human rights and the rule of law. Both the Security Council and the General Assembly have consistently endorsed the protection of human rights as an integral component of any effective counter-terrorism policy, and I welcome the attention the Council has devoted to this topic. Several States — including those that have been victimized by terrorism — are eager to implement their obligations under the counter-terrorism frameworks but lack the resources and other capacities to do so. Capacity-building is, therefore, a priority for the United Nations. Considering the gravity of the situation in the Sahel-Maghreb region, I am committed to working with the region's leaders on strengthening State capacity for counter-terrorism. In Central Asia, the United Nations is already working on capacity-building in the areas of law enforcement, criminal justice and international cooperation. I would also like to stress the importance of supporting victims of terrorism.

One may characterize the criminal activity of terrorists in several ways. However, terrorists do violate the human rights of their victims, i.e., terrorism per se constitutes a violation of human rights, because, ultimately, terrorism reduces to a false understanding of heroism and justice. In the light of the Platonic approach to justice which I have defended in the present book, true heroism does not consist in on one's endurance of hardship or audaciousness, even though such attitudes presuppose a lot of psychological strength. The quality of a soul is not tested in a struggle for power, because, if heroism were identified with warlike achievements, then heroism would have no place, and, in fact, would be nullified under conditions of peace or after the accomplishment of a war hero's mission. If we identify heroism with warlike achievements or with competition in general, then, apart from war or competition, there is no other activity which can nourish a heroic consciousness, and, thus, the end of war or competition for power becomes synonymous to the end of heroism. In the light of the Platonic approach to justice which I have defended in the present book, heroism signifies an attempt to achieve the unity of the self and of humanity at a higher level of consciousness. Hence, a real hero is a person who has the courage — irrespective of his historical conditions — to seek the ultimate meaning of existence, instead of compromising with the values and the terms of the historical becoming. A real hero is a person who has the courage to maintain his spiritual autonomy from the historical becoming.

A real hero refuses to subordinate the spirit to historical expediencies, but he is not a renunciate. On the contrary, a real hero undertakes his historical responsibilities while remaining spiritually independent from historical results, since he acknowledges that the end of history is not a historical goal. In other words, such a person is historically active, but his existential hopes are not exhausted in history. Hence, for such a person, the end does not justify the means.

For Plato, the primary purpose of philosophy is not to establish practical procedures, as if it were a manual of moral *practices* or an elixir of magical political achievements, but to establish *criteria* of action, lead to psychic harmony and safeguard the spiritual autonomy of the human being. On other hand, those who approach truth pragmatically and acknowledge a practical — namely, historical (as opposed to metaphysical) — goal as the ultimate meaning of life cannot refute the essence of terrorism and totalitarianism and, in fact, they are prone to terrorism and totalitarianism. Fyodor Dostoyevsky, in the fifth book of his novel *The Brothers Karamazov*[301], narrates the myth of the Holy Inquisitor, which helps one understand why those people who reduce the ultimate meaning of life to a practical regulation of things, i.e., they attempt to transform a metaphysical idea into a societal regime, lead humanity to totalitarianism and terror. According to this myth, one of the Karamazov brothers tells his bother about a dream, a vision, which unfolds "in Spain, in Seville, in the most terrible time of the Inquisition, when fires were lighted every day to the glory of God". Christ reappears at that very moment; he proceeds to perform several miracles and is arrested by the Grand Inquisitor who instantly puts Christ in jail. The next day, the Grand Inquisitor visits Christ in his cell, and the dialogue unfolds; in fact, it is a monologue by the Grand Inquisitor explaining his cosmo-theory to Christ. The Grand Inquisitor tells Christ that the greatest gift of freedom was also an incredible burden for people and the Inquisition succeeded in lifting that terrible burden:

> For fifteen centuries we have been wrestling with Thy freedom, but now it is ended and over for good. Dost Thou not believe that it's over for good? Thou lookest meekly at me and deignest not even to be wroth with me. But let me tell Thee that now, to-day, people are more persuaded than ever that they have perfect freedom, yet they have brought their freedom to us and laid it humbly at our feet.

301 F. Dostoyevsky, *The Brothers Karamazov*, trans. C. Garnett, New York: Penguin Books, 1958, Book V, Chapter 5.

And now that the freedom was banished:

> for the first time it has become possible to think of the happiness of men. Man was created a rebel; and how can rebels be happy?

The Grand Inquisitor proceeds to challenge Christ about the three questions in "the temptations":

> For in those three questions the whole subsequent history of mankind is, as it were, brought together into one whole, and foretold, and in them are united all the unsolved historical contradictions of human nature. At the time it could not be so clear, since the future was unknown; but now that fifteen hundred years have passed, we see that everything in those three questions was so justly divined and foretold, and has been so truly fulfilled, that nothing can be added to them or taken from them.

The first temptation was that Christ had a choice of giving people bread and establishing himself as the King of the world, but he rejected that temptation claiming that "Man does not live by bread alone" and granting humanity freedom. The Grand Inquisitor argues that this decision Christ made had tragic consequences:

> Yet in this question lies hid the great secret of this world. Choosing 'bread', Thou wouldst have satisfied the universal and everlasting craving of humanity — to find someone to worship. So long as man remains free he strives for nothing so incessantly and so painfully as to find someone to worship. But man seeks to worship what is established beyond dispute, so that all men would agree at once to worship it. For these pitiful creatures are concerned not only to find what one or the other can worship, but to find community of worship is the chief misery of every man individually and of all humanity from the beginning of time. For the sake of common worship they've slain each other with the sword. They have set up gods and challenged one another, 'Put away your gods and come and worship ours, or we will kill you and your gods!' And so it will be to the end of the world, even when gods disappear from the earth; they will fall down before idols just the same. Thou didst know, Thou couldst not but have known, this fundamental secret of human nature, but Thou didst reject the one infallible banner which was offered Thee to make all men bow down to Thee alone — the banner of earthly bread; and Thou hast rejected it for the sake of freedom and the bread of Heaven. Behold what Thou didst further. And all again in the name of freedom! I tell Thee that man is tormented by no greater anxiety than to find someone quickly to whom he can hand over that gift of freedom with which the ill-fated creature is born. But only one who can appease their conscience can take over their freedom. In bread there was offered Thee an invincible banner; give bread, and man will worship thee, for nothing is more certain than bread... But what happened? Instead of taking men's freedom from them,

Thou didst make it greater than ever! Didst Thou forget that man prefers peace, and even death, to freedom of choice in the knowledge of good and evil? Nothing is more seductive for man than his freedom of conscience, but nothing is a greater cause of suffering. And behold, instead of giving a firm foundation for setting the conscience of man at rest for ever, Thou didst choose all that is exceptional, vague and enigmatic; Thou didst choose what was utterly beyond the strength of men, acting as though Thou didst not love them at all — Thou who didst come to give Thy life for them! Instead of taking possession of men's freedom, Thou didst increase it, and burdened the spiritual kingdom of mankind with its sufferings for ever.

The Grand Inquisitor proceeds to the second temptation, and he ridicules Christ, telling him that he made all the wrong choices including the rejection of miracles in the second temptation, again for the sake of freedom:

There are three powers, three powers alone, able to conquer and to hold captive for ever the conscience of these impotent rebels for their happiness those forces are miracle, mystery and authority... Thou didst not come down from the Cross when they shouted to Thee, mocking and reviling Thee, 'Come down from the cross and we will believe that Thou art He'. Thou didst not come down, for again Thou wouldst not enslave man by a miracle, and didst crave faith given freely, not based on miracle. Thou didst crave for free love and not the base raptures of the slave before the might that has overawed him for ever.

In the third temptation, Christ has rejected the role of an Earthly King to the mortals. This is the most devastating challenge to Christ by the Grand Inquisitor, who argues that the Papacy has assumed the role of Caesar for the sake of humankind:

Hadst Thou taken the world and Caesar's purple, Thou wouldst have founded the universal state and have given universal peace. For who can rule men if not he who holds their conscience and their bread in his hands? We have taken the sword of Caesar, and in taking it, of course, have rejected Thee and followed him. Oh, ages are yet to come of the confusion of free thought, of their science and cannibalism. For having begun to build their tower of Babel without us, they will end, of course, with cannibalism. But then the beast will crawl to us and lick our feet and spatter them with tears of blood. And we shall sit upon the beast and raise the cup, and on it will be written, 'Mystery'.

Finally, the Grand Inquisitor mocks the idea of truth, and he argues that the religious establishment which he represents has managed to substitute its authority for the absolute good, by covering the ontological gap which characterizes a world which is not spiritually united by the absolute good and in the absolute good:

> They will be convinced that we are right, for they will remember the horrors of slavery and confusion to which Thy freedom brought them. Freedom, free thought, and science will lead them into such straits and will bring them face to face with such marvels and insoluble mysteries, that some of them, the fierce and rebellious, will destroy themselves, others, rebellious but weak, will destroy one another, while the rest, weak and unhappy, will crawl fawning to our feet and whine to us: 'Yes, you were right, you alone possess His mystery, and we come back to you, save us from ourselves!'

A historical object as such has only one significance — namely, that significance which is dictated by nature or by established historical conventions — and it can be approached only in utilitarian terms, and not in terms of a personal relationship. On the other hand, for a person who refuses to subordinate his spirit to historical necessities, the significance of every historical object is a matter of personal choice. The Platonic approach to justice deters totalitarianism because it refuses to transform the spirit into a historical institution, i.e., it keeps the spirit continuously transcendental and, therefore, irreducible to practice. Hence, within the framework of Plato's philosophy, one's relationship with the absolute good is always personal and, hence, free, and not determined by any logical or other necessities. On the other hand, terrorism is a form of totalitarianism, and, therefore, a violation of human rights, because it wishes to transform the spirit into practice. The ultimate aim of totalitarianism is to eliminate theoretical thought from human life — in accordance with Marx's eleventh thesis on Feuerbach: "Philosophers have hitherto only interpreted the world in various ways; the point is to change it"[302] — and to establish the absolute domination of practice, historical action. Therefore, terrorists, by being absolutely 'practical' persons, refuse to accept the ethos and the norms of the Geneva Conventions, which make clear that, in any armed conflict, the rights of the parties to the conflict to choose methods or means of warfare are not unlimited.

When the human being (a person or a people) internalizes its historical condition in a negative sense and believes that the ultimate meaning of its existence is the achievement of a historical goal, then it justifies the evil and allows its consciousness to take the side of the evil. This metaphysi-

---

302 Karl Marx's "Theses on Feuerbach" was first written in 1845. The English translation was first published in the Lawrence and Wishart edition of *The German Ideology* in 1938.

cal attitude — namely, this ontological gap — caused many socialist and national-liberation movements to degenerate and become inhuman, even though they followed a humanistic rhetoric, and also it caused various religious communities to endorse negative attitudes towards human rights and declare 'holy' wars.

From the previous analysis, it follows that the essence of terrorism is the subjugation of the spirit to historical necessities. Hence, terrorism is not conducted only by non-state actors but also by states. The fundamental characteristic of a terrorist is not his political, legal, or ideological status, but his absolute commitment to the pursuit of his historical vindication and his refusal to recognize any trans-historical principles and values. In other words, at a fundamental level, terrorism is a mental attitude.

Therefore, the core of counter-terrorist legislation and policy should be a methodical restriction of the actors' rights to choose the methods or means of conflict, irrespective of the cause of each conflict. In other words, the foundation of the counter-terrorist legislation and policy should be the spirit's autonomy from historical necessities.

4.7 The ideational structure of the European integration project

As John Ruggie has argued, "the building blocks of international reality are ideational as well as material"[303]. In fact, our understanding of the world is based on a dialectical relationship between material elements and ideational elements. However, during the Cold War, ideas were usually looked down on by IR scholars. This was mainly due to two reasons. The first reason is that, in general, the study of ideas is an arduous task — since ideas are often seen as "too vague, amorphous, and constantly evolving"[304] — whereas policy-makers, usually, "are shaped by a style of life that inhibits reflectiveness"[305]. Second, certain positivist formulations of the rational-choice theory, which emphasize the rational behaviours of actors irrespective of their identities and value system, were exercising a dominant power on the scholarly discipline of International Relations throughout the Cold

303 J.G. Ruggie, "What Makes the World Hang Together? Neo-Utilitarianism and the Social Constructivist Challenge", *International Organization*, Vol.52, 1998, p. 879.
304 S. Berman, *The Social Democratic Moment: Ideas and Politics in the Making of Interwar Europe*, Cambridge, Mass.: Harvard University Press, 1998, p. 16.
305 H.A. Kissinger, "The Policymaker and the Intellectual", in: J.N. Rosenau (ed.), *International Politics and Foreign Policy*, New York: The Free Press of Glencoe, 1961, p. 274.

War[306]. However, the end of the Cold War and the emergence of a new, complex world system gave rise to a new awareness of the influence of ideational elements on politics[307]. The European integration project is a characteristic case of the influence of ideational elements on politics.

The European integration project is not merely the result of material elements, such as interest rates, exchange rates and external threats. The attempt of the European Union to diffuse political, economic and legal norms is intimately related to values, which constitute the ideational basis of the European integration project. Thus, some scholars, such as T. Diez[308] and C. Parsons[309], try to understand the European Union in terms of the EU policymakers' value systems and ultimate goals, and some other scholars, such as J.T. Checkel[310], emphasize acculturation processes within the framework of the European Union.

On 25 March 1957, the Treaty of Rome was signed by the Heads of Government of France, Belgium, Luxembourg, West Germany, the Netherlands and Italy, culminating long negotiations between them for the reconstruction of the European continent after World War II. The Treaty of Rome was the founding treaty of the European Economic Community (EEC), which later became the European Union (EU), and it established four institutions — namely: a Commission, a Council of Ministers, a European Parliament and a European Court of Justice. A major further step along the path to the political unification of Europe was made with the creation of the European Union (EU) by means of the Treaty of Maastricht. Although the Treaty was signed in Maastricht on 7 February 1992, a number of obstacles in the ratification process meant that it did not enter into force until 1st November 1993. The Treaty refers to itself as "a new stage in the process of creating an ever closer union among the peoples of Europe". Moreover, the Amsterdam Treaty, which was signed on 2 October 1997, and entered into force on 1 May

---

306 See: C. Hay, *Political Analysis — A Critical Introduction*. New York: Palgrave, 2002, p. 196.

307 See: C. Hay, op. cit. (ref. 306), pp. 198-199.

308 T. Diez, "Speaking Europe: The Politics of Integration Discourse", in: T. Christiansen, K.E. Jorgensen, and A. Wiener (eds), *The Social Construction of Europe*, London: Sage, 2001.

309 C. Parsons, "Showing Ideas as Causes: The Origins of the European Union", *International Organization*, Vol. 56, 2002, pp.47-84.

310 J.T. Checkel, "Social Construction and European Integration", in: T. Christiansen, K.E. Jorgensen, and A. Wiener (eds), *The Social Construction of Europe*, London: Sage, 2001.

1999, amending the Treaty of Maastricht, meant mainly a greater emphasis on citizenship and the rights of individuals and an attempt to implement a European area of freedom, security and justice, according to Article 2 of the Treaty of Maastricht. Through Article 6(1) of the Treaty of Amsterdam, the European Union declares itself to be established on the principles of freedom, democracy, the rule of law and respect for human rights and fundamental freedoms.

According to the Treaty of Rome, the status of 'European Citizen' confers four special rights: (1) the freedom to move and take up residence anywhere in the Union; (2) the right to vote and stand in local government and European Parliament elections in the country of residence; (3) diplomatic and consular protection from the authorities of any Member State where the country of which a person is a national is not represented in a non-Union country (Article 20 of the Rome Treaty); (3) the right of petition and appeal to the European Ombudsman. Following the entry into force of the Treaty of Amsterdam, the status of 'European Citizen' also confers the following rights: (1) the right to address the European institutions in any one of the official languages and to receive a reply written in the same language; (2) the right to access the documents of the European Parliament, the Council and the Commission, subject to certain conditions (Article 255 of the Rome Treaty); (3) the right to non-discrimination between EU citizens on the basis of nationality (Article 12 of the Rome Treaty) and to non-discrimination on the basis of gender, race, religion, handicap, age or sexual orientation; (4) equal access to the Community's civil service.

The most ambitious federalist initiatives undertaken by the European Union are the Treaty Establishing a Constitution for Europe and the Charter of Fundamental Rights of the European Union, which enshrines certain political, social, and economic rights for EU citizens and residents into EU law. As Joschka Fischer, German Foreign Minister, stated in the *Daily Telegraph* on 27 November 1998: "The creation of a single European state bound by one European constitution is 'the decisive task of our time'". In addition, Dr Johannes Rau, President of the Federal Republic of Germany, stated at the European Parliament on 4 April 2001:

> We need a European Constitution. The European Constitution is not the 'final touch' of the European structure; it must become its foundation. The European Constitution should prescribe that... we are building a Federation of Nation-States... The first part should be based on the Charter of Fundamental Rights proclaimed at the

European summit at Nice... If we transform the EU into a Federation of Nation-States, we will enhance the democratic legitimacy... We should not prescribe what the EU should never be allowed to... I believe that the Parliament and the Council of Ministers should be developed into a genuine bicameral parliament.

However, the rejection of the EU Constitution in two democratic referenda in 2005 did not end this "grandiose project"[311]. In fact, just hours after France's 'Non', Jean-Claude Juncker, Prime Minister of Luxembourg and warm supporter of the EU Constitution, declared: "The European process does not come to an end today"[312]. Additionally, President of the European Commission José Manuel Barroso stated: "What is important is to recommit ourselves to this vision of Europe"[313].

The need to review the EU's constitutional framework was highlighted in a declaration annexed to the Treaty of Nice in 2001. The Treaty of Lisbon, which was signed by the EU member states on 13 December 2007, and entered into force on 1 December 2009, is intended to make sure that European Union regulations and directives do not contradict the European Convention on Human Rights, which was integrated into the text of the rejected EU Constitution and was legally binding. Moreover, in its Preamble, the Lisbon Treaty presents the European Union as a cultural community and not only as a family of nations; in particular, the Preamble of the Lisbon Treaty includes the following statement:

> Drawing inspiration from the cultural, religious and humanist inheritance of Europe, from which have developed the universal values of the inviolable and inalienable rights of the human person, freedom, democracy, equality and the rule of law...

In addition, Article 2 of the Lisbon Treaty states the following: "The Union's aim is to promote peace, its values and the well-being of its peoples". "In the 15th century, Portuguese sailors used to set sail from Lisbon to explore the still uncharted waters of the world", said European Parliament President Jerzy Buzek, speaking ahead of a visit to Lisbon on 1 December 2009, and, "today" that "we are living in a new globalized world", "we Europeans have a new chart to guide us — the Lisbon Treaty". Moreover, Buzek

311 N. Watt, "EU Constitution a Grandiose Project That Failed, Says Beckett", *The Guardian*, 18 October 2006.

312 See: K. Bennhold and G. Bowley, "Charter 'Not Dead', EU Insists", *International Herald Tribune*, 31 May 2005.

313 See: G. Parker, "Would a Constitution by Another Name Smell Sweeter?", *The Financial Times*, 29 May 2006.

added that "the Treaty of Lisbon represents an increase in democracy and efficiency in the European Union" and that it "gives a huge boost to the powers of the directly-elected European Parliament".

Ian Manners, who is admittedly the father of the of the concept of 'normative power Europe', has emphasized that the European Union is not trying to fill any geopolitical gap, since it is not oriented towards a state-like model of 'ordinary power Europe'. In fact, for Manners, it is "necessary" to argue for a different consideration of "EU's normative power in world politics" and to "displace the State as the centre of concern", until "the unhealthy concentration on how much like a State the EU looks" — as in old 'power' and 'capabilities' debates — is definitively put aside[314]. Therefore, from this perspective, EU's role in international relations must be seen as one of 'normalization', spreading "common principles" disregarding "Westphalian conceptions" of balance-of-power arrangements, since the EU has "the unique ability to shape conceptions of 'normal' in international relations"[315] — an ideational perspective, far beyond the arguments of the 'school' of political realism. Additionally, as G. Therborn has argued, EU has the capability to "tell the other parts of the world what... institutions they should have", and its political and economic structure is strong enough in order to support its huge potential of political influence by setting up a normative framework of international relations[316].

First of all, committing oneself to the vision of Europe means that one understands the historical background of the idea of European Unity. This idea has been developed in order to promote peace and prosperity in Europe through pan-European institutions.

William Penn (1644 -1718), an English real estate entrepreneur, philosopher and founder of the State of Pennsylvania in North America, was an early champion of democracy and religious freedom who articulated a plan for the unification of Europe. In particular, in his *An Essay towards the Present and Future Peace of Europe by the Establishment of an European Dyet, Parliament, or Estates* (1693), Penn recognizes the devastating effects of war and the desirableness of peace, and he argues that justice is the truest means of peace and furthermore that justice is the purpose and the fruit of government, because

---

314 I. Manners, "Normative Power Europe: A Contradiction in Terms?", *Journal of Common Market Studies*, Vol. 40, 2002, p. 239.

315 I. Manners, op. cit. (ref. 314), p. 239.

316 G. Therborn, "Europe in the Twenty-First Century", in: P. Gowan and P. Anderson (eds), *The Question of Europe*, London: Verso, 1997.

government itself is the result of society, and society "first came from a rea-sonable design in men of peace"; therefore, for the same reason, the society of the European states must be governed by some form of pan-European government. In Penn's own language:

> He must not be a Man but a Statue of Brass or Stone whose Bowels do not melt when he beholds the bloody Tragedies of this War... So that in the Contraries of Peace we see the Beauties and Benefits of it; ... What can we desire better than Peace, but the Grace to use it?... I shall proceed to the next Point: What is the best Means of Peace... As Justice is a Preserver, so it is a better Procurer of Peace than War. Tho' 'Pax quaeritur bello', be an usual saying, 'Peace is the end of War',... yet the Use generally made of that expression shews us, that properly and truly speaking, Men seek their Wills by War rather than Peace... If we look over all the Stories of all Times, we shall find the Aggressors generally moved by Ambition; the Pride of Conquest and Greatness of Dominion more than Right... Government is an Expedient against Confusion; a Restraint upon all Disorder; just Weights and an even Balance; that one may not injure another or himself by Intemperance... No Man is Judge in his own Cause, which ends the Confusion and Blood of so many Judges and Executioners. For out of Society every Man is his own King, does what he lists, at his own Peril. But when he comes to incorporate himself, he sub-mits that Royalty to the Conveniency of the Whole, from whom he receives the Returns of Protection. So that he is not now his own Judge or Avenger, neither is his Antagonist, but the Law, in indif-ferent hands between both. And if he is Servant to others that be-fore was free, he is also served of others that formerly owed him no Obligation. Thus while we are not our own, every Body is ours, and we get more than we lose, the Safety of the Society being the Safety of the Particulars that constitute it. So that while we seem to sub-mit to, and hold all we have from Society, it is by Society that we keep what we have. Government then is the Prevention and Cure of Disorder, and the Means of Justice, as that is of Peace: For this Cause they have Sessions, Terms, Assizes and Parliaments, to over-rule Men's Passions and Resentments.... I have thus briefly treated of Peace, Justice, and Government, as a necessary Introduction, be-cause the Ways and Methods by which Peace is preserved in par-ticular Governments will help those Readers, most concerned in my Proposal, to conceive with what Ease and Advantage the Peace of Europe might be procured and kept; which is the End designed by me, with all Submission to those interested in this little Treatise... Now if the Sovereign Princes of Europe, who represent that Society or Independent State of Men that was previous to the Obligations of Society, would, for the same Reason that engaged Men first into Society, viz: Love of Peace and Order, agree to meet by their Stated Deputies in a General Dyet, Estates, or Parliament, and there estab-lish Rules of Justice for Sovereign Princes to observe one to another; and thus to meet Yearly, or once in Two or Three Years at farthest,

or as they shall see Cause, and to be Styled The Sovereign or Imperial Dyet, Parliament, or State of Europe; before which Sovereign Assembly should be brought all Differences depending between one Sovereign and another, that cannot be made up by private Embassies, before the Sessions begins,... Europe would quietly obtain the so much desired and needed PEACE to Her harassed Inhabitants; no Sovereignty in Europe, having the Power, and therefore cannot show the Will to dispute the Conclusion.[317]

In the same spirit, Richard Nikolaus Eijiro von Coudenhove-Kalergi (1894-1972), an Austrian politician, geopolitician, philosopher and count of Coudenhove-Kalergi, founded the first popular movement for a unified Europe. In Coudenhove-Kalergi's own words:

This is the European Question: the mutual hatred of Europeans for each other poisons the international atmosphere and is a perpetual worry to even the most peace-loving countries of the world... The European Question will be resolved only by the union of the peoples of Europe... Only the reconstruction of Europe, undertaken broadmindedly, on federalist and democratic bases can put right economically the fragmentation of Austria-Hungary and the mutilation of Germany. Statesmen who are better in at tearing down rather than building up are dilettanti and demagogues. They must vanish from the political scene and make room for constructive leaders... There is only one radical way to resolve the problem of European frontiers equitably and lastingly: not redrawing the frontiers but suppressing them.[318]

Moreover, Jean Omer Marie Gabriel Monnet (1888-1979), who is regarded by many as a chief architect of European Unity, explained the need for the unification of Europe as follows:

There will be no peace in Europe if States are reconstituted on a basis of national sovereignty with all that implies for in terms of prestige politics and economic protectionism. If the nations of Europe adopt defensive positions again, huge armies will be necessary again. Under the future peace treaty, some nations will be allowed to re-arm; others will not. That was tried in 1919; we all know the result. Intra-European alliances will be formed; we know what they are worth. Social reform will be impeded or blocked by the sheer weight of military budgets. Europe will be reborn in fear. The nations of Europe are too circumscribed to give their people the pros-

---

317 W. Penn, *An Essay towards the Present and Future Peace of Europe by the Establishment of an European Dyet, Parliament, or Estates* (first published in 1693), in: T. Salmon and Sir W. Nicoll (eds), *Building European Union — A Documentary History and Analysis*, Manchester: Manchester University Press, 1997, p. 3 ff., sections I-IV.

318 R. Von Coudenhove-Kalergi, *Pan-Europe* (first published in 1923), in: T. Salmon and Sir W. Nicoll (eds), *Building European Union — A Documentary History and Analysis*, Manchester: Manchester University Press, 1997, pp. 7-9.

perity made possible, and hence necessary, by modern conditions. They will need larger markets. And they will have to refrain from using a major proportion of their resources to maintain 'key' industries needed for national defence and made mandatory by the concept of sovereign, protectionist States, as we know them before 1939. Prosperity and vital social progress will remain elusive until the nations of Europe form a federation of a 'European entity' which will forge them into a single economic unit.[319]

Furthermore, commitment to the vision of the European Union implies awareness of a common European culture and hence commitment to common values. The French philosopher, essayist and poet Paul Valéry has summarized the cardinal values of the European civilization and culture as follows:

> I shall consider as European all those peoples who in the course of history have undergone the three influences I shall name. The first is that of Rome. Wherever the Roman Empire has ruled and its power has asserted itself; and further, wherever the Empire has been the object of fear, admiration, and envy; wherever the weight of the Roman sword has been felt; wherever the majesty of Roman institutions and laws, or the apparatus and dignity of its magistrate have been recognized or copied, and sometimes even incongruously aped — there is something European. Rome is the eternal model of organized and stable power... Then came Christianity... But while the Roman conquest had affected only political man and ruled the mind only in its external habits, the Christian conquest aimed at and gradually reached the depths of consciousness... I shall do no more than remind you of some of the features of its influence. In the first place it introduced subjective morality, and above all it brought about the consolidation of moral thought. This new unity took its place alongside the juridical unity contributed by Roman law; in both cases, abstract analysis tended to make regulations uniform. Let us go beyond that. The new religion imposed self-examination... Christianity proposed to the mind the most subtle, the greatest, and indeed the most fruitful problems. Whether it were a question of the value of testimony, the criticism of texts, or the sources and guarantees of knowledge; of the distinction between faith and reason, and the opposition that arises between them, or the antagonism between faith, deeds, and works; a question of freedom, servitude, or grace; of spiritual and material power and their mutual conflict, the equality of men, the status of women — and how much else — Christianity educated and stimulated millions of minds, making them act and react, century after century. However, this is not yet a finished portrait of us Europeans. Something is still missing from

319 J. Monnet, *Algiers Memorandum* (first published in 1943), in: T. Salmon and Sir W. Nicoll (eds), *Building European Union — A Documentary History and Analysis*, Manchester: Manchester University Press, 1997, p. 21.

our make-up. What is missing is that marvellous transformation to which we owe, not the sense of public order, the cult of the city and of temporal justice; nor even the depth of our consciousness, our capacity for absolute ideality, and our sense of an eternal justice... what is missing is rather that subtle yet powerful influence to which we owe the best of our intelligence, the acuteness and solidity of our knowledge, as also the clarity, purity, and elegance of our arts and literature: it is from Greece that these virtues came to us... What we owe to Greece is perhaps what has most profoundly distinguished us from the rest of humanity. To her we owe the discipline of the Mind, the extraordinary example of perfection in everything. To her we owe the method of thought that tends to relate all things to man, the complete man. Man became for himself the system of reference to which all things must in the end relate. He must therefore develop all the parts of his being and maintain them in a harmony as clear and even as evident as possible. He must develop both body and mind. As for the mind, he must learn to defend himself against its excesses and its reveries, those of its products which are vague and purely imaginary, by means of scrupulous criticism and minute analysis of its judgments, the rational separation of its functions, and the regulation of its forms. From this discipline, science was to emerge — our science, that is to say, the most characteristic product and the surest and most personal triumph of our intellect. Europe is above all the creator of science. There have been arts in all countries, there has been true science only in Europe.[320]

In other words, according to Paul Valéry, the fundamental principles which underpin the European civilization are the rule of law, the metaphysically founded humanism of Christianity, and the spirit of science.

The rule of law, the first component of the European civilization, is an ancient ideal, and it has been studied by ancient Greek philosophers such as Plato and Aristotle. According to Plato's *Laws* and *Republic*, where the law is subject to some other authority and has none of its own, the collapse of the state is not far off, whereas, if law is the master of the government and the government is its slave, then the situation is full of promise and men enjoy all the blessings that the Divine Reason showers on a state. Likewise, Aristotle, in his *Politics*, endorsed the rule of law, writing that "law should govern", and those in power should be "servants of the laws".

In the 1st century BC, Cicero, in his book entitled *De re publica*, condemned the king who does not abide by the law as a representative of political despotism who "is the foulest and most repellant creature imaginable". According to Cicero, no one can be properly called a man who renounces

---

320 P. Valéry, *History and Politics*, in: *The Collected Works of Paul Valéry*, ed. J. Matthews, trans. D. Folliot and J. Matthews, New York: Pantheon Books, 1962, Vol. 10, part I.

every legal tie or every civilized partnership with the entire humanity. Cicero was a contemporary of Julius Caesar and was writing during a period in which the Roman republic's rule of law and order were giving place to the autocratic rule, i.e., the rule of the stronger[321]. In his book entitled *De legibus*, Cicero defines the rule of law as follows: "a magistrate's function is to take charge and to issue directives which are right, beneficial, and in accordance with the laws. As magistrates are subject to the laws, the people are subject to the magistrates. In fact, it is true to say that a magistrate is a speaking law, and a law a silent magistrate". In other words, Cicero emphasizes that it is the law that rules, not the individual which happens to be the magistrate. Thus, Cicero contrasted rule under an autocratic regime with living under a body of law for a free community[322].

In the 20th century, the concept of the rule of law was embedded in the Charter of the United Nations. In its Preamble, one of the aims of the UN is "to establish conditions under which justice and respect for the obligations arising from treaties and other sources of international law can be maintained". A primary purpose of the Organization is "to maintain international peace and security... and to bring about by peaceful means, and in conformity with the principles of justice and international law, adjustment or settlement of international disputes or situations which might lead to a breach of the peace". In addition, the *Universal Declaration of Human Rights* of 1948, the historic international recognition that all human beings have fundamental rights and freedoms, recognizes that:

> [I]t is essential, if man is not to be compelled to have recourse, as a last resort, to rebellion against tyranny and oppression, that human rights should be protected by the rule of law.

For the UN, the Secretary-General defines the rule of law as follows:

> [A] principle of governance in which all persons, institutions and entities, public and private, including the State itself, are accountable to laws that are publicly promulgated, equally enforced and independently adjudicated, and which are consistent with international human rights norms and standards. It requires, as well, measures to ensure adherence to the principles of supremacy of law, equality before the law, accountability to the law, fairness in the application of the law, separation of powers, participation in decision-

---

321 See: E. Rawson, *Intellectual Life in the Late Roman Republic*, London: Duckworth, 1985, ch. 19.
322 See: A.E. Douglas, *Cicero*, Oxford: Clarendon Press, 1968, and H.F. Jolowicz and B. Nicholas, *Historical Introduction to the Study of Roman Law*, Cambridge: Cambridge University Press, 1972.

making, legal certainty, avoidance of arbitrariness and procedural and legal transparency[323].

Christianity, the second component of the roots of the European civilization, provided an incarnated archetype of the Platonic Perfect Being — namely, Jesus Christ — thus showing that every human being is a potential god and discriminating the Biblical spirituality from the selfish historical expediencies of the Pharisees and from the Jewish ethnocentrism (and thus we read in Matthew 23:38 that Jesus Christ said to the Jews: "Behold, your house is left unto you desolate"). According to the creation narrative in Genesis, in the mystery of creation, God made a 'vessel' in man to receive the gift of the love and immortal life of God. The vessel is the human mind, which is the image of God. "And God made man. According to the image of God He made him"[324]. The earliest Church Fathers teach that, from the beginning, man was made permanently in the 'image' with a reasoning mind, free will, and self-rule or power over himself. However, as Theophilus of Antioch[325], Irenaeus of Lyons[326] and many other Church Fathers have explained, "the destiny of man was for him not to remain in the state in which God made him, since he was made to become perfect and, thus, to be divinized. He was made needing to acquire perfection, not because he was made flawed in nature and morally deficient but because moral perfection is achieved only in total freedom"[327]. In other words, according to those Church Fathers, in Paradise, the Forebears of humanity were not endowed from the start with all possible wisdom and knowledge, i.e., their perfection was not a realized one but a potential one. Thus, their fall is not a penalty imposed on them by God according to some legalistic formula, but it is the result of their failure to realize their potential[328]. In psychological terms, man's state in 'Paradise'

---

323 United Nations, *Report of the Secretary-General — The Rule of Law and Transitional Justice in Conflict and Post-Conflict Societies*, New York, 2004.

324 Genesis 1:27.

325 Theophilus of Antioch (died ca. 183-185 AD) is one of the precursors of that group of writers who, from Irenaeus to Cyprian, not only break the obscurity which rests on the earliest history of the Christian Church, but alike in the East and in the West carry it to the front in literary eminence.

326 Irenaeus of Lyons (2nd century -202 AD) was an early Church Father and apologist, and his writings were formative in the early development of Christian theology. He was a disciple of Polycarp, who was a disciple of John the Evangelist.

327 J.S. Romanides, *The Ancestral Sin*, trans. G.S. Gabriel, Ridgewood, NJ: Zephyr Publishing, 2002, p. 126.

328 At this point, I must mention that, in the Middle Ages, many theologians interpreted the concept of sin as disobedience to God's authority and thus they argued

refs to a state in which man follows a path of perfection guided by the knowledge of the Perfect Being, i.e., God, who is the Prototype of man's creation, and 'sin' is nothing else apart from the perpetration of a mistake by man during his evolutionary course towards perfection.

From the perspective of Christianity, Plato's Perfect Being was incarnated in Jesus Christ, and thus it became more easily and more fully understood by people, especially by those who were not able to delve into difficult ideational studies. Christ represents the Divine Archetype of man as he is restored to his God-oriented path to perfection and deification. Gregory the Theologian[329] writes: "[Today] I am glorified with Him..., today I am quickened with Him,... let us honour our Archetype". Similarly, John of Damascus[330], speaking of the deification of man, refers to the Divine image in man as it is "mingled" with Christ the "Archetype".

According to the classical Greek thought, philosophy is the path, the ascent to deification. Plato, in the tenth book of the *Republic*, writes that the righteous man will not be neglected by God, and that man, "by the practice of virtue, will be likened unto god so far as that is possible for man"[331]. Plato's understanding of philosophy is echoed in the writings of the Neoplatonists. Ammonius of Alexandria argues that "philosophy is likeness in God

---

that the Fall of Man was a penalty imposed on him by God. This legalistic interpretation conflicts openly with the humanistic interpretation of the concept of sin and the Fall of Man by the earliest Greek Church Fathers. According to the latter, the commitment of 'sin' means the commitment of a mistake by man during his progressive struggle for perfection, and the Fall of Man is simply the consequence of failure and not the damnation of humanity. Therefore, the Enlightenment-derived thought has trouble with the Biblical concept of sin only when the latter is interpreted in legalistic terms, and not when it is interpreted according to the humanistic theology of the earliest Greek Church Fathers.

329 Gregory the Theologian, "First Oration: On Easter and His Reluctance", in: P. Schaff and H. Wace (eds), *A Select Library of Nicene and Post-Nicene Fathers*, 1905, Vol. 7, p. 203. Gregory the Theologian (also known as Gregory of Nazianzus) was a 4th century Archbishop of Constantinople. He made a significant impact on the shape of Trinitarian theology among both Greek- and Latin-speaking theologians, and he is known as the "Trinitarian Theologian".

330 John of Damascus, "Homilia in Transfigurationem Domini" (Homily on the transfiguration of the Lord), *Patrologia Graeca*, Vol. 96, col. 552C. John of Damascus (born in ca. 676 and died between 754-784) epitomized in a single work (*De fide orthodoxa*) the teachings of the great ecclesiastical writers who have gone before him, and his work has always been held in the highest esteem in both the Roman and the Greek Churches.

331 Plato, *Republic*, X.12.613.

so far as that is possible for man"[332]. Similarly, the philosopher Themistius argues that "philosophy is nothing else than assimilation to God to the extent that it is possible for man"[333]. Thus, one of the earliest Greek Church Fathers, Justin the philosopher and martyr (died ca. 165) taught that God can be discovered through the writings of Greek philosophers, and he emphasized that Plato's teachings or the doctrines of the Stoics, the poets and the prose authors of Greek antiquity, were not contrary to Christ's: "For each, through his share in the divine spermatic Logos, spoke well... Whatever has been spoken aright by any man belongs to us Christians"[334].

Finally, science, the third component of the European civilization, signifies an activity of consciousness whose aim is to build theories which bring consciousness closer and closer to reality. Reality is not merely an object statically and partially conceived by scientific minds; instead, reality is a goal towards which the scientific consciousness is oriented in a dynamic way. In particular, the scientific consciousness pursues steadily to annihilate the distance between itself and reality, as I argued in Chapter 3. According to the ancient Greek scientific thought, there is a distinction between *empeiria*, i.e., knowledge or skill acquired through practice, and *episteme*, i.e., methodic knowledge, which required being able as to give reasons why something was the case and to acknowledge the purpose of things. A typical example for the Greeks was the difference between the knowledge of a few folk remedies for disease and the medical science, according to which — as Hippocrates argued — each disease has a natural cause which is the object of the medical science.

The above components of the European civilization — namely, the Roman legal tradition, the Greek scientific tradition, and the metaphysically grounded humanism of Christianity — show that Europe is not only a geographical, geo-economic and geo-political reality but also an idea. Meanwhile, in Europe, public commitment in cultural policy is being undermined by the tendency of neo-liberal ideologists to reduce values to the economic concept of price and to subjugate cultural production to market mechanisms. But, as Klaus Held has argued, the European integration project cannot be grounded only on political and economic co-operation of the

---

332 Ammonius, *Ammonius in Porphyrii Isagogen sive V Voces*, ed. A. Busse, Berlin, 1891, IV, Section III.

333 Themistius, *Orationes quae supersunt*, eds N. Schenkl, G. Downey, and A.F. Norman, Leipzig: Bibliotheca Teubneriana, 1965-74, 21.32d.

334 Justin, *Apologia*, I.46, II.13, ed. Bibliotheke Hellenon Pateron, vol. 3, Athens, 1955.

EU member states, without any intrinsic common bonds; without common values, the European integration project would be foredoomed to failure[335]. The foundations of the European civilization are not only deeply compatible but also deeply connected with the universal theory of human rights which I propose in the present book based on my interpretation of Plato's philosophy. In fact, Plato's philosophy — as I interpreted it in Chapter 3 — provides solutions to the ontological gaps of modernity, thus making possible the building of an ontologically grounded humanistic world order. Therefore, to the extent that the European Union will insist on having spiritual, and not only economic, requests from itself and will fully endorse and assimilate the universalistic character of human rights, the European integration project can be significantly enriched by the spirit of Plato and can set the standards for the building of a humanistic world order.

4.8 From ideology to cultural anthropology

The different levels of knowledge which we studied in Chapter 3 do not signify ideological issues and differences. The term 'ideology' was coined by Destutt de Tracy in 1796 to designate a systematic evaluative and 'corrective' approach to the sensationalist grounds of concepts[336], and, its modern use in social and political theory is intimately related to a mocking metonymic use of the term to stand for all politically-oriented symbolic systems which exaggerate their importance in the constitution and transformation of the world. Ideologies and ideological differences are temporal phenomena and thus are swept away by time, irrespective of how intensely they are followed by people in each historical segment. On the other hand, Plato studies different levels of knowledge as different ways in which people understand the human being and its existential end, and he argues that the manner in which a person understands the human being and its existential end is the outcome of the degree to which it partakes of the absolute being, i.e., it reflects its progress in the knowledge of the absolute good, which, in religious language, is called the divine. Without that knowledge which connects the human being with a trans-historical and trans-temporal truth,

335 K. Held, "The Origin of Europe with the Greek Discovery of the World", *Epoche*, Vol. 7, 2002.

336 See: R.H. Cox, *Ideology, Politics, and Political Theory*, Belmont, Calif.: Wadsworth, 1969; G. Lichtheim, *The Concept of Ideology, and Other Essays*, New York: Random House, 1967.

which is the ultimate source of the significance of all things, no people can live a meaningful life. A people which lacks that knowledge which connects the human being with a trans-historical and trans-temporal truth (Plato's absolute good) can only survive by suffering nihilistically under the yoke of historical becoming until the moment of its historical annihilation.

For Plato, there is no such thing as a pure subject. The human being exists as a partaker of the absolute being, and, therefore, the term 'person' does not mean 'personality' — i.e., the individual presence of a human being in its social environment — but it means the universality of each individual human being, a universality which is due to the participation of the individual human being in the absolute being. The universality of each individual human being endows society with a peculiar spiritual significance, because, from this perspective, society is not based on an instinctive assemblage of live organisms but on the spiritual unity of individuals who are partakers of the same truth. By being partakers of the same truth, persons become partakers of one another. From this perspective, therefore, freedom is not restricted to the safeguarding of the rights of the individual, but it signifies the reconciliation between the rational and the supra-rational within the moral consciousness of the individual. To the extent that one has a deep feeling of moral responsibility, the 'other' exists in his mind not as an object but as a part of his own self, since they are both members of the same spiritual end.

Z. Brzezinski has correctly pointed out that:

> a society in which self-gratification is the norm is also a society in which there are no longer any criteria for making moral judgments... In a society that culturally emphasizes the maximization of individual satisfactions and the minimization of moral restraints, civic freedom tends to be elevated into a self-validating absolute. *In other words, civic freedom is divorced from a notion of civic responsibility.*[337]

Within the framework of the Platonic philosophy which I defend in the present book, society is constituted on the grounds of truth and not on the grounds of rights. From this perspective, tradition is not an ideological matter, but it is an anthropological prototype which is being transmitted from one generation to another as a spiritual norm. Plato's anthropological prototype is the human being as partaker of the absolute being, as a being-in-the-process-of-perfection.

---

337 Z. Brzezinski, op. cit. (ref. 244), pp. 67, 69

In the medieval era, the scholastics, by considering that the term idea is equivalent to the term concept, proposed another anthropological prototype — namely, a rationally self-assured individual. As a reaction against the scholastics' rationalism, many scholars of the Reformation proposed an alternative anthropological prototype — namely, an individual who is self-assured through his/her sense of duty which is manifested in pious tasks.

The above three anthropological prototypes represent three different ways of understanding the end of life: from the perspective of the Platonic approach to spirituality which I propose in the present book, the end of life is to harmonize one's mind with the absolute being, or the Good; for the scholastics, the end of life is to attain the integration of one's consciousness through power and in terms of power (in this case, 'power' refers to the rational capacity of the intellect); for pietism, the end of life is to subordinate one's existence to the categorical imperative of the moral duty and the well-disciplined society.

The human being which understands the ultimate purpose of its life as its unification with the absolute being, the Good, is the divinized man, the man-god. The revelation of the great secret of the man-god is the essence of Jesus Christ's ministry. The liberty of the god-man is the divine law itself, and thus it soars above all human laws and all conventional religious obligations. As Christ said, the law is made for man and not man for the law. That which others understand as the categorical imperative of the moral duty and the well-disciplined society, the god-man terms his good pleasure. He practices justice because this is the way he exists, and he understands corrective punishment as a benefit, and not as an act of vengeance. It is towards this spiritual autonomy that the human being can advance by progressing through the different levels of knowledge which we studied in Chapter 3.

The person whose aim is to attain the above spiritual autonomy is neither a radical nor a neo-liberal. Radicals — e.g., the so-called Ricardian socialists[338] and the Levellers[339] — want to change historical institutions in order to avoid reflecting on their own selves and personal shortcomings and, thus, avoid changing themselves. In a sense, radicals attempt to hide

---

338 The Ricardian socialists are a group of radicals writing in the 1820s and 1830s. The term itself was used as the title of a book written by Esther Lowenthal in 1911. B. Burkitt argues that, if the criterion of inclusion is to have been influenced by David Ricardo, then Karl Marx himself must be included in the Ricardian socialists, and N. Thompson argues that the only Ricardian socialist is Marx. See: B. Burkitt, *Radical Political Economy*, Brighton: Wheatsheaf, 1984; N. Thompson, *The People's Science: The Popular Political Economy of Exploitation and Crisis 1816-34*, Cambridge: Cambridge University Press, 1984.
339 The term Levellers refers to a radical political movement acting during the English Civil War. See: J. Frank, *The Levellers*, New York: Russell & Russell, 1969.

their personal shortcomings behind their proposals for institutional reforms. Therefore, often, the socialist programmes for the expansion of the economic role of the state provide political refuge and moral legitimacy to emotions of envy and anger against the rich and they encourage persons who make inefficient decisions and do not care for improving their qualifications to continue following the same attitudes.

Neo-liberals want to change historical institutions and treat innovation as a value in itself because their will is disorientated, i.e., they rather do not know exactly what they want. Therefore, under a neo-liberal regime, capitalism leads to a continuous production of new goods which are produced not because they have been demanded by the consumers but because marketing techniques will make the consumers buy them, since the mob's criteria of action are blurred and thus easily manipulated through advertising and propaganda. Moreover, Benjamin R. Barber has described the ontological gap of the neo-liberals' consumer capitalism as follows:

> There is of course endless talk about giving people 'what they want', and how the market 'empowers' consumers. The market, indeed, does not tell us what to do; it gives us what we want — once it gets through telling us what it is that we want. It promises liberty and happiness while, in truth, delivering neither. More to the point, consumerism encourages a kind of civic schizophrenia, a disorder that divides the citizen into opposing fragments and denies legitimacy to the part that we understand to be 'civic' or 'public'. The market treats choice as fundamentally private, a matter not of determining some deliberative 'we should' but only of enumerating all the 'wants' that we harbor as private consumers and creatures of personal desire. Yet private choices inevitably do have social consequences and public outcomes. When these derive from purely personal preferences, the results are often irrational and unintended, at wide variance with the kind of society we might choose through democratic deliberation. Such private choices, though technically 'free', are quite literally dysfunctional with respect to our values and norms. Privatization means the choices we make eventually determine the social outcomes we must suffer together, but which we never directly choose in common. This explains how a society without villains or conspirators, composed of good-willed but self-seeking individuals, can produce a culture that so many of its members despise. Consumer capitalism... generates thinking on the model of the narcissistic child, infantilizing consumers to the point where puerility is not simply an option; it is a mandate.[340]

---

340 B.R. Barber, "Shrunken Sovereign: Consumerism, Globalization, and American Emptiness", *World Affairs*, Spring 2008.

The person whose aim is to attain the spiritual autonomy which — according to Plato's terminology — corresponds to the level of knowledge called intelligence is characterized by a peculiar form of conservatism. I am calling this form of conservatism 'peculiar' because I want to distinguish it from the religiously-inspired pessimism of the paradigmatic representatives of the French conservatism — e.g., Joseph de Maistre and Charles Maurras — and from the skepticism of the paradigmatic representatives of the British conservatism[341]. The person whose aim is to attain the spiritual autonomy which corresponds to the Platonic notion of intelligence is conservative not because he lacks imagination but because he thinks carefully and deeply about the consequences that every change will have for himself and the others. Such a person wants to conserve everything that has value, and, thus, he has a deep sense of fairness. Hence, this form of conservatism means personal responsibility and authentic creativity, and, in this case, authentic creativity means continuous expansion of the spirit.

The term 'conservative' consists of the prefix con-, the Latin root servat, and the suffix -ive. The prefix con- is derived from the Latin word *cum*, which means 'with' or 'together'. The Latin verb *servare* means to preserve, guard, protect, etc. *Servatus* is the perfect passive participle form of the verb *servare*, and some words that are used in modern English with a derivative of the root *servatus* in them are observe and preserve. The suffix -ive is an adjectival suffix — derived from the Latin suffix -ivus — and it means 'relating to' or 'belonging to'. Thus, there is a deep conceptual relationship between the term 'conservative' and the term 'consciousness', since, at a fundamental level, *servare* implies that one is fully aware of something or someone, and, with the prefix con-, it implies self-awareness and responsibility. A 'Platonic' conservative, therefore, is not a 'cultural fossil' but a deeply responsible person who carefully evaluates the practical and the moral content of the actions that he plans to undertake. This sense of responsibility endows such a conservative person with authoritativeness. On the other hand, persons who assume positions of authority without having this sense of responsibility have authority without authoritativeness and, thus, they become agents of barbarism. Hence, for instance, in the 21st century, it has become clear that the more the principle of self-gratification becomes an

---

341 See: H. Cecil, *Conservatism*, London: Thornton Butterworth, 1912; N. O'Sullivan, *Conservatism*, London: Dent, 1976.

end in itself in the West the less the West becomes capable of maintaining the preponderant authority in the management of international affairs[342].

The form of conservatism which is based on the interpretation of Platonism which I defend in the present book implies that the way to peace in international affairs is not to apply between nations the power politics balancing, which is marked by a legacy of failure — since it failed even between patriarchal families and between ancient city-states — but to extend from nations to the world humanistic norms which treat the human being as a partaker of the absolute being, i.e., as a being-in-the-process-of-perfection, and, therefore, as a bearer of an innate, trans-historical, value. The Austro-Hungarian sociologist of law Eugen Ehrlich[343] has pointed that no community can have law without norms and that these norms are never given by any particular facts in any society, such as the economic ones, the political ones, the climate, etc. The norms are not determined by any particular facts given inductively by observation; instead, they are determined by what Ehrlich termed "the inner order" of the facts. Thus, there is never a legal, political, or economic society except when all these facts of that society are ordered by common normative, i.e., ideational, principles. Hence, we cannot have a science of politics or of international politics without a specification first of the normative inner order of the individual nations and then of the relations between the different national inner orders. Ehrlich called this normative inner order of each society or nation its living law, and he argued that, in order for positive law to be effective, it must correspond to the ethos of the underlying normative inner law.

Therefore, an effective humanistic approach to international politics is intimately related to the following three things: First, one must specify the normative inner order of each international actor. This means that one has to classify international actors according to Plato's four levels of knowledge. Then one will be able to know the qualitative aspects of each international actor's behavior, i.e., its dominant motives and values. Second, one must determine the relation between the normative inner order of each international actor and the rest of the world. Third, the international actors (state and non-state ones) who defend the universalistic character of human rights and treat the human being as a bearer of an innate, trans-historical

---

342 Z. Brzezinski, op. cit. (ref. 244), p. 73.
343 E. Ehrlich, *Fundamental Principles of the Sociology of Law*, trans. W.L. Moll, Cambridge, Mass.: Harvard University Press, 1936.

value, must operate collectively in order to educate-acculturate the rest of the members of the international system by framing foreign policy of nations and the institutions of the world society in the light of a humanistic cosmopolitanism, thus transforming the exercise of political power into the application of a higher civilizing programme.

What does the term 'a higher civilizing programme' mean? Given the arguments I have put forward in the present book, 'a higher civilizing programme' implies a deeper relationship with truth. Truth does not consist only in a manner of giving account and determining the logical structure of an object. As I have already explained, for the classical Greek philosophers, truth signifies a deeper reality which comes to light, i.e., the revelation of a deeper reality. Therefore, according to Plato, the term idea is different from the term concept, and, within the framework of Platonism, truth transcends logicism. However, when, especially due to the rationalist theologians and philosophers, people started treating truth as a means of achieving psychological and intellectual security, truth assumed a more stable logical form, which, gradually, limited the spiritual horizon of the human being, since the truth of rationalism could not accommodate emotion and will. In the 19th and the 20th centuries, people realized that truth does not merely refer to the objectivity of things, but it is intimately related to our personal experiences. In other words, our relationship with truth is determined not only by the accuracy of our analytical endeavours but also by the manner in which we experience things[344].

---

344 This is something of which modern natural scientists are aware, too. Apart from the real objects of which the natural scientist has direct knowledge, there are — for, instance, at sub-atomic level — behaviours which oblige modern physics to use concepts which are formulated in a subjective manner. Such terms as ions, photons, gravitons, etc. do not correspond to any indisputable form of reality; instead, they are elements of nominalistic systems and they are used for the formulation of scientific hypotheses. Niels Bohr, who made foundational contributions to understanding atomic structure and quantum mechanics, is reported to have said to Werner Heisenberg, who was another great pioneer of quantum physics: "When it comes to atoms, language can be used only as in poetry. The poet, too, is not nearly so concerned with describing facts as with creating images" (Quoted in:J. Bronowski, *The Ascent of Man*, Boston: Little, 1974, p. 340). Moreover, in the same spirit, Alfred Whitehead, who co-authored the epochal *Principia Mathematica* with B. Russell, argued that "nature is a structure of evolving process. The reality is the process. It is nonsense to ask if the color red is real. The color red is ingredient in the process of realisation. The realities of nature are the apprehensions in nature, that is to say, the events in nature" (A. Whitehead, *Science and the Modern World*, New York: Macmillan, 1944, p. 106).

From the perspective of the theory of knowledge which I presented in Chapter 3, since our relationship with truth is not static but dynamic, the quest for truth urges us not only to improve our logical-analytical skills but also to become more responsible beings. Truth signifies the manner in which we integrate ourselves into reality, and there is a dialectical relationship between the reality of consciousness and the reality of the external world, which urges us to follow a 'critical' attitude, according to the fourfold dialectic which I analyzed in Section 3.5. Therefore, we are personally responsible for the manner in which we integrate ourselves into reality — i.e., for our relationship with truth — because we are personally responsible for the manner in which we understand the reality of our consciousness and the reality of the external world.

As I have already argued in the present book, truth cannot be fully formalized. Every attempt to achieve an absolute logical formalization of truth leads either to logical fallacies or to fanaticism, despotism and identity-based conflicts (e.g., ethnic and religious wars). On the other hand, the awareness of the dynamic character of truth does not justify nihilism. For, even though humans' relationship with truth is subject to change, the quest for truth can remain stable. For instance, ten different people may seek truth in ten different ways respectively, but the very fact that they seek truth is the basis on which they can build a real society between themselves. The fact that people experience their relationship with truth in a subjective manner does not imply that truth itself is a subjective concept. On the contrary, the quest for an inter-subjective truth is the foundation of humans' sociability. This is the essence of a truth-centred, post-nihilistic civilization.

A truth-centred civilization is a creative alternative to nihilism, because, by contrast with nihilism, a truth-centred civilization allows humans to reflect on themselves and thus achieve self-knowledge and become more authentically sociable and responsible beings. The most important spiritual problem of a nihilist is that he has not a means of reflecting on himself. Therefore, a nihilist has a tragic difficulty in achieving self-knowledge. For, in order for one to achieve trustworthy knowledge of himself, he needs a transcendental truth (Plato's absolute good), which can operate as a trustworthy existential mirror. If one attempts to know himself by himself and in himself, then, sooner or later, he will come across a spiritual dead end, because he will come across the limits of logic, i.e., he will realize what Gödel has proved mathematically — namely, that logic is not in control of itself, and, therefore, the truth, the ultimate meaning, of a thing transcends the logical form of the given thing. Hence, in order for one to achieve complete self-knowledge, he needs a spiritual 'Archimedean point' outside himself. The broader a truth is the more effective it is as an existential mirror of the human being.

Thus, when a religious or an ethnic mythological system operates as a link between the human being and an absolute, inter-subjective, truth, it chisels the rock of the human psyche and thus makes the human being more sociable and more responsible. On the other hand, when a religious or an ethnic mythological system fixates the human mind in a particular logical conception of the world and of the self — which is manifested through religious fanaticism/fundamentalism, legalistic normative formulas, and nationalism — then it leads to spiritual dead ends, which in their turn lead to identity-based conflicts.

Identity-based conflicts are not a result of humans' quest for an absolute truth. On the contrary, identity-based conflicts are an outcome of a crisis in the relationship between man and truth, a crisis which consists in the attempt of certain communities to stop the human being's endless evolutionary itinerary towards its unification with an absolute truth and to imprison the human mind in a particular logical form of the world and of the self and, thus, in a sense, to 'freeze' history. Therefore, identity-based conflicts are caused by people who have lost their deep spiritual link with the absolute as mystery and want to transform truth into a closed logical system, and not by people who understand truth as an absolute reality which transcends every historical construction.

A truth-centred civilization implies that the essence of truth cannot be manipulated by any particular person or particular community of persons, and that the essence of truth is a mystery which can be experienced in a personal manner. As it has been shown by Gabriel Marcel, the distinction between the terms 'problem' and 'mystery' is one that hinges on the notion of participation:

> A problem is something which I meet, which I find completely before me, but which I can therefore lay siege to and reduce. But a mystery is something in which I am myself involved, and it can therefore only be thought of as a sphere where the distinction be-

tween what is in me and what is before me loses its meaning and initial validity.[345]

Marcel often describes a mystery as a "problem that encroaches on its own data"[346], and, therefore, such a 'problem' is, in fact, 'meta-problematic', in the sense that it is a question in which the identity, and, hence, the personal responsibility, of the questioner is an issue. This type of relationship with truth rules out every form of logical fallacy, fanaticism and spiritual despotism, and, additionally, it makes the consciousness of the human being more sensitive and more sociable. From this perspective, the dynamic character of the humans' relationship with truth does not signify cognitive or moral instability, but it signifies a deepening in their relationship with truth. A truth becomes 'deeper' not when it becomes 'more accurate' or 'more particular', but when it becomes 'broader', i.e., capable of covering a bigger part of reality. This awareness rules out fanaticism, fundamentalism, and spiritual despotism.

4.9 Normative political thought and a global cultural diplomacy

I have already argued that normative political theory presupposes that the members of a political system participate in the same spiritual reality, i.e., in a universal truth, which is the foundation of society. It is exactly for this reason that I have argued that Plato's philosophy — as I interpreted it in Chapter 3 — provides the most adequate approach to normative political thought. Intimately related to the Platonic approach to normative political thought which I defend in the present book is the development of a global cultural diplomacy which would be able to acculturate the members of the international system into a universal value system. From this perspective, cultural diplomacy is the business or art of developing and deploying an international educational programme and thus influencing mentalities on a global scale.

As I explained in Section 4.1, culture consists of the answers that a collective consciousness (human community) gives to questions about the quality of collective life, i.e., about the spiritual underpinnings of society. In other words, culture answers the following question: 'Which quality of

---

345 G. Marcel, *Being and Having*, trans. K. Farrer, Westminister: Dacre Press, 1949, p. 117.
346 G. Marcel, *The Philosophy of Existentialism*, trans. M. Harari, New York: Carol Publishing Group, 1995, p. 19.

life is the end of our society?' Thus, as I argued in Section 4.1, culture is the qualitative cover of a polity.

Therefore, given this definition of culture, we can make a very important distinction between two different ways of understanding the relationship between culture and politics. I shall call the first way of understanding the relationship between culture and politics 'substantial' and the second 'pragmatic'. A paradigmatic representative of the 'substantial' way of understanding the relationship between culture and politics is Aristotle. According to Aristotle's *Nicomachean Ethics*, Book IV, 1122B, the purpose of correct/good reasoning is the creation of correct/good societal relationships between people. In other words, rationality, i.e., the exercise of reason, interests Aristotle in order to achieve the most complete societal relationships possible, i.e., in order to establish a polity on the spiritual unity of its members. For Aristotle, polity is a historical-institutional manifestation of society, where society means the participation of a group of people in the same world of meanings, or values. As I noted in Chapters 2 and 3, Aristotle argues that reason — which is, potentially, whatever the soul can conceive or think — can be distinguished into creative reason and passive reason. In passive reason, concepts are merely potential, and passive reason operates in the medium of sensuous images. On the other hand, active reason is pure actuality, and, in it, the intellectual activity of the soul and its object are united. Therefore, Aristotle understands 'substantial truth' as a transition from potentiality to actuality, i.e., as the natural or spiritual perfection of a being, and not as an abstraction of a given being. From the perspective of Aristotle's philosophy, society is based on the love for the perfection of the absolute being, or the divine, i.e., on an attraction to archetypal forms of harmony and rationality.

On the other hand, one of the first paradigmatic representatives of the 'pragmatic' way of understanding the relationship between culture and politics was Thomas Aquinas. Even though Aquinas was inspired by Aristotle's theory of correct reasoning, i.e., logic, he radically departed from the essence of Aristotelianism, because Aquinas gave priority to the practical organization of life over the quest for the end (ultimate meaning) of life. Thus, whereas Aristotle was interested in logic as a means by which one can pursue a form of qualitative perfection — i.e., participation in the absolute good through inner life and virtue — Thomas Aquinas was interested in logic as a means by which one can pursue a form of quantitative perfection

— i.e., maximize a utility function by achieving specific quantifiable goals and by complying with specific positivistic formulations of religion. In particular, for Thomas Aquinas, logic was a means by which one could defeat his opponents, impose his thought on others, eliminate doubt, and achieve self-assurance. The first priority of Aristotelianism is the quest for the ultimate meaning of life, and, from this perspective, politics *per se* is of secondary significance vis-à-vis culture, since politics is a means of serving culture, i.e., the progress of the human spirit. The first priority of Thomas Aquinas is the quest for an effective practical organization of life, i.e., for effective institutions. The end of Aristotelianism is social harmony, whereas the end of Thomism is individual power. Hence, Thomism cultivated a legalistic form of religious life, as opposed to the mystical-philosophical form of religious life cultivated by Greek Church Fathers, such as Gregory of Nyssa and Maximus the Confessor, who combined the spirituality of the classical Greek thought with the Gospel of Christ.

The 'pragmatic' way of understanding the relationship between culture and politics dominated scholasticism. Thus, the scholastic philosophers and theologians characterized certain institutions and historical entities as 'holy', and they reduced the relationship between the human being and the perfect being into a relationship between the human being and 'holy' historical entities and institutions. Thus, instead of experiencing his relationship with the perfect being, or the divine, as the fullest experience of freedom, the human being whose spiritual life was practically organized by the scholastics' legalistic religious formulas experienced religion as spiritual oppression. This spiritual oppression, gradually, gave birth to various forms of reaction. Hence, other social forces — such as the civil class — who were also struggling for power, attempted to substitute their own pragmatic model of social organization for the one which had been established by the scholastics. Thus, the social forces which started competing with the scholastics for power treated historical entities and institutions which were compatible with their own pragmatic goals as 'holy' and often refused to accept the scholastics' views about the 'holiness' of certain historical entities and institutions. For instance, the civil class, gradually, gave rise to a civilization which was based on the (implicit) 'holiness' of the economic market and its commandments as well as on the (implicit) 'holiness' of a utilitarian approach to individual rights. In fact, exactly because the civil class's approach to individual rights was utilitarian, it was often manipulated by political and economic elites in order to justify social injustice and inhuman behaviours on the basis of the safeguarding of the rights of the individual.

Furthermore, the 'pragmatic' way of understanding the relationship between culture and politics underpins those modern political theories which treat cultural diplomacy as a delicate instrument of power politics. Robert J. Williams' comparative study of the international cultural programmes of Canada and Australia helps one understand the intimate relationship between cultural diplomacy and international cultural relations as well as the connection between cultural diplomacy and foreign policy goals within the framework of contemporary international relations. Williams distinguishes between two approaches to government international cultural programmes and policies: (i) Autonomist approach: within the framework of this approach, international cultural relations facilitate the achievement of cultural policy objectives. (ii) Auxiliary approach: within the framework of this approach, the conduct of cultural diplomacy aims at facilitating the achievement of foreign policy objectives. According to the autonomist approach to cultural diplomacy, "the pursuit of international cultural relations has a rationale and a viability somewhat distinct from the mainstream of foreign policy"[347]. According to the auxiliary approach, cultural diplomacy "is heavily influenced by foreign policy considerations, to the extent that the priorities for cultural programmes will be established on the basis of such criteria as cementing strategic or commercial affiliations, or offsetting sympathy which might lie with a potential adversary, or achieving co-ordinated appeals to influential opinion-leaders or decision-makers"[348]. However, both approaches to cultural diplomacy have a common element: the "extension of the understanding and appreciation of one society by another through the achievements of 'cultural agents'"[349]. In other words, such approaches to cultural diplomacy are alien to any humanistic cosmopolitan ideal and underpin the intensification of the 'individuality', as opposed to the 'sociability', of the members of the international system.

Joseph Nye, Jr, has identified cultural diplomacy with "soft power". According to Nye, cultural diplomacy is the best example of the so-called soft

---

347 R.J. Williams, "International Cultural Programmes: Canada and Australia Compared", in: A.F. Cooper (ed.), *Canadian Culture: International Dimensions*, Waterloo, Ont.: Centre on Foreign Policy and Federalism, University of Waterloo/ Wilfred Laurier University, 1985, p. 87.
348 R.J. Williams, op. cit. (ref. 347), p. 87.
349 R.J. Williams, op. cit. (ref. 347), p. 86.

power, i.e., the possibility of communicating, via the conduit of culture, of values and ideas, which is in contrast to hard power, i.e., one that uses military instruments[350]. However, as it has been pointed by Paul Cammack[351], if cultural diplomacy is identified with soft power, it reduces to an advanced form of propaganda, it is not substantially based on any humanistic cosmopolitan ideal, and it remains heavily dependent upon hard power.

For instance, the theory of soft power has been used by the Turkish Foreign Minister Ahmet Davutoğlu in order to articulate his theory of "Neo-Ottomanism", which is an attempt to promote the international power of Turkey based on its unique geography and historical past. Thus, "Neo-Ottomanism" shows clearly that the theory of soft power is based on a geopolitical way of thinking and, in fact, that the theory of soft power is an attempt to support the pursuit of geopolitical interests by advanced forms of propaganda. Furthermore, "Neo-Ottomanism", which is the Turkish version of soft power, keeps many members of the political elite of the 21st century Turkey obsessed with their Ottoman past, and thus reduces their ability of assimilating the dynamics of the future.

At the dawn of the 21st century, globalization and the information revolution have clearly shown that the communication of conscious beings with each other makes time operate as a multiplier of space, by transcending all spatial barriers and divisions. Paul Virilio, observing the collision of science fiction with the present, describes aspects of this conflict, defined by dromology, the logic of speed, as eradicating the dimension of time utterly: "the conquerors of the Time war, that ultimate mythic Odyssey in which the invaders will to overlordship... exerted not upon geographical distances, but in perturbations of a spatio–temporal vortex", "making the future no longer appear to exist by having it happen now"[352]. Additionally, Sproull and Kiesler argue that the "consequences of new technology can be usefully thought of as first-level, or efficiency, effects and second-level, or social system, effects... Advances in networking technologies now make it possible to think of people, as well as databases and processors, as resources on a network... These technologies can change how people spend their time and what and whom they know and care about. The full range of payoffs, and

---

350 J.S. Nye, Jr., *The Paradox of American Power*, Oxford: Oxford University Press, 2002, p. 8.

351 P. Cammack, "Smart Power and US Leadership: A Critique of Joseph Nye", *49th Parallel — An Interdisciplinary Journal of North American Studies*, Vol. 22, 2008, pp. 4-20.

352 P. Virilio, *The Information Bomb*, London: Verso, 2000, pp. 89, 94.

the dilemmas, will come from how the technologies affect how people can think and work together — the second-level effects"[353].

Neither space nor time exists without the human being. If, therefore, an international actor conquers space, but fails to 'conquer' the human factor, i.e., if his cultural superiority is not acknowledged by the others, then spatial conquests will be annihilated by time. The collapse of colonialism is a characteristic case in point. The major European colonial powers, e.g., Great Britain, Spain and France, were mentally orientated towards looting the natural resources of other nations, focused on geopolitical plans deprived of any significant thought about culture, and they lacked a proposal for life which could be internationally attractive. These cultural characteristics of the European colonial powers were the ultimate causes of the failure of the colonial system to survive for long time.

George Washington advised Americans: "Associate with men of good quality if you esteem your own reputation; for it is better to be alone than in bad company", and: "Happiness and moral duty are inseparably connected". On the other hand, the commitment of many Western policy-makers and political theorists, such as Robert McNamara, Henry Kissinger, Zbigniew Brzezinski, Robert D. Kaplan, and George F. Kennan, to a geopolitical way of thinking which subjugates values and generally cultural issues to power politics and ephemeral geopolitical and geoeconomic interests has made the West perpetrate very costly political mistakes and endorse short-sighted approaches to its interests.

For instance, in 1953, American covert operatives ("Operation Ajax") helped overthrow Iran's left-leaning government and restored the Shah to power. The CIA had funded ayatollahs, mobilized the religious right and engineered a sophisticated propaganda campaign to successfully further its aims, but, finally, Iran's religious leaders were among the first to turn against the United States and they established a theocratic constitution in December 1979. Moreover, during the Cold War, the United States provided staggering quantities of aid to anti-Marxist Islamic extremists, who were fighting against the Soviet Union, but, in the post-Cold War era, those very same extremists became America's next great enemy.

In the 21st century, many Western policy-makers and political theorists have difficulties in understanding that many forms of 'Westernization' of

---

353 L. Sproull and S. Kiesler, *Connections: New Ways of Working in the Networked Organization*, Cambridge, Mass.: MIT Press, 1991, pp. 15-16.

Islam do not reflect a substantial cultural transformation of Islamic societies, but they merely signify that certain Islamic forces adopt Western modes of political and economic communication and utilize Western political and economic institutions and technological infrastructures, without adopting the substantive content of the Western humanistic culture itself. As R. Labévière has put it:

> Taking advantage of economic liberalization, many former chiefs of the 'holy war' have now transmuted into businessmen. They make up an 'Islamo-business' world that has colonies in various sectors: Islamic financial institutions, Islamic garment industries, humanitarian and benevolent organizations, private schools, and so on... They represent a globalization of Islam, de-territorialized, in an approach that has been uncoupled from the Middle East.[354]

In fact, the 'Westernization' of Islam means that Islamic entities (social institutions, organizations, nations, etc.) are linking up with modern worldwide networks, but this does not mean that the 'Westernized' Islamic entities conform to the substantive content of Western modernity. Therefore, many movements of Islamic modernism remain anchored in Islamic communitarianism. Furthermore, some influential Muslim scholars completely reject every principle that does not have its origins in the Qur'an[355].

Additionally, in the 21st century, political analysts and decision-makers who despise value-driven foreign policy and endorse the power monism of the traditional theory of Realpolitik argue that the United States' policy of 'constructive engagement' towards China, which sought to integrate Beijing into, rather than isolate it from the international system, strengthened the influence and the power of so-called pragmatists in the Chinese Communist Party and created the economic, diplomatic and political framework within which China's economic transformation could occur. This analysis fails to recognize that China's economic transformation by the 'pragmatists' of the Chinese Communist Party does not mark the establishment of a free-market economic system in China, but it reflects the selfish economic calculations of an authoritarian Chinese political and economic elite which identifies its interests with the established system of state-regulated capitalism and uses capitalist institutions in order to expand its power internationally. Therefore, far from reflecting high diplomatic skills, the 'pragmatic' policy

---

354 R. Labévière, *Dollars for Terror — The United States and Islam*, trans. M. DeMers, New York: Algora Publishers, 2000, p. 11.

355 See: Khurshid Ahmad (ed.), *Islam — Its Meaning and Message*, The Islamic Foundation, 2nd Edition, 1980.

of the United States towards the communist China reflects the misunder-standing of reality by the supporters of the 'school' of political realism. In general, in the West, modern political life is often characterized by what one could call a 'pragmatic fallacy', which is a short-sighted practicalism that wants to eliminate political discourse and value-driven politics. Prag-matism is a protection against ignorance and a cover for moral abdication. It makes very little sense for those who know how to articulate a successful strategy and who take their values seriously.

In his *Republic*, Plato argues that politics would betray itself if its aim did not include the moral improvement of the individual and the society. In fact, in the *Republic*, 340c, Plato has posed a crucial political question which has been evaded by the supporters of Realpolitik and political pragmatism: "was this how you meant to define what is right, that it is that which *seems* to the stronger to be his interest, whether it *really* is or not?".

Geopolitical calculations can yield power, indeed. But even the most ingenious geopolitical calculations will end up in failure if they are not combined with a cultural proposal which can claim ecumenical authority and be internationally attractive; for, they will be defeated by time. Culture leads to a dynamic understanding of space and unites it with time, like a work of art, whose truth is continuously formed and reformed over time. In fact, the ability of the Greco-Roman (Byzantine) Empire to survive for more than one thousand years was based on the ability of that empire to integrate its subjects into an ecumenical culture which could meet the fundamental existential quests of diverse peoples.

The commitment of a civilization to a pragmatic way of thinking about the relationship between culture and politics has dramatic consequences. The societal relations between persons reduce to a corporate association of individuals who voluntarily undermine their existential otherness — their personhood — due to the requests of a "social contract". This situation is a consequence of the substitution of a legalistic model of social organization for the spiritual unity which emanates from Plato's and Aristotle's 'substan-tial' approach to the relationship between culture and politics.

From the perspective of what I have called a 'substantial' approach to the relationship between culture and politics, society signifies the participation of a human community in the same existential purpose, i.e., the perfection/divinization of the human being. On the other hand, if one's approach to the relationship between culture and politics is pragmatic, i.e., if the spirit is reduced to an institution, then the term 'society' has declined to an arithmetic sum total, an abstract interpretation of a total of undifferentiated units. Furthermore, in a civilization which is founded on a pragmatic approach to the relationship between culture and politics, we can never talk about social unity, but only about social conventions and compromises, because, in such a civilization, society is the outcome of the interaction between selfish individuals struggling for survival and historical power.

In the ancient democracy of Athens — which was based on what I have called a 'substantial' approach to the relationship between culture and politics — the freedom and dignity of the person were being conceived neither as a quest for individual self-assurance or self-gratification, nor as a defence against the power of the state; instead, they were being conceived as a consequence of the participation of the citizens in the collective achievement of communal relations. For, the ancient Greek polity was founded on an ontological (existential) request: the pursuit of the truth of life, and, for the ancient Greeks, truth means the imitation and the fulfilment of the logical harmony of the cosmos, the transformation of a set of historical/natural entities into a meaningful world ('cosmos'). For the ancient Greeks, truth is not exhausted in objectivity or logical self-assurance. From Heraclitus to the Neo-Platonists, knowledge of truth was intimately related to an event of social unity: "everything that we share, we know to be true; what we have that is peculiar to us, we know to be false"[356]. For the ancient Greeks, the ultimate stage of knowledge corresponds to the experience of a universal truth, which exactly because it is universal, and hence it cannot be manipulated by any individual, operates as the foundation of social unity.

As shown in the previous analysis, the creation of a humanistic cosmopolitan political system depends on the endorsement of what I have called a 'substantial' — as opposed to pragmatic — approach to the relationship between culture and politics. Plato's philosophy — as it was explained in Chapter 3 — provides the most trustworthy and effective philosophical framework within which human rights can acquire an absolute status, irrespective of historical conditions and pragmatic-utilitarian political expediencies.

---

356 Heraclitus, *Frag. Diels-Kranz I*, pp.148, 29-30.

BIBLIOGRAPHY

A'la Mawdudi, A., *Human Rights in Islam*, Leicester: The Islamic Foundation, 1980

Alain (pseudonym of Émile-August Chartier), *Préliminaires à la mythologie*, Paris: Paul Hartmann, Éditeur, 1943

Amonius, *Ammonius in Porphyrii Isagogen sive V Voces*, ed. A. Busse, Berlin, 1891, IV, Section III

Annan, K., *We the Peoples: the Role of the United Nations in the 21ˢᵗ Century* — Report of the Secretary-General, New York: UN General Assembly Edition, March 2000

Aris, R., *History of Political Thought in Germany from 1789 to 1815*, London: Allen & Unwin, 1936

Aristotle, *Collected Works*, Penguin and Oxford University Press

Artz, F.B., *The Mind of the Middle Ages*, Chicago: University of Chicago Press, 1980

Ashley, R.K., "Living on Borderlines: Man, Poststructuralism and War", in: J. Der Derian and M. Shapiro (eds.), *International/Intertextual Relations: Postmodern Readings in World Politics*, Lexington: Lexington Books, 1989

Ashley, R., and Walker, R.B.J. (eds.), Special Issue *International Studies Quarterly*, Vol. 34, No. 3, September 1990

Ashley, R., and Walker, R.B.J., "Speaking the Language of Exile: Dissidence in International Studies", Special Issue *International Studies Quarterly*, Vol. 34, No. 3, September 1990

Ashley, R., and Walker, R.B.J., "Reading Dissidence/Writing the Discipline: Crisis and the Question of Sovereignty in International Studies", Special Issue *International Studies Quarterly*, Vol. 34, No. 3, September 1990

Atkinson, A., *Pushing 'Reset' on Sustainable Development*, Sustainable Development Insights, The Frederick S. Pardee Center for the Study of the Long Range Future, October 2009

Bakhtin, M., *The Dialogic Imagination*, Austin: University of Texas Press, 1981

Barber, B.R., "Shrunken Sovereign: Consumerism, Globalization, and American Emptiness", *World Affairs*, Spring 2008

Beitz, C.R., *Political Theory and International Relations*, Princeton: Princeton University Press, 1979

Bennhold, K., and Bowley, G., "Charter 'Not Dead', EU Insists", *International Herald Tribune*, 31 May 2005

Bergson, H., *The Creative Mind*, tr. M.L. Andison, New York: The Citadel Press, 1992

Berkeley, G., *Of the Principles of Human Knowledge*, in: *The Works of George Berkeley, Bishop of Cloyne*, eds A.A. Luce and T.E. Jessop, London: Thomas Nelson and Sons, 1948-1957

Berman, S., *The Social Democratic Moment: Ideas and Politics in the Making of Interwar Europe*, Cambridge, Mass.: Harvard University Press, 1998

Bronowski, J., *The Ascent of Man*, Boston: Little, 1974

Brouwer, L.E.J., *Life, Art, and Mysticism*, trans. W.P. van Stigt, *Notre Dame Journal of Formal Logic*, Vol. 37, No. 3, 1996

Brown, C., *International Relations Theory — New Normative Approaches*, New York: Harvester-Wheatsheaf, 1992

Brown, C., Nardin, T., and Rengger, N. (eds.), *International Relations in Political Thought*, Cambridge: Cambridge University Press, 2002

Brzezinski, Z., *Out of Control — Global Turmoil on the Eve of the 21st Century*, New York: Macmillan, 1993

Burkitt, B., *Radical Political Economy*, Brighton: Wheatsheaf, 1984

Callon, M., "Whose Impostures? Physics at War with the Third Person", *Social Studies of Science*, Vol. 29, 1999

Cammack, P., "Smart Power and US Leadership: A Critique of Joseph Nye", *49th Parallel — An Interdisciplinary Journal of North American Studies*, Vol. 22, 2008

Casement, A., *Carl Gustav Jung*, London: Sage, 2001

Cecil, H., *Conservatism*, London: Thornton Butterworth, 1912

Checkel, J.T., "Social Construction and European Integration", in: T. Christiansen, K.E. Jorgensen, and A. Wiener (eds.), *The Social Construction of Europe*, London: Sage, 2001

Chua, A., *Day of Empire — How Hyperpowers Rise to Global Dominance and Why They Fall*, New York: Doubleday, 2007

Cimbala, S.J. (ed.), *Artificial Intelligence and National Security*, Lexington: Lexington Books, 1987

Code, A., "Aristotle's Metaphysics as a Science of Principles", *Revue Internationale de Philosophie*, Vol. 51, 1997

Commission on Global Governance, *Our Global Neighborhood*, Oxford: Oxford University Press, 1995

Cox, R.H., *Ideology, Politics, and Political Theory*, Belmont, Calif.: Wadsworth, 1969

Curley, E., *Behind the Geometric Method*, Princeton: Princeton University Press, 1988

Davis, C.T., "An Early Florentine Political Theorist: Fra Remigio de Girolami", *Proceedings of the American Philosophical Society*, Vol. 104, 1960

Dawson, J.W., Jr., "Gödel and the Limits of Logic", *Scientific American*, Vol. 280, No. 6, 1999

Dawson, J.W., Jr., *Logical Dilemmas: The Life and Work of Kurt Gödel*, Wellesley Mass.: A.K. Peters, 1997

Der Derian, J., and Shapiro, M. (eds.), *International/Intertextual Relations: Postmodern Readings in World Politics*, Lexington: Lexington Books, 1989

Descartes, R., *Rules for the Direction of our Native Intelligence* (originally published in 1628), in: *Descartes: Selected Philosophical Writings*, trans. J. Cottingham, R. Stoothoff and D. Murdoch, Cambridge: Cambridge University Press, 1988

Descartes, R., *Meditations*, in *Descartes: Selected Philosophical Writings* (originally published in 1641), trans. J. Cottingham, R. Stoothoff and D. Murdoch, Cambridge: Cambridge University Press, 1988

Deubner, L., *Iamblichi de vita Pythagorica*, Leipzig: Teubner, 1937

Diez, T., "Speaking Europe: The Politics of Integration Discourse", in: T. Christiansen, K.E. Jorgensen, and A. Wiener (eds.), *The Social Construction of Europe*, London: Sage, 2001

Dodds, E.R. (ed.), *Plato: Gorgias*, Oxford: Oxford University Press, 1959

Dostoyevsky, F., *The Brothers Karamazov*, trans. C. Garnett, New York: Penguin Books, 1958

Douglas, A.E., *Cicero*, Oxford: Clarendon Press, 1968

Dunne, T., "A British School of International Relations", in: J. Hayward, B. Barry, and A. Brown (eds.), *The British Study of Politics in the Twentieth Century*, Oxford: Oxford University Press, 2003

Eckhart, M., *Meister Eckhart: The Essential Writings*, trans. R.B. Blakney, New York: HarperCollins, 1957

Ehrlich, E., *Fundamental Principles of the Sociology of Law*, trans. W.L. Moll, Cambridge, Mass.: Harvard University Press, 1936

Eichengreen, B., Rose, A.K., and Wyplosz, C., "Contagious Currency Crises", *Scandinavian Journal of Economics*, Vol. 98, 1996

European Commission, *European Sustainable Cities*, Report by the Expert Group on Urban Environment, Brussels, 1996

Feuerbach, L.A., *Principles of the Philosophy of the Future* (originally published in 1843), trans. M.H. Vogel, Library of Liberal Arts, Indianapolis: Bobbs-Merrill, 1966

Feuerbach, L.A., *The Essence of Christianity* (originally published in 1854), trans. G. Eliot, Amherst, NY: Prometheus Books, 1989

Fichte, J.G., *The Popular Works of Johann Gottlieb Fichte*, trans. W. Smith, 2 vols, London: Thoemmes, 1999

Finnis, J., *Natural Law and Natural Rights*, Oxford: Clarendon Press, 1980

Fleck, D. (ed.), *The Handbook of International Humanitarian Law*, Oxford: Oxford University Press, 2008

Foucault, M., *Language, Counter-Memory, Practice*, ed. D.F. Bouchard, Ithaca, NY: Cornell University Press, 1977

Foucault, M., *The Order of Things — An Archaeology of the Human Sciences*, trans. A. Sheridan, New York: Pantheon, 1970

Foucault, M., "Nietzsche, Genealogy, History", in: P. Rabinow (ed.), *The Foucault Reader*, Harmondsworth: Peregrine Books, 1986

Foucault, M., *Les Mots et les Choses*, Paris: Gallimard, 1996

Frank, J., *The Levellers*, New York: Russell & Russell, 1969

Freud, S., *Civilization and Its Discontents*, trans. J. Rivière, London: Hogarth, 1930

Fromm, B., "Science Wars and Beyond", *Philosophy and Literature*, Vol. 30, 2006

Frost, M., *Ethics in International Relations — A Constitutive Theory*, Cambridge: Cambridge University Press, 1986

George, A.L., "The Operational Code; a Neglected Approach to the Study of International Political Leaders and Decision-Making", *International Studies Quarterly*, Vol. 13, No. 2, 1969

George, J., and Campbell, D., "Patterns of Dissent and the Celebration of Difference: Critical Social Theory in International Relations", in: R. Ashley and R.B.J. Walker (eds.), Special Issue *International Studies Quarterly*, Vol. 34, No. 3, September 1990

Gibson, J., *Locke's Theory of Knowledge and its Historical Relations*, Cambridge: Cambridge University Press, 1968

Gödel, K., "Some Basic Theorems on the Foundations of Mathematics and Their Implications", in: K. Gödel, *Collected Works*, Volume III, eds S. Feferman, J.W. Dawson Jr., W. Goldfarb, C. Parsons, and R.N. Solovay, Oxford: Oxford University Press, 1995

Gordon, J., and Shortliffe, E.H., "A method for Managing Evidential Reasoning in a Hierarchical Hypothesis Space: A Retrospective", in: D.G. Bobrow (ed.), *Artificial Intelligence in Perspective*, Amsterdam: MIT Press/Elsevier Science Publishers, 1994

Gregory the Theologian, "First Oration: On Easter and His Reluctance", in: P. Schaff and H. Wace (eds.), *A Select Library of Nicene and Post-Nicene Fathers*, 1905, Vol. 7

Groom, A.J.R., and Powell, D., "From World Politics to Global Governance — A Theme in Need of a Focus", in: A.J.R. Groom and M. Light (eds.), *Contemporary International Relations: A Guide to Theory*, London: Pinter, 1994

Gross, P., and Levitt, N., *Higher Superstition: The Academic Left and Its Quarrels with Science*, Baltimore: Johns Hopkins University Press, 1994

Hao Wang, *A Logical Journey — From Gödel to Philosophy*, Cambridge, Mass.: MIT Press, 1996

Hart, H.L.A., "Are There Any Natural Rights?", *Philosophical Review*, Vol. 64, 1955

Hart, H.L.A., *Essays on Bentham, Jurisprudence and Political Theory*, Oxford: Clarendon Press, 1982

Hay, C., *Political Analysis — A Critical Introduction*. New York: Palgrave, 2002

Heath, T.L., *The Thirteen Books of Euclid's Elements*, Cambridge: Cambridge University Press, 1908

Hegel, G.W.F., *Phenomenology of Spirit* (originally published in 1807), trans. A.V. Miller, Delhi: Motilal Banarsidass, 1998

Hegel, G.W.F., *Philosophy of Right* (originally published in 1821), trans. T.M. Knox, Oxford: Oxford University Press, 1942

Held, K., "The Origin of Europe with the Greek Discovery of the World", *Epoche*, Vol. 7, 2002

Hempel, C., "Reasons and Covering Laws in Historical Explanation", in: P. Gardiner (ed.), *The Philosophy of History*, Oxford: Oxford University Press, 1974

Hempel, C., *Philosophy of Natural Science*, Englewood Cliffs, NJ: Prentice-Hall, 1966

Hobbes, T., *Leviathan*, ed. C.B. Macpherson, Harmondsworth: Penguin, 1968

Homer, *Odyssey*, trans. R. Fitzgerald, New York: Vintage, 1961

Horkheimer, M., and Adorno, T., *Dialectic of Enlightenment — Philosophical Fragments*, Stanford: Stanford University Press, 2002

Houtart, F., "The Multiple Crisis and Beyond", *Globalizations*, Vol. 7, 2010

Howard, R.E., *Human Rights in Commonwealth Africa*, Totowa: Rowman and Littlefield, 1986

Hsiung, J.C. (ed.), *Human Rights in East Asia — A Cultural Perspective*, New York: Paragon, 1985

Hume, D., *An Inquiry Concerning Human Understanding* (originally published in 1748), Indianapolis, IN: Bobbs- Merrill, 1955

Humphreys, A., "One Official's 'Refugee' Is Another's 'Terrorist'", *National Post*, 17 January 2006

Jackson, R.H., "The Situational Ethics of Statecraft", in: C.J. Nolan (ed.), *Ethics and Statecraft — The Moral Dimension of International Affairs*, Westport: Praeger, 1995

Jaffee, M.S., *Early Judaism*, Upper Saddle River, NJ: Prentice Hall, 1997

Jaeger, W., *Paideia — The Ideals of Greek Culture*, Oxford: Oxford University Press, 1945

Jaynes, E.T., *Probability Theory — The Logic of Science*, Cambridge: Cambridge University Press, 2003

Jefferson, T., "Thomas Jefferson to Elbridge Gerry", 1801, Memorial Edition, Vol. 10

Jefferson, T., "Thomas Jefferson to Dr Maese", 1809, Memorial Edition, Vol. 12

Jefferson, T., "Thomas Jefferson to Thomas Law", 1814, Memorial Edition, Vol. 14

Jefferson, T., "Thomas Jefferson to John Adams", 1816, Memorial Edition, Vol. 15

Jellinek, G., *Die Lehre von den Staatenverbindungn*, 1882

John of Damascus, "Homilia in Transfigurationem Domini" (Homily on the transfiguration of the Lord), *Patrologia Graeca*, Vol. 96

Jolowicz, H.F., and Nicholas, B., *Historical Introduction to the Study of Roman Law*, Cambridge: Cambridge University Press, 1972

Jung, C.G., "The Relations Between the Ego and the Unconscious", in: J. Campbell (ed.), *The Portable Jung*, New York: Penguin Books, 1971

Kaminsky, G., Lizondo, S., and Reinhart, C.M., "Leading Indicators of Currency Crises", IMF Staff Papers, Vol. 45, 1998

Kant, I., *Collected Works*: Königlichen Preussischen (later Deutschen) Akademie der Wissenschaften (ed.), Kants gesammelte Schriften, Berlin: Georg Reimer (later Walter De Gruyter). English edition of Kant's works: P. Guyer and A. Wood (eds.), *The Cambridge Edition of the Works of Immanuel Kant*, Cambridge: Cambridge University Press

Kaplan, M.A., "Problems of Theory Building and Theory Confirmation in International Politics", in: K. Knorr and S. Verba (eds.), *The International System*, Princeton: Princeton University Press, 1961

Kathrani, P., "A Decade of Change: A Case for Global Morality, Dialogue and Transnational Trust-Building", *Jurisprudence*, Vol.4, 2009

Kelly, P.J., Utilitarianism and Distributive Justice — Jeremy Bentham and the Civil Law, Oxford: Oxford University Press, 1990

Kelman, H., "Kairos — The Auspicious Moment", *American Journal of Psychoanalysis*, Vol. 29, 1969

Kerferd, G.B., *The Sophistic Movement*, Cambridge: Cambridge University Press, 1981

Khurshid Ahmad (ed.), *Islam — Its Meaning and Message*, The Islamic Foundation, 2nd Edition, 1980

Kierkegaard, S., *The Kierkegaard Reader*, ed. J. Chamberlain and J. Rée, Oxford: Blackwell, 2001

Kissinger, H.A., *The Necessity of Choice: Prospects of American Foreign Policy*, Garden City, New York: Doubleday & Co., 1962

Kissinger, H.A., "The Policymaker and the Intellectual", in: J.N. Rosenau (ed.), *International Politics and Foreign Policy*, New York: The Free Press of Glencoe, 1961

Kissinger, H.A., *A World Restored — Europe after Napoleon: The Politics of Conservatism in a Revolutionary Age*, New York: Grosset and Dunlap, 1964

Kissinger, H.A., "Reflections on a Partnership: British and American Attitudes to Postwar Foreign Policy", *Executive Intelligence Review*, 11 January 2002

Knight, K., *Aristotelian Philosophy — Ethics and Politics from Aristotle to MacIntyre*, London: Polity Press, 2007

Labévière, R., *Dollars for Terror — The United States and Islam*, trans. M. DeMers, New York: Algora Publishers, 2000

Lahart, J., "Bernanke's Bubble Laboratory — A Princeton Protégés of Fed Chief, Study the Economics of Manias", *The Wall Street Journal*, 16 May 2008

Laos, N.K., *Topics in Mathematical Analysis and Differential Geometry*, London: World Scientific Publishing Co., 1998

Lavelle, L., *De l'être*, Paris: Aubier, 1947

Lavelle, L, *De l'acte*, Paris: Aubier, 1937

Leibniz, G., *New Essays on Human Understanding* (originally published in 1704), in *Leinbiz: Philosophical Writings*, ed. G.H.R. Parkinson, trans. M. Morris and G.H.R. Parkinson, London: J.M. Dent & Sons, 1973

Lévi-Strauss, C., *The Raw and the Cooked*, trans. John and Doreen Weightman, Chicago: The University of Chicago Press, 1969

Lévi-Strauss, C., *Structural Anthropology*, trans. C. Jacobson, New York: Basic Books, 1963

Lévy-Bruhl, L., *Primitive Mentality* (originally published in 1922), New York: AMS Press, 1978

Lichtheim, G., *The Concept of Ideology, and Other Essays*, New York: Random House, 1967

Liddell, Scott and Jones, *Greek-English Lexicon*, 9th Edition

Lovelock, J.E., *Gaia — A New Look at Life on Earth*, Oxford: Oxford University Press, 1979

Luther, M., *Martin Luther: Selections from His Writings*, ed. J. Dillenberger, Garden City, NJ: Doubleday, 1961

Lyotard, J.-F., *The Postmodern Condition: A Report on Knowledge*, trans. G. Bennington and B. Massumi, Minneapolis: University of Minnesota Press, 1984

Mackie, J.L., *Hume's Moral Theory*, London: Routledge & Kegan Paul, 1980

Manners, I., "Normative Power Europe: A Contradiction in Terms?", *Journal of Common Market Studies*, Vol. 40, 2002

Mannheim, K., "Historicism", in: *Essays on the Sociology of Knowledge*, London: Routledge & Kegan Paul, 1952

Marcel, G., *Being and Having*, trans. K. Farrer, Westminister: Dacre Press, 1949

Marcel, G., *The Philosophy of Existentialism*, trans. M. Harari, New York: Carol Publishing Group, 1995

Marrou, H.I., *St Augustine and His Influence through the Ages*, New York: Harper Torch, 1957

Martin, R., "The Two Cities of Augustine's Political Philosophy", *Journal of the History of Ideas*, Vol. 33, 1972

Marx, K., *Selected Writings*, ed. D. McLellan, Oxford: Oxford University Press, 1977

Marx, K., *A Contribution to the Critique of Political Economy* (original edition of 1859), trans. N.I. Stone, New York: International Library Publishing, 1904

Maurois, A., *Alain*, Paris: Gallimard, 1963

M'Baye, K., "Human Rights in Africa", in: K. Vasak and P. Alston (eds.), *The International Dimensions of Human Rights*, Westport: Greenwood Press, 1982

McCabe, M.M., *Plato's Individuals*, Princeton: Princeton University Press, 1994

Mesquita, B.de, *The War Trap*, New Haven: Yale University Press, 1981

Michelet, J., *Histoire de France au XVIIE Siècle*, Tome VII: Renaissance, Paris: Chamerot, 1857 (published in English by Elibron Classics, Adamant Media Corporation, in 2006)

Michon, C., *Nominalisme: La théorie de la signification d'Occam*, Paris: J. Vrin, 1994

Mill, J.S., "A Few Words on Nonintervention", *Dissertations and Discussions*, Vol. 3, London: Longmans, 1873

Monnet, J., *Algiers Memorandum* (first published in 1943), in: T. Salmon and Sir W. Nicoll (eds.), *Building European Union — A Documentary History and Analysis*, Manchester: Manchester University Press, 1997

Moore, G.E., *Principia Ethica*, Cambridge: Cambridge University Press, 1903

Morgenthau, H.J., *Scientific Man Versus Power Politics*, Chicago: University of Chicago Press, 1946

Moutsopoulos, E., *Kairos et alternance: d' Empédocle à Platon*, Athènes: Académie d'Athènes, 1989

Murray, C.J.(ed.), *Encyclopedia of the Romantic Era: 1760-1850*, New York: Fitzroy Dearborn, 2004

Nardin, T., *Law, Morality, and the Relations of States*, Princeton: Princeton University Press, 1983

Navari, C., "Intervention, Nonintervention and the Construction of the State", in: I. Forbes and M. Hoffman (eds.), *Political Theory, International Relations and the Ethics of Intervention*, London: Macmillan, 1993

Nersessian, E., and Kopff, R.G., Jr. (eds.), *Textbook of Psychoanalysis*, Washington, DC: American Psychiatric Press, 1996

Nicholson, M., *Causes and Consequences in International Relations — A Conceptual Study*, London: Pinter, 1996

Nickel, J., *Making Sense of Human Rights — Philosophical Reflections on the Declaration of Human Rights*, Berkeley: University of California Press, 1987

Nietzsche, F., *Beyond Good and Evil* (originally published in 1886), trans. W. Kaufmann, New York: Vintage Books, 1989

Nietzsche, F., *On the Genealogy of Morality* (first published in 1887), trans. M. Clark and A.J. Swensen, Indianapolis: Hackett Publishing Co., 1998

Noer, T.J., "Henry Kissinger's Philosophy of History", *Modern Age*, Spring 1975

Norris, C., *Derrida*, London: Fontana, 1987

Nye, J.S., Jr., *The Paradox of American Power*, Oxford: Oxford University Press, 2002

Oakeshott, M.J., *On Human Conduct*, Oxford: Clarendon Press, 1975

O'Connor, D.J., *Aquinas and Natural Law*, London: Macmillan, 1967

Onians, R.B., *The Origins of European Thought about the Body, the Mind, the Soul, the World, Time, and Fate*, New York: Arno Press, 1973

O'Sullivan, N., *Conservatism*, London: Dent, 1976

Parfit, D., *Reasons and Persons*, Oxford: Clarendon Press, 1984

Parker, G., "Would a Constitution by Another Name Smell Sweeter?", *The Financial Times*, 29 May 2006

Parsons, C., "Showing Ideas as Causes: The Origins of the European Union", *International Organization*, Vol.56, 2002

Parsons, S., Gmytrasiewicz, P., and Wooldridge, M. (eds.), *Game Theory and Decision Theory in Agent-Based Systems*, Norwell, Mass.: Kluwer Academic Publishers, 2002

Penn, W., *An Essay towards the Present and Future Peace of Europe by the Establishment of an European Dyet, Parliament, or Estates* (first published in 1693), in: T. Salmon and Sir W. Nicoll (eds.), *Building European Union — A Documentary History and Analysis*, Manchester: Manchester University Press, 1997

Phillips, A., *On Filtration*, Cambridge, Mass.: Harvard University Press, 1994

Plato, *Collected Works*, Penguin and Oxford University Press

Polya, G., *How to Solve It*, Princeton: Princeton University Press, 1973

Prigogine, I., and Stengers, I., *Order out of Chaos — Man's New Dialogue with Nature*, New York : Bentam, 1984

Rashdall, H., *Ethics*, London: T.C. & E.C. Jack, 1913

Rawls, J., *A Theory of Justice*, Oxford: Oxford University Press, 1972

Rawson, E., *Intellectual Life in the Late Roman Republic*, London: Duckworth, 1985

Reiss, H.J. (ed.), *Kant's Political Writings*, Cambridge: Cambridge University Press, 1979

Reiss, H.S. (ed.), *The Political Thought of the German Romantics 1793-1815*, Oxford: Blackwell, 1955

Robbins, L., *An Essay on the Nature and Significance of Economic Science*, 2nd edn, London: Macmillan, 1935

Romanides, J.S., *The Ancestral Sin*, trans. G.S. Gabriel, Ridgewood, NJ: Zephyr Publishing, 2002

Rorty, R., *Objectivity, Relativism and Truth: Philosophical Papers*, Vol. I, Cambridge: Cambridge University Press, 1991

Rorty, R., "Human Rights, Rationality and Sentimentality", in: *Truth and Progress*, Cambridge: Cambridge University Press, 1998

Ross, W.D., *Foundations of Ethics*, Oxford: Oxford University Press, 1939

Ross, W.D., *The Right and the Good*, Oxford: Oxford University Press, 1930

Rubinstein, N., "Political Theories in the Renaissance", in: A. Chastel et al., *The Renaissance: Essays in Interpretation*, London: Methuen, 1982

Ryan, J.A., *Economic Justice — Selections from Distributive Justice and a Living Wage*, ed. H.R. Beckley, Louisville, Kentucky: Westminister John Knox Press, 1996

Ruggie, J.G., "What Makes the World Hang Together? Neo-Utilitarianism and the Social Constructivist Challenge", *International Organization*, Vol.52, 1998

Ryan, A., *J.S. Mill*, London: Routledge & Kegan Paul, 1974

Sachs, J., Tornell, A., and Velasco, A., "Financial Crises in Emerging Markets: The Lessons from 1995", *Brookings Papers on Economic Activity*, New York: The Brookings Institution, Vol. 27, 1996

Schopenhauer, A., *Essays of Schopenhauer*, ed. S.H. Dircks, The Floating Press, 2010

Shaw, M.N., *International Law*, fifth edition, Cambridge: Cambridge University Press, 2003

Shue, H., *Basic Rights — Subsistence, Affluence, and U.S. Foreign Policy*, second edition, Princeton: Princeton University Press, 1996

Smith, C., *Contemporary French Philosophy*, London: Methuen & Co., 196Snyder, R.C., "Game Theory and Analysis of Political Behavior", in: .J.N. Rosenau (ed.), *International Politics and Foreign Policy*, New York: The Free Press of Glencoe, 1964

Spade, P.V., *Five Texts on the Mediaeval Problem of Universals*, Indianapolis: Hackett Publishing, 1994

Sproull, L., and Kiesler, S., *Connections: New Ways of Working in the Networked Organization*, Cambridge, Mass.: MIT Press, 1991

Stacey, D., *Strategic Management and Organizational Dynamics*, London: Pitman, 1993

Stalin, J., *Dialectical and Historical Materialism*, New York: International Publishers, 1977

Sterne, L., *The Life and Opinions of Tristram Shandy, A Gentleman* (originally published in 1759-1767), Middlesex: Penguin, 1976

Taylor, C., *Hegel*, Cambridge: Cambridge University Press, 1975

Themistius, *Orationes quae supersunt*, eds N. Schenkl, G. Downey, and A.F. Norman, Leipzig: Bibliotheca Teubneriana, 1965-74

Therborn, G., "Europe in the Twenty-First Century", in: P. Gowan and P. Anderson (eds.), *The Question of Europe*, London: Verso, 1997

Thompson, N., *The People's Science: The Popular Political Economy of Exploitation and Crisis 1816-34*, Cambridge: Cambridge University Press, 1984

Tuck, R., *Natural Rights Theories*, Cambridge: Cambridge University Press, 1979

United Nations, *Guidance Note of the Secretary-General — United Nations Approach to Transitional Justice*, New York, 2010

United Nations, *Report of the Secretary-General — The Rule of Law and Transitional Justice in Conflict and Post-Conflict Societies*, New York, 2004

Valéry, P., *History and Politics*, in: *The Collected Works of Paul Valéry*, ed. J. Matthews, trans. D. Folliot and J. Matthews, New York: Pantheon Books, 1962

Van Ham, P., "The Rise of the Brand State: The Postmodern Politics of Image and Reputation", *Foreign Affairs*, Vol. 80, 2001

Virilio, P., *The Information Bomb*, London: Verso, 2000

Voltaire, F.M.A. de, *Essay on the Manners of Nations*, 1756

Von Coudenhove-Kalergi, R., *Pan-Europe* (first published in 1923), in: T. Salmon and Sir W. Nicoll (eds.), *Building European Union — A Documentary History and Analysis*, Manchester: Manchester University Press, 1997

Von Neumann, J., and Morgenstern, O., *Theory of Games and Economic Behavior*, Princeton: Princeton University Press, 1944

Waldrop, M.M., *Complexity: The Emerging Science at the Edge of Order and Chaos*, London: Viking, 1992

Walton, D., *Appeal to Popular Opinion*, Pennsylvania: The Pennsylvania University Press, 1999

Waltz, K.N., *Theory of International Politics*, New York: McGraw-Hill, 1979

Watt, N., "EU Constitution a Grandiose Project That Failed, Says Beckett", *The Guardian*, 18 October 2006

Weber, M., *The Protestant Ethic and the Spirit of Capitalism*, London: Allen & Unwin, 1930

Webster's New World College Dictionary, 4th Edition.

Weisheipl, J., *Friar Thomas D' Aquino — His Life, Thought and Works*, Oxford: Blackwell, 1974

White, D.J., *Decision Theory*, Chicago: Aldine, 1969

Whitehead, A., *Science and the Modern World*, New York: Macmillan, 1944

Williams, A.T., "Taking Values Seriously: Towards a Philosophy of EU Law", *Oxford Journal of Legal Studies*, Vol. 29, 2009

Williams, I.A., *Kairology — A Time for Personal Development*, New Zealand: Phantom Publishing, 2008

Williams, R.J., "International Cultural Programmes: Canada and Australia Compared", in: A.F. Cooper (ed.), *Canadian Culture: International Dimensions*, Waterloo, Ont.: Centre on Foreign Policy and Federalism, University of Waterloo/ Wilfred Laurier University, 1985

Wiseman, G., "Pax Americana: Bumping into Diplomatic Culture", *International Studies Perspectives*, Vol. 6, 2005

Wolter, A.B., *Duns Scotus on the Will and Morality*, Washington, DC: The Catholic University of America Press, 1986

Woolhouse, R.S. and Francks, R., *Leibniz: Philosophical Texts*, Oxford: Oxford University Press, 1998

ACKNOWLEDGMENTS

The ideas expressed in this book were shaped by my academic research and philosophical attitude, refined by my work as a political consultant, and reinforced by methodic observations and analyses of different countries and cultures around the world.

In the following paragraphs, I will cite the persons who have helped me develop my intellectual armour by the institutions where I encountered them. This list is not exhaustive by any means, but it is representative. At the University of La Verne (California), Professor Themistocles M. Rassias (currently Professor at the National Technical University of Athens) introduced me in advanced mathematical analysis and helped me complete my book *Topics in Mathematical Analysis and Differential Geometry* (World Scientific Publishing Co.), and Professor Rehavia U. Yakovee opened to me the world of international politics and the mathematical models of arms races and arms acquisition patterns. At the University of Rousse (Bulgaria), Professor Svetoslav Jordanov Bilchev, hosted me, co-operated with me in preparing and publishing research papers in mathematical modeling and discussed with me interesting problems in game theory and cybernetics. At the University of Kent's London Centre of International Relations, Professor Hazel Smith and Professor Michael Nicholson played a key role in my international-political education, and they helped me complete a research project entitled *Theory Construction and Empirical Relevance in International Relations*. At the Royal Institute of International Affairs (Chatham House), Mr

William Hopkinson, former Head of the Chatham House's International Security Programme, opened to me the scholarly charity of this prestigious institution in 1999. At the Academy of Athens, the gifted philosopher Professor Evangelos Moutsopoulos' work broadened my thought in the fields of ontology, cognition and ethics, and Professor Moutsopoulos contributed some of his thoughts to my research project *International Relations as an Object of Science*. The Chairman of the Saint Elias Seminary and Graduate School (Virginia), Bishop Seraphim, has been particularly encouraging and supportive towards my interdisciplinary research and teaching interests in philosophy, politics and spirituality, and his institution has awarded me the honorary degree of Doctor of Divinity. At the Business Schools of European University (Switzerland) and the Free European School of Economics (Germany), Dr Dirk Craen, President of the first, and Dr Friedrich Frei, Rector of the latter, have given me creative opportunities to accomplish my goals in business education and research. Additionally, at the European University's Athens Postgraduate Programme, where I have taught European politics and economics and decision-making, my students and interdisciplinary colleagues have offered me useful intellectual challenges.

Professor Dr George J. Hagerty, Provost of the Hellenic American University, has carefully read the final draft of my manuscript and has expressed his appreciation through his Foreword to the present book. Mrs Jenny Pavlakou-Panagiotopoulou, English language teacher at Gnosi School in Greece, proofread the manuscript of this book. Furthermore, my gratitude extends to my parents, who played an important role in the development of my scholarly intuition.

My greatest thanks are to Algora Publishing for their persuasive advice which helped me define more sharply my main theses as well as for their patience which allowed me to delve deeply and freely into the elusive yet critical interdependence between culture, political thought and international affairs and to utilize sufficient resources in order to produce the present book.

INDEX